Jean

MW01608377

THE FAMILY TREES OF THE KINGS OF FRANCE

The engravings used in this book have been taken from
l'Histoire de France Populaire
by Henri Martin
published in 1876 by Furne et Jouvet

Translated by Angela Moyon

EDITIONS JEAN-PAUL GISSEROT
10, rue Gracieuse, 75005 Paris

BIBLIOGRAPHY

- Père Anselme de SAINTE-MARIE, *Histoire de la maison royale de France,* Paris, Editions du Palais royal, re-edited 1967.
- BLUCHE, François (Dir.), *Dictionnaire du Grand Siècle*, Paris, Fayard, 1990.
- Numerous biographies of the kings of France, in particular those published by Fayard
- BOURNAZEL, Eric; VIVIEN, Germaine; and GOUNELLE Max, *Les grandes dates de l'histoire de France*, Paris, Larousse, 1993.
- BOUYER, Christian, *Dictionnaire des reines de France*, Paris, Perrin, 1992.
- "Nouvelle histoire de la France médiévale" collection, Paris, Seuil, Points histoire, Vols. 1 to 5, 1990.
- EGINHARD, *Vie de Charlemagne*, trans. by Louis Halphen, Paris, Les Belles Lettres, 1967.
- FAVIER, Jean (Dir.) *Chronique de la France et des Français*, Paris, Larousse, 1987.
- FAVIER, Jean, *Dictionnaire de la France médiévale*, Paris, Fayard, 1993.
- GEARY Patrick J., *Le monde mérovingien. Naissance de la France*, Paris, Flammarion, "Histoires", 1989.
- LEJEUNE, Paule, *Les reines de France*, Paris, Vernal-Philippe Lebaud, 1989.
- LEWIS Andrew, *Le sang royal. La famille capétienne et l'Etat, France Xe-XIVe siècles*, Paris, Gallimard, "Bibliothèque des histories", 1986.
- MAUREPAS, Arnaud de; ROBERT, Hervé; THIBAULT, Pierre, *Les grands hommes d'Etat de l'histoire de France*, Paris, Larousse, "Essentiels", 1989.
- MOURRE Michel (Dir.), *Dictionnaire encyclopédique d'histoire*, 8 volumes, Paris, Bordas, 2nd edition, 1989.
- RICHE, Pierre, *Les Carolingiens, une famille qui fit l'Europe*, paris, Hachette-Littérature, 1983.
- SIRJEAN, Gaston, *Encyclopédie généalogique des maison souveraines du monde*, Paris, Ed. Sirjean, 3 volumes, 1959-1963.
- SONNET, Martine; CHARMASSON, Thérèse; and LELORRAIN Anne-Marie, *Chronologie de l'histoire de France*, Paris, P.U.F., 1994.
- Abbé SUGER, *Vie de Louis VI le Gros,* trans. by Henri Waquet, Paris, Les Belles Lettres, 1964.
- TULARD, Jean (Dir.), *Dictionnaire Napoléon*, Paris, Fayard, 1989.
- VAN KERREBROUCK, Patrick (Dir.), *Nouvelle histoire généalogique de l'auguste maison de France*, Villeneuve d'Ascq, 3 volumes, 1990-1993.

© 2002 Editions Jean-Paul GISSEROT. Ce livre a été imprimé et façonné par Pollina
85400 Luçon N°L98270
Imprimé en France

THE MEROVINGIANS

The first dynasty of Frankish kings reigned over Gaul from 481 to 751 A.D. It gets its name from Merovech, Clovis' grandfather. The founder of the dynasty was Clovis I, King from 481 to 511 A.D, who, thanks to his many victories, was the first King of all the Franks.

Since Germanic tradition demanded that a kingdom be divided between the heirs, Clovis' kingdom was later split up and, over the 6th century, three kingdoms gradually came into being – Neustria, Austrasia and Burgundy. They engaged in a long power struggle. The kingdom of the Franks was only reunified for short periods, during the reigns of Chlotar I (558-561), Chlotar II (613-629) and Dagobert I (632-639).

After 639 A.D, the Merovingian monarchy swiftly fell into a decline and real power passed to the Mayors of the Palace who succeeded in making their positions hereditary in Austrasia, through the Pippinides dynasty. This was the period of the "Sluggard Kings". Eventually, in 751 A.D, the Mayor of the Palace Pepin the Short removed the last Merovingian King, Childeric III from power and seized the throne. This marked the end of the first royal dynasty.

Brunehault's death (613)

THE MEROVINGIAN DYNASTY

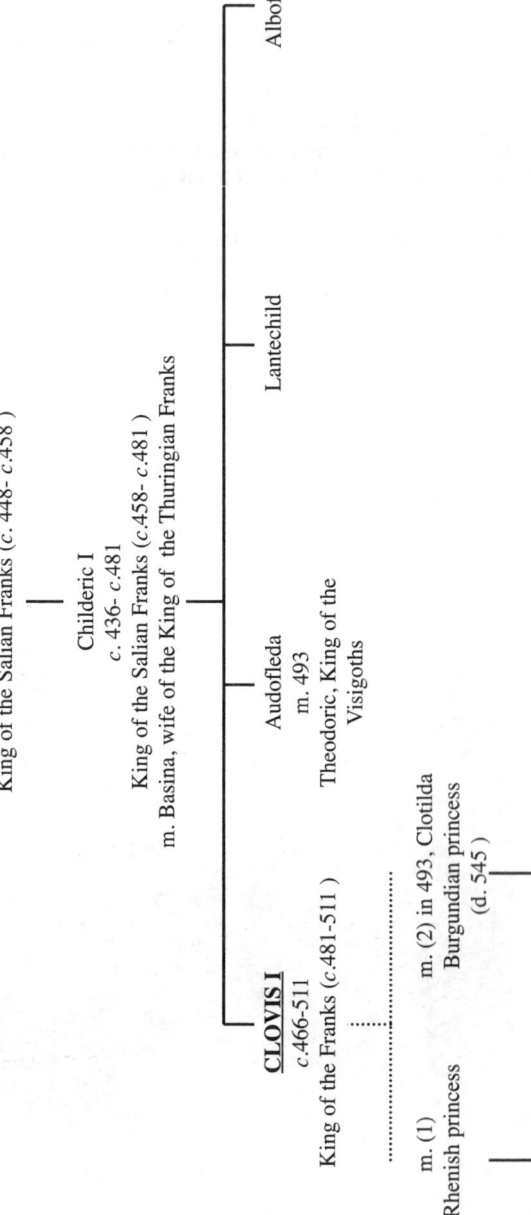

Merovech
died c. 458
King of the Salian Franks (c. 448- c.458)

Childeric I
c. 436- c.481
King of the Salian Franks (c.458- c.481)
m. Basina, wife of the King of the Thuringian Franks

Albofleda

Lantechild

Audofleda
m. 493
Theodoric, King of the Visigoths

CLOVIS I
c.466-511
King of the Franks (c.481-511)

m. (1)
Rhenish princess

m. (2) in 493, Clotilda
Burgundian princess
(d. 545)

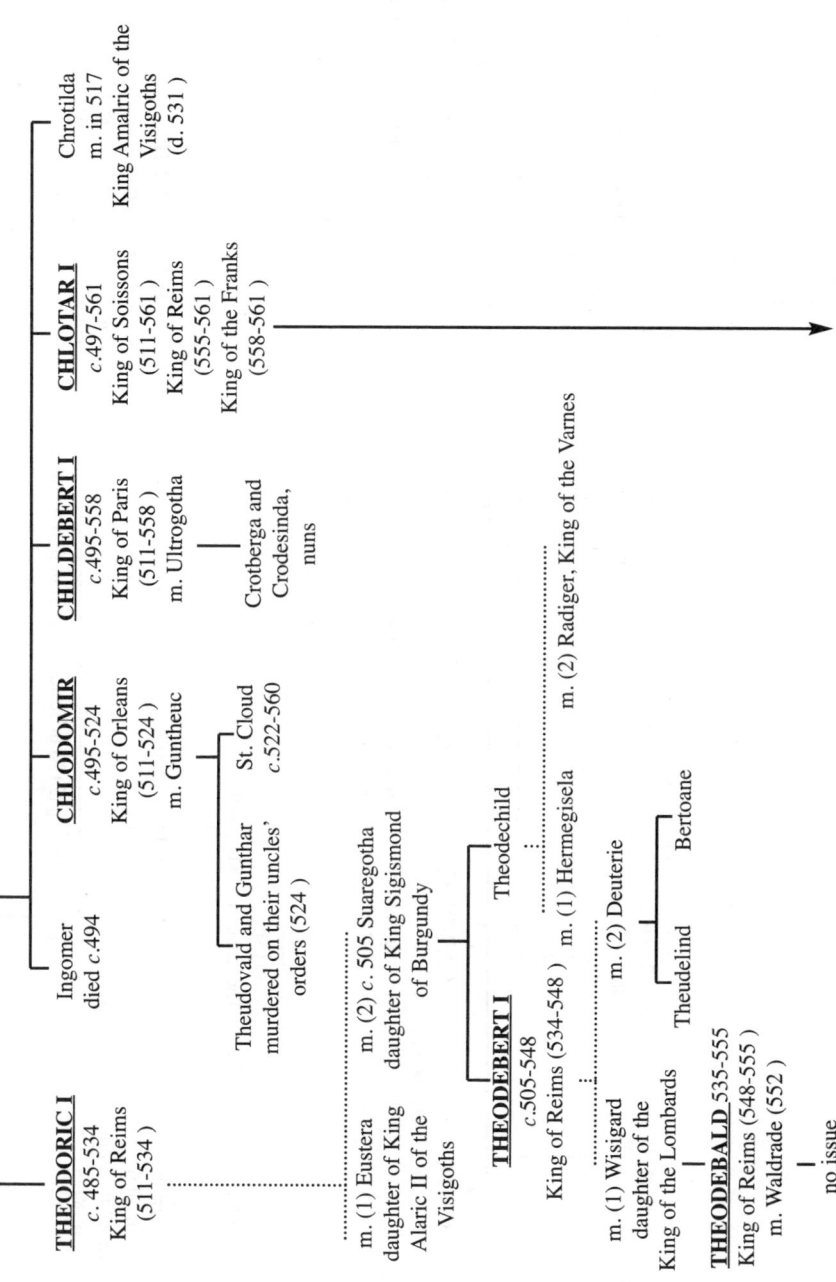

THEODORIC I
c. 485-534
King of Reims
(511-534)

Ingomer
died *c.* 494

CHLODOMIR
c. 495-524
King of Orleans
(511-524)
m. Guntheuc

CHILDEBERT I
c. 495-558
King of Paris
(511-558)
m. Ultrogotha

CHLOTAR I
c. 497-561
King of Soissons
(511-561)
King of Reims
(555-561)
King of the Franks
(558-561)

Chrotilda
m. in 517
King Amalric of the
Visigoths
(d. 531)

Theudovald and Gunthar
murdered on their uncles'
orders (524)

St. Cloud
c. 522-560

Crotberga and
Crodesinda,
nuns

m. (1) Eustera
daughter of King
Alaric II of the
Visigoths

m. (2) *c.* 505 Suaregotha
daughter of King Sigismond
of Burgundy

Theodechild

m. (1) Hermegisela   m. (2) Radiger, King of the Varnes

THEODEBERT I
c. 505-548
King of Reims (534-548)

m. (2) Deuterie

Theudelind   Bertoane

m. (1) Wisigard
daughter of the
King of the Lombards

THEODEBALD 535-555
King of Reims (548-555)
m. Waldrade (552)

no issue

5

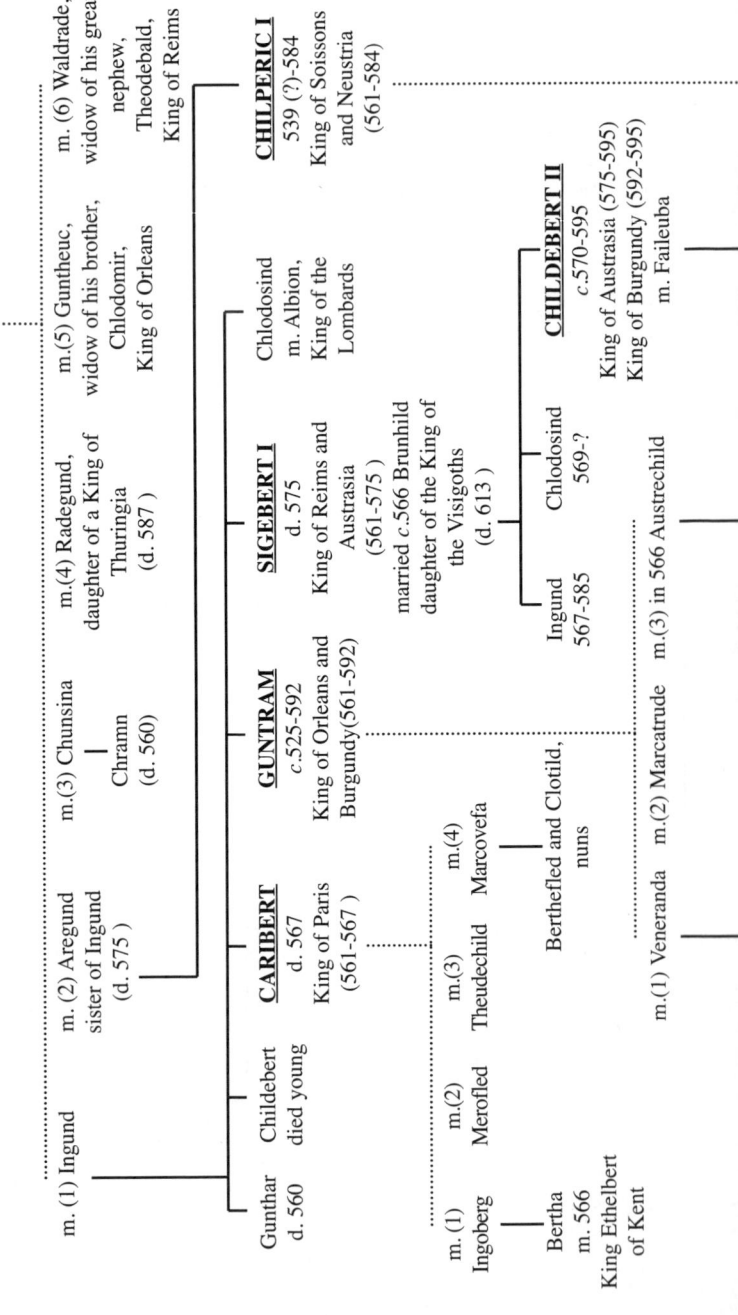

CHLOTAR I

m. (1) Ingund

m. (2) Aregund sister of Ingund (d. 575)

m.(3) Chunsina

m.(4) Radegund, daughter of a King of Thuringia (d. 587)

m.(5) Guntheuc, widow of his brother, Chlodomir, King of Orleans

m. (6) Waldrade, widow of his great-nephew, Theodebald, King of Reims

Chramm (d. 560)

CHILPERIC I 539 (?)-584 King of Soissons and Neustria (561-584)

Chlodosind m. Albion, King of the Lombards

SIGEBERT I d. 575 King of Reims and Austrasia (561-575) married c.566 Brunhild daughter of the King of the Visigoths (d. 613)

GUNTRAM c.525-592 King of Orleans and Burgundy(561-592)

CARIBERT d. 567 King of Paris (561-567)

Guunthar d. 560

Childebert died young

CHILDEBERT II c.570-595 King of Austrasia (575-595) King of Burgundy (592-595) m. Faileuba

Chlodosind 569-?

Ingund 567-585

m.(3) in 566 Austrechild

m.(2) Marcatrude

m.(1) Veneranda

m.(4) Marcovefa

m.(3) Theudechild

Berthefled and Clotild, nuns

m.(2) Merofled

m. (1) Ingoberg

Bertha m. 566 King Ethelbert of Kent

6

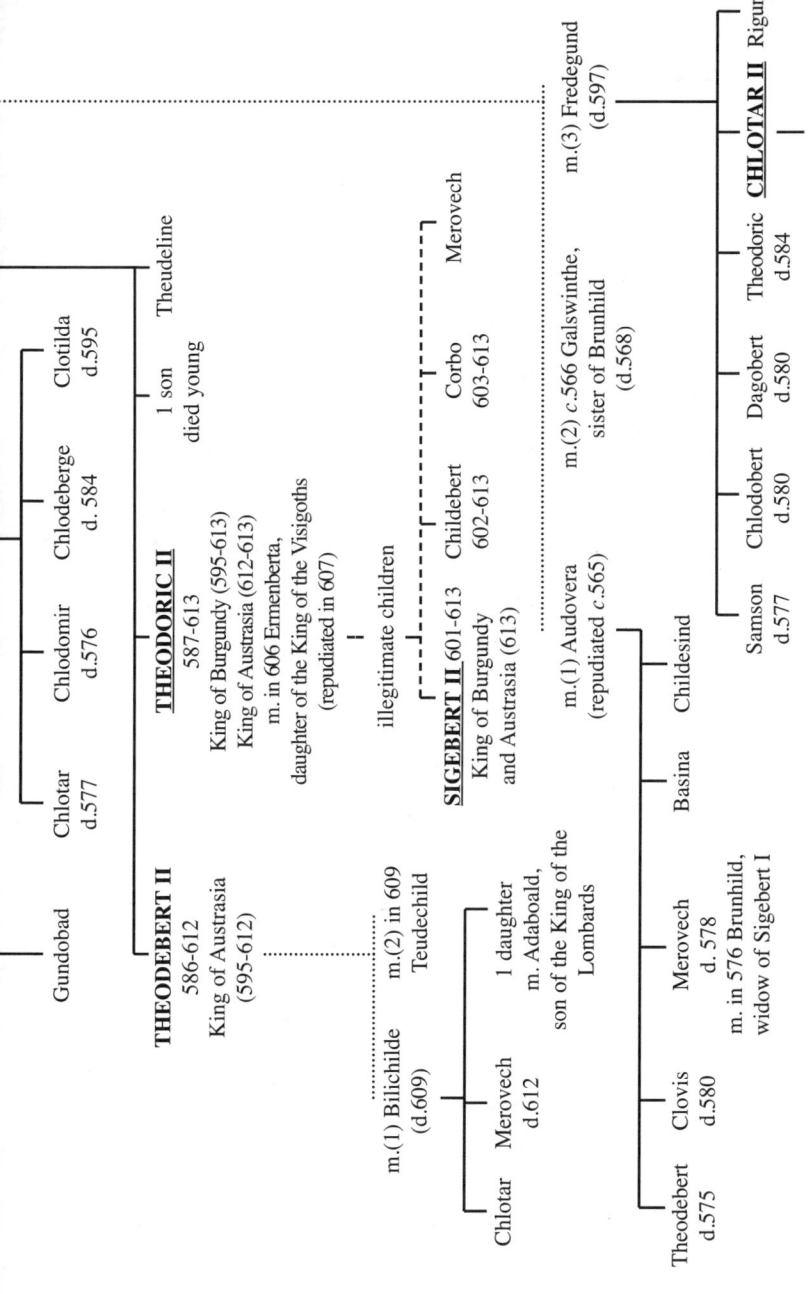

Gundobad

Chlotar d.577   Chlodomir d.576   Chlodeberge d. 584   Clotilda d.595

Theudeline

1 son died young

THEODEBERT II
586-612
King of Austrasia
(595-612)

THEODORIC II
587-613
King of Burgundy (595-613)
King of Austrasia (612-613)
m. in 606 Ermenberta,
daughter of the King of the Visigoths
(repudiated in 607)

illegitimate children

Merovech

Childebert 602-613   Corbo 603-613

m.(1) Bilichilde (d.609)   m.(2) in 609 Teudechild

Chlotar   Merovech d.612

1 daughter m. Adaboald, son of the King of the Lombards

SIGEBERT II 601-613
King of Burgundy
and Austrasia (613)

m.(1) Audovera (repudiated c.565)   m.(2) c.566 Galswinthe, sister of Brunhild (d.568)   m.(3) Fredegund (d.597)

Theodebert d.575   Clovis d.580   Merovech d. 578 m. in 576 Brunhild, widow of Sigebert I

Basina   Childesind

Samson d.577   Chlodobert d.580   Dagobert d.580   Theodoric d.584   **CHLOTAR II**   Rigunth

7

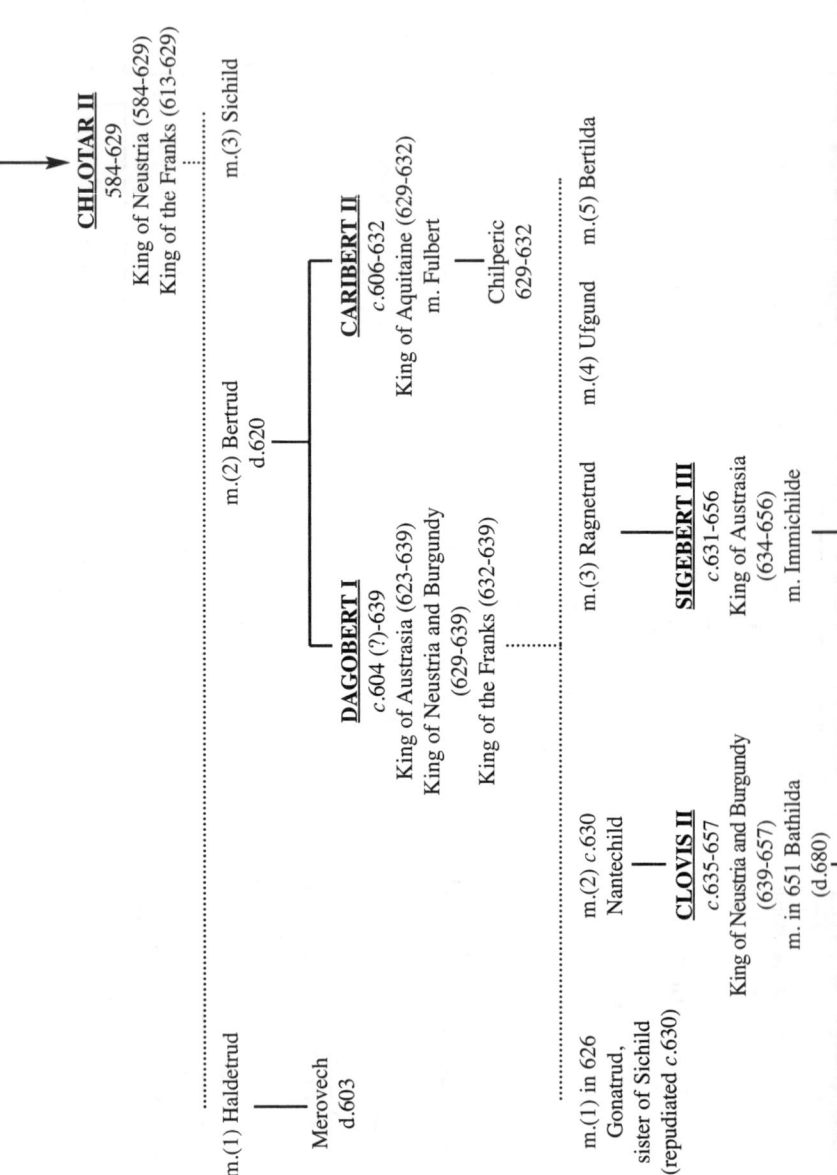

CHLOTAR II
584-629
King of Neustria (584-629)
King of the Franks (613-629)

m.(1) Haldetrud   m.(2) Bertrud   m.(3) Sichild
d.620

Merovech
d.603

DAGOBERT I
c.604 (?)-639
King of Austrasia (623-639)
King of Neustria and Burgundy (629-639)
King of the Franks (632-639)

CARIBERT II
c.606-632
King of Aquitaine (629-632)
m. Fulbert

Chilperic
629-632

m.(1) in 626   m.(2) c.630   m.(3) Ragnetrud   m.(4) Ufgund   m.(5) Bertilda
Gonatrud,   Nantechild
sister of Sichild,
(repudiated c.630)

CLOVIS II
c.635-657
King of Neustria and Burgundy (639-657)
m. in 651 Bathilda (d.680)

SIGEBERT III
c.631-656
King of Austrasia (634-656)
m. Immichilde

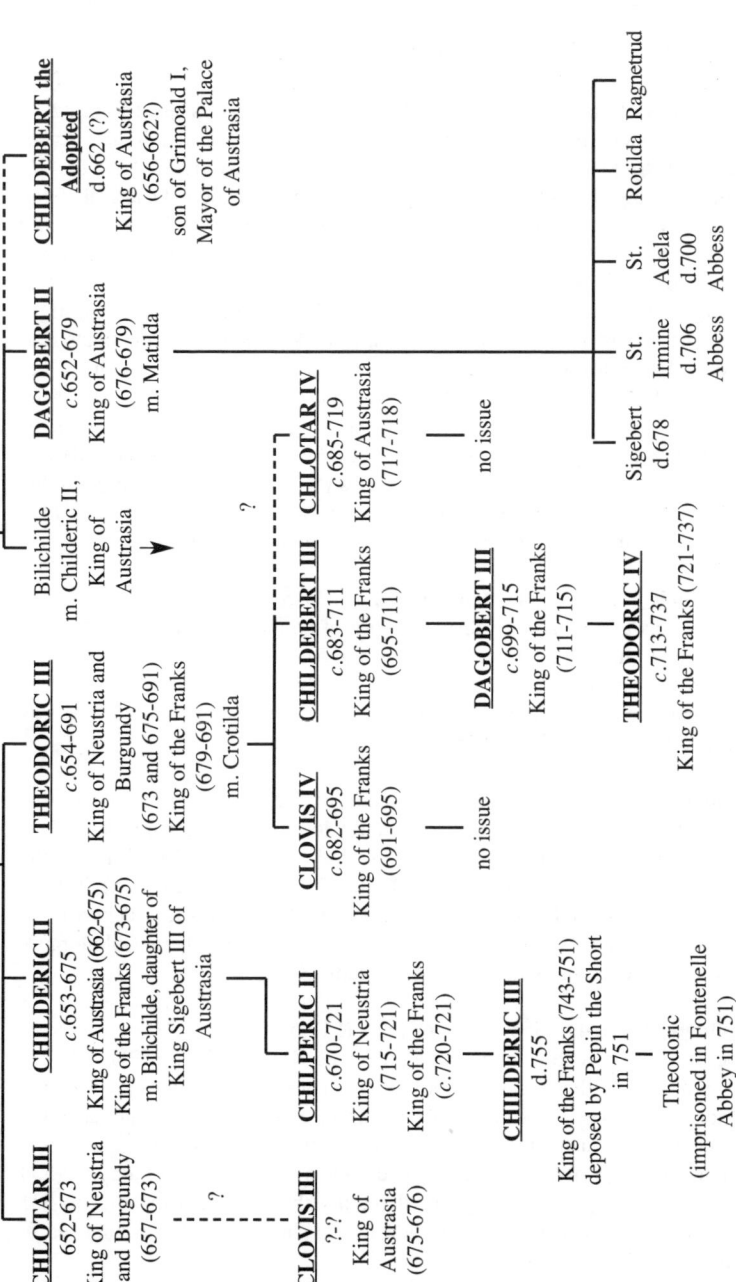

CHLOTAR III
652-673
King of Neustria
and Burgundy
(657-673)

CLOVIS III
?-?
King of
Austrasia
(675-676)

CHILDERIC II
c.653-675
King of Austrasia (662-675)
King of the Franks (673-675)
m. Bilichilde, daughter of
King Sigebert III of
Austrasia

CHILPERIC II
c.670-721
King of Neustria
(715-721)
King of the Franks
(c.720-721)

CHILDERIC III
d.755
King of the Franks (743-751)
deposed by Pepin the Short
in 751
—
Theodoric
(imprisoned in Fontenelle
Abbey in 751)

THEODORIC III
c.654-691
King of Neustria and
Burgundy
(673 and 675-691)
King of the Franks
(679-691)
m. Crotilda

CLOVIS IV
c.682-695
King of the Franks
(691-695)
—
no issue

CHILDEBERT III
c.683-711
King of the Franks
(695-711)

DAGOBERT III
c.699-715
King of the Franks
(711-715)

THEODORIC IV
c.713-737
King of the Franks (721-737)

Bilichilde
m. Childeric II,
King of Austrasia →

?

CHLOTAR IV
c.685-719
King of Austrasia
(717-718)
—
no issue

DAGOBERT II
c.652-679
King of Austrasia
(676-679)
m. Matilda

**CHILDEBERT the
Adopted**
d.662 (?)
King of Austrasia
(656-662?)
son of Grimoald I,
Mayor of the Palace
of Austrasia

Sigebert
d.678

St.
Irmine
d.706
Abbess

St.
Adela
d.700
Abbess

Rotilda Ragnetrud

END OF THE MEROVINGIAN DYNASTY

9

Clovis I (c. 466-511). King of the Franks (c. 481-511)

Clovis, the son of Childeric I and Basina, succeeded his father as King of the Salian Franks of Tournai c. 481 A.D. Much of his reign was spent fighting, in an effort to extend his kingdom. In 486, he defeated Syagrius, the last representative of Rome, near Soissons. He defeated the Alemanni in Tolbiac in 496, vanquished King Gondebaud of Burgundy near Dijon c. 500 A.D. and defeated and killed Alaric II, King of the Visigoths, in Vouillé in 507 A.D. He gradually unified the kingdom of the Franks until it covered nearly all of Gaul, from the Pyrenees to the Rhine. Clovis married a Roman Catholic Burgundian princess, Clotilda, in 493 and this brought him the support of the bishops in his fight against the Aryan heresy followed by the leaders of the Burgundians and Visigoths. Under his wife's influence, Clovis had himself baptised with several thousand of his soldiers (c. 498). His conversion brought him the support of the Catholics who saw him as the only legitimate king and he then instigated policies jointly with the Church. Clovis was not only the conqueror of the Aryans; he was also the protector of new monasteries (St. Genevieve's Abbey). On his death in 511, in accordance with Germanic tradition, his kingdom was divided between his four sons Theodoric, Chlodomir, Childebert and Chlotar.

Theodoric I (c. 485-534). King of Reims (511-534).

Theodoric was Clovis I's eldest son, born of an unknown Rhenish princess. He received a share of his father's kingdom in 511 A.D. with Reims as its capital. With his brothers, he took part in a number of campaigns against the Burgundians and conquered Thuringia in 531. On his death in 534 A.D, he was succeeded by his son, Theodebert I.

Chlodomir (c. 495-524). King of Orléans. (511-524).

Chlodomir, the second son of Clovis and Clotilda, became King of Orléans upon his father's death in 511 A.D. Chlodomir was killed fighting the Burgundians with his brothers, at the Battle of Vézeronce (524 A.D.). Two of his sons, Theobald and Gontaire, were killed by their uncles, Childebert I and Chlotar I, who then shared the kingdom of Orléans between them. Chlodomir's third son succeeded in escaping and he became St. Cloud.

Childebert I (c. 495-558). King of Paris (511-558).

The third son of Clovis and Clotilda became King of Paris in 511 A.D. He was involved in the assassination of the sons of his deceased brother, Chlodomir, and took Chartres and Orléans in 524 A.D. With Chlotar I and Theodebert I, he instigated an increasing number of campaigns against the Burgundians and, when they were quelled, took over part of their kingdom (534 A.D). He also fought the Visigoths, defeating their leader, Amalaric, in 531 A.D. When he died without a male heir in 558, his kingdom was annexed to that of his brother, Chlotar I.

Chlotar I (c. 497-561). King of Soissons (511-561), King of Reims (555-561), King of the Franks (558-561).

Clovis I's fourth son became King of Soissons in 511 A.D. when the kingdom of the Franks was divided up. With his brothers, he fought the Burgundians and ordered the assassination of two of Chlomodir's sons before taking over part of Chlodomir's erstwhile kingdom (524 A.D). He conquered Thuringia in 531 A.D. with Theodoric I. When his grand-nephew, Theodebald, King of Reims, died in 555 A.D, he took over Theodebald's kingdom then did the same thing in 558 on the death of his brother, Childebert I. In doing so, he became sole ruler of all the Frankish states. However, the unity of the Frankish kingdom lasted only a short time. On Chlotar I's death, it was again divided between his four sons.

Theodebert I (c. 505-548). King of Reims (534-548).

Theodebert, Clovis I's grandson, succeeded his father, Theodoric I, in 534 A.D. as King of Reims. With his uncles, he succeeded in conquering the Burgundian kingdom. He forced the Ostrogoth king, Vitiges, to hand over Provence then conquered Northern Italy in 539 A.D. He was succeeded by his son, Theodebald.

Theodebald (535-555). King of Reims (548-555).

Theodebert I's son and heir became King of Reims in 548, at the age of thirteen. However, his poor health prevented him from playing an effective role and he died, childless, at the age of twenty. His kingdom was then annexed to that of Chlotar I, the last surviving son of Clovis I.

Caribert (?-567). King of Paris (561-567).

Chlotar I's eldest son became king of Western Gaul, with Paris as its capital, in 561 A.D. He was a bigamist and excommunicated. He died in 567, leaving only daughters, and his kingdom was divided between his brothers.

Guntram (c. 525-592). King of Orléans and Burgundy (561-592).

Chlotar I's second son became King of Orléans and Burgundy in 561 A.D. He tried to put a halt to the dissension between his brothers, Sigebert I and Chilperic I, who began warring in 570 A.D. He instigated campaigns against the Bretons, Basques and Visigoths. Having no male heir, he adopted his nephew, Childebert II, King of Austrasia, who became his successor under the terms of the Treaty of Andelot (587 A.D). He was generous towards churches and abbeys and was beatified.

Sigebert I (?-575). King of Reims and Austrasia (561-575).

Chlotar I's third son received Austrasia, with Reims as its capital, as his inheritance. He launched several expeditions against the Avars. In 566 A.D, he married Brunhild, daughter of the King of the Visigoths, while his brother, Chilperic I, married her sister, Galswinthe. The latter's murder in 568 A.D. brought the brothers into conflict. Sigebert I succeeded in conquering almost all

Chilperic I's kingdom. Just as he had taken Paris and been proclaimed King of Neustria, he was assassinated on the orders of Fredegund, his brother's new wife. He was succeeded by his son, Childebert II.

Chilperic I (539?-584). King of Soissons and Neustria (561-584).

Chlotar I's fourth son received the kingdom of Soissons when his father died. Chilperic was a very complex person. He was literate and a patron of the performing arts but was also a tyrant who was fond of debauchery. In 566 A.D, he married Galswinthe, the sister of Brunhild, his brother Sigebert I's wife. However he had her strangled by Fredegund whom he took as his second spouse (568 A.D.). The assassination led to a long war between the two kingdoms. Chilperic I was defeated by the Austrasians in 575 A.D. but was saved by the death of his brother. He died in mysterious circumstances in his villa in Chelles in 584 A.D. and was succeeded by his son, Chlotar II.

Childebert II (c. 570-595). King of Austrasia (575-595), King of Burgundy (592-595).

Childebert, the son of Sigebert I and Brunhild, succeeded his father on the throne of Austrasia at the age of five, in 575 A.D, but because of his young age remained under his mother's tutelage. He was adopted by his uncle, Guntram, King of Burgundy, whom he succeeded in 592 A.D. under the terms of the Treaty of Andelot (587 A.D.), thereby uniting Austrasia, Burgundy and the Orléans and Paris regions. He died shortly afterwards, in 595 A.D, possibly as a result of poisoning by his wife Faileuba. His states were divided between his two sons, Theodebert II and Theodoric II.

Chlotar II (584-629). King of Neustria (584-629), King of the Franks (613-629).

Chlotar, the son of Chilperic I and Fredegund, was only a few months old when his father was murdered and his mother acted as Regent in Neustria until 597 A.D. She defended the kingdom against the King of Austrasia, Childebert II, but Chlotar II was defeated by Childebert's sons, Theodebert II and Theodoric II in 604 A.D. and lost almost all his territory. However, after their deaths in 612 and 613, he had Brunhild and King Sigebert II executed and took over their kingdoms, becoming sole King of the Franks. His reign was a period of prosperity marked by the emergence of landed gentry. Chlotar II appointed a Mayor of the Palace to head each of the three kingdoms (Neustria, Austrasia and Burgundy). In 614 A.D, he convened a meeting of leading noblemen and a council in Paris and published an Edict of Peace.

Theodebert II (586-612). King of Austrasia (595-612).

Theodebert was the son and heir of Childebert II. He received the kingdom of Austrasia on the death of his father in 595 A.D. but remained under the domination of his grandmother, Brunhild, whom he succeeded in removing from his Court in 599 A.D. With his brother, Theodoric II, he reinstigated the struggle against the kingdom of Neustria and, once they had defeated Chlotar II, they took over much of his territory (600-604). However, the two brothers then took up arms against each other. Theodebert II was defeated in Toul and Tolbiac in 612 A.D. He was shut up in a monastery on the orders of his grandmother, Brunhild, and murdered with his son, Mérovée.

Theodoric II (587-613). King of Burgundy (595-613), King of Austrasia (612-613).

Childebert's second son received the kingdoms of Orléans and Burgundy on his father's death in 595 A.D. He reigned under the control of his grandmother, Brunhild, who had been exiled from Austrasia by his brother, Theodebert II. The two brothers fought and defeated King Chlotar II of Neustria (604 A.D). Then, with Brunhild's encouragement, Theodoric turned on his brother, defeating him in Toul and Tolbiac in 612 A.D. and taking over the kingdom of Austrasia.

Sigebert II (601-613). King of Burgundy and Austrasia (613).

Sigebert, illegitimate son of Theodoric II, succeeded his father in 613 A.D. but the Mayor of the Palace, fearing that he would be manipulated by his great-grandmother, Brunhild, because of his young age, handed them both over to Chlotar II, King of Neustria, who had them murdered a few months later. Sigebert II's kingdom was then annexed to Neustria.

Dagobert I (c. 604?-639). King of Austrasia (623-639), King of Neustria and Burgundy (629-639), King of the Franks (632-639).

Dagobert, the eldest son of Chlotar II and Bertrude, received the kingdom of Austrasia from his father in 623 A.D, under the control of Bishop Arnoul of Metz. When Chlotar II died in 629 A.D, Dagobert I received Neustria and Burgundy, leaving Aquitaine for his brother, Caribert II. When Caribert died in 632 A.D, Dagobert reunited the Frankish kingdom and took Paris as its capital. He was the last great Merovingian king, imposing his authority on the aristocracy and attracting talented counsellors such as Ely or Didier. He defeated the Basques, Bretons, Visigoths and Lombards but failed to quell the Slavs and he signed a peace treaty with the Byzantine Emperor, Heraklius, in 631 A.D. He received the full backing of the Catholic Church for he continued to convert pagans and create or extend numerous monasteries (e.g. Saint-Denis). In 634 A.D, he appointed his son, Sigebert III, King of Austrasia; this shows a certain push for independence on the part of the Austrasian people. Then, before his death, he took steps to organise his succession by giving Neustria and Burgundy to his other son, Clovis II. It was during his reign that two families were united – the family of Pepin, Mayor of the Palace in Austrasia, and the family of Bishop Arnoul of Metz who founded the Carolingian dynasty.

Caribert II (c. 606-632). King of Aquitaine (629-632).

Caribert, the son of Chlotar II and brother of Dagobert I, received the kingdom of Aquitaine from Dagobert upon the death of their father. He reigned there for three years.

Sigebert III (c. 631-656). King of Austrasia (634-656).

Sigebert, Dagobert I's son, was appointed King of Austrasia in 634 A.D. by his father and remained so after the latter's death. However, he put the government of his territory in the hands of to Bishop Cunibert of Cologne and Duke Adalgesil of Austrasia and, later, appointed Pippin of Landen and Grimoald as Mayors of the Palace. He founded Ludon Monastery in the Ardenne Forest. In 643 A.D, Sigebert III, who had no children, adopted Grimoald's son, Childebert. However, c. 652, Sigebert finally had a son, Dagobert II, who was exiled by Grimoald when the king died in 656 A.D. so that Grimoald's own son could accede to the throne.

Clovis II (c. 635-657). King of Neustria and Burgundy (639-657).

Clovis, another of Dagobert's sons, succeeded him in 639 A.D. as monarch of the kingdom of Neustria and Burgundy, under the control of his mother, Nantechilde, and two successive Mayors of the Palace, Aega and Erchinoald. In 651 A.D, he married the future St. Bathilda. He was succeeded by his son, Chlotar III.

Childebert the Adopted (?-662?). King of Austrasia (656-662?).

Childebert was the son of Grimoald, Mayor of the Palace of Austrasia, but was adopted by King Sigebert III in 643 A.D. and placed on the throne in 656 A.D. by his own father, in place of Dagobert II, the son of the deceased monarch, who was forced into exile. Childebert and his father, Grimoald, were then eliminated by the Elders of Neustria, probably in 662 A.D.

Chlotar III (652-673). King of Neustria and Burgundy (657-673).

When Clovis II died in 657 A.D, his eldest son, Chlotar, was given the kingdom of Neustria and Burgundy but because of his young age reigned under the control of his mother, Bathilda. Ebroin, who became Mayor of the Palace in 658 A.D, eventually seized total power.

Childeric II (c. 653-675). King of Austrasia (662-675), King of the Franks (673-675).

Childeric was the second son of Clovis II, and the brother of Chlotar III, King of Neustria and Burgundy. He became King of Austrasia in 662 A.D. after the elimination of Childebert the Adopted and his father, Grimoald, Mayor of the Palace. He reigned under the control of his aunt, Immichilde. In 673 A.D, he removed King Theodoric III of Neustria and Burgundy from power and placed all the Frankish states under his own authority. He was assassinated in 675 A.D. by the Elders of Neustria in Lognes Forest.

Theodoric III (c. 654-691). King of Neustria and Burgundy (673 and 675-691), King of the Franks (679-691).

Clovis II's third son acceded to the throne of Neustria and Burgundy in 673 A.D. after the death of his brother, Chlotar III. Theodoric was made king by Ebroin, Mayor of the Palace, but was almost immediately overthrown by

Childeric II, King of Austrasia, at the instigation of the kingdom's leading noblemen. Theodoric was shut up in Saint-Denis. When Childeric II died in 675, Theodoric III was re-established on the throne but reigned under Ebroin's control. The death of King Dagobert II of Austrasia in 679 A.D. made him King of all the Franks. Ebroin's murder in 680 dealt a fatal blow to Neustria and its troops were defeated at Tertry in 687 A.D. by Pippin of Heristal, Mayor of the Palace of Austrasia. Government of the three kingdoms then passed into Pippin's hands although he left Theodoric on the throne.

Clovis III (? - ?). King of Austrasia (675-676).
When Childeric II of Austrasia died in 675, Clovis III mounted the throne. He was presented as Chlotar III's son but neither his genealogy nor his existence have ever been proven and he only reigned for one year.

Dagobert II (c. 652-679). King of Austrasia (676-679).
Dagobert II was exiled to an Irish monastery by Grimoald, Mayor of the Palace, in 656 A.D. upon the death of his father, Sigebert III. He was recalled to the throne in 676 A.D. but was assassinated three years later.

Clovis IV (c. 682-695). King of the Franks (691-695).
Theodoric III's eldest son succeeded him in 691 A.D. on the throne of all three kingdoms but he left the Mayor of the Palace, Pippin of Heristal, to govern the countries. He died shortly afterwards, at the age of thirteen.

Childebert III (c. 683-711). King of the Franks (695-711).
Theodoric III's second son became King of the Franks in 695 A.D. on the death of his brother, Clovis IV, but also reigned under the control of Pippin of Heristal, Mayor of the Palace. Pippin launched a number of campaigns against the Friesians and Alemanni. When Childebert III died, he was succeeded by his son, Dagobert III.

Dagobert III (c. 699-715). King of the Franks (711-715).
Dagobert, the son of Childebert III, succeeded his father at the head of the three Frankish kingdoms in 711 A.D, at the age of twelve. However, power still lay in the hands of the Mayor of the Palace, Pippin of Heristal, who died in 714 A.D.

Chilperic II (c. 670-721). King of Neustria (715-721), King of the Franks (c. 720-721).
Chilperic II, Childeric II's son, was placed on the throne of Neustria in 715 A.D. on the death of Dagobert III by Rainfroi, Mayor of the Palace, in an effort to counter the influence of Charles Martel, Mayor of the Palace in Austrasia. Charles Martel, however, defeated the Neustrians in 717 and 719 and Chilperic II was obliged to acknowledge him as Mayor of the Palace in Neustria. Charles Martel then recognised Chilperic as King of the Franks c. 720 A.D.

Chlotar IV (c. 685-719). King of Austrasia (717-718).

This Merovingian king, who has never been proven to be the son of Theodoric III, was placed on the throne of Austrasia by Charles Martel, Mayor of the Palace, in 717 A.D. to counter King Chilperic II of Neustria.

Theodoric IV (c. 713-737). King of the Franks (721-737).

Although Theodoric, Dagobert III's son, succeeded Chilperic II in 721 A.D, he reigned under the total control of Charles Martel, Mayor of the Palace. The latter launched countless campaigns against the Friesians and Saxons, forced Thuringia and Bavaria to surrender and halted the Saracen advance in Poitiers (732 A.D). When Theodoric IV died, Charles Martel left the Merovingian throne vacant. He himself died in 741 A.D.

Childeric III (? – 755). King of the Franks (743-751).

Childeric, the son of Chilperic II, entered holy orders but became King of the Franks in 743 A.D. after the throne had been left vacant for six years. He was placed on the throne by Pepin the Short and Carloman, both of them Mayors of the Palace and both Charles Martel's sons and successors. Childeric was the last Merovingian king. He was deposed by Pepin the Short in 751 A.D. and was imprisoned, on Pepin's orders, in Saint-Bertin Abbey where he died a few years later. Meanwhile, Pepin ruled in his place. Childeric's son, Theodoric, was imprisoned in Fontenelle Abbey. This marked the end of the Merovingian dynasty.

Battle of Poitiers (732)

THE PIPPINIDS

This dynasty gets its name from Pepin (or Pippin) the Short, Mayor of the Palace then King of the Franks (751-768). It derived from the union of two aristocratic Frankish families in Austrasia. Members of the family succeeded each other as Mayors of the Palace from the 7th century on, beginning with Pippin of Landen. The rise of the Pippinids coincided with a weakening of the Merovingian monarchy, through Pepin of Heristal, Charles Martel and Pepin the Short.

Pepin the Short, who was assured of support from the papacy, overthrew the last Merovingian king, Childeric III, in 751 A.D. and had himself declared King of the Franks by an assembly of noblemen. His son, Charlemagne, gave his name to the Carolingian dynasty.

THE PIPPINID DYNASTY
(ancestors of Pepin the Short)

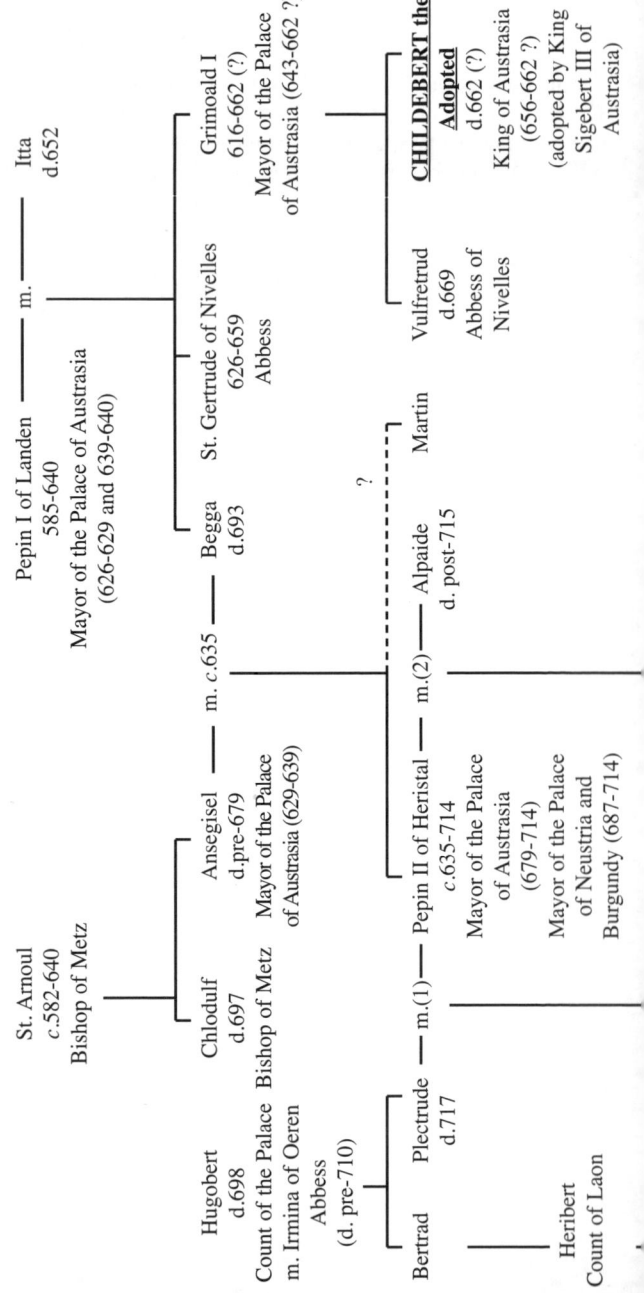

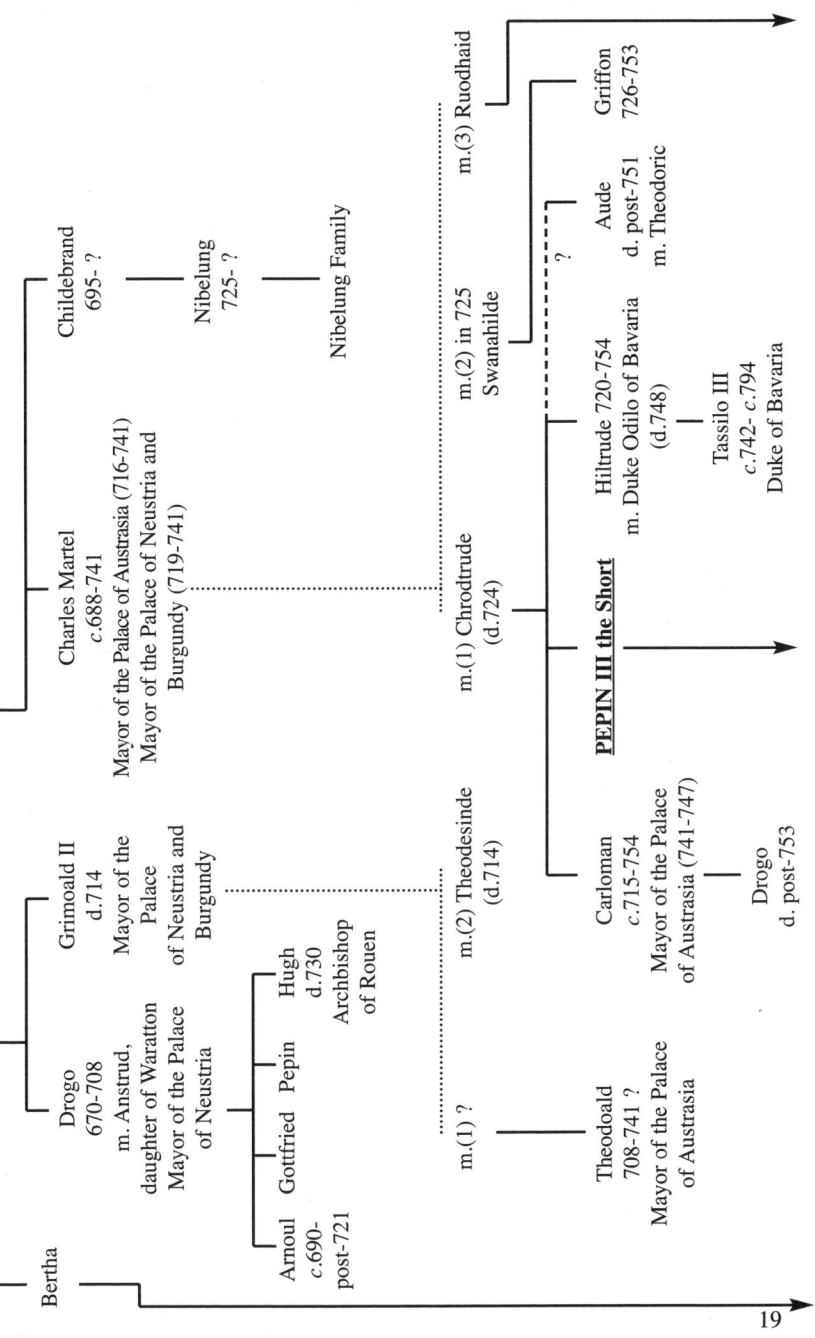

Bertha

Drogo
670-708
m. Anstrud, daughter of Waratton
Mayor of the Palace of Neustria

Arnoul
c.690-
post-721

Gottfried

Pepin

Hugh
d.730
Archbishop
of Rouen

Grimoald II
d.714
Mayor of the
Palace
of Neustria and
Burgundy

m.(1) ?

m.(2) Theodesinde
(d.714)

Theodoald
708-741 ?
Mayor of the Palace
of Austrasia

Charles Martel
c.688-741
Mayor of the Palace of Austrasia (716-741)
Mayor of the Palace of Neustria and
Burgundy (719-741)

Childebrand
695- ?

Nibelung
725- ?

Nibelung Family

m.(1) Chrodtrude
(d.724)

m.(2) in 725 Swanahilde

m.(3) Ruodhaid

Carloman
c.715-754
Mayor of Austrasia (741-747)

Drogo
d. post-753

PEPIN III the Short

Hiltrude 720-754
m. Duke Odilo of Bavaria
(d.748)

Tassilo III
c.742- c.794
Duke of Bavaria

?

Aude
d. post-751
m. Theodoric

Griffon
726-753

19

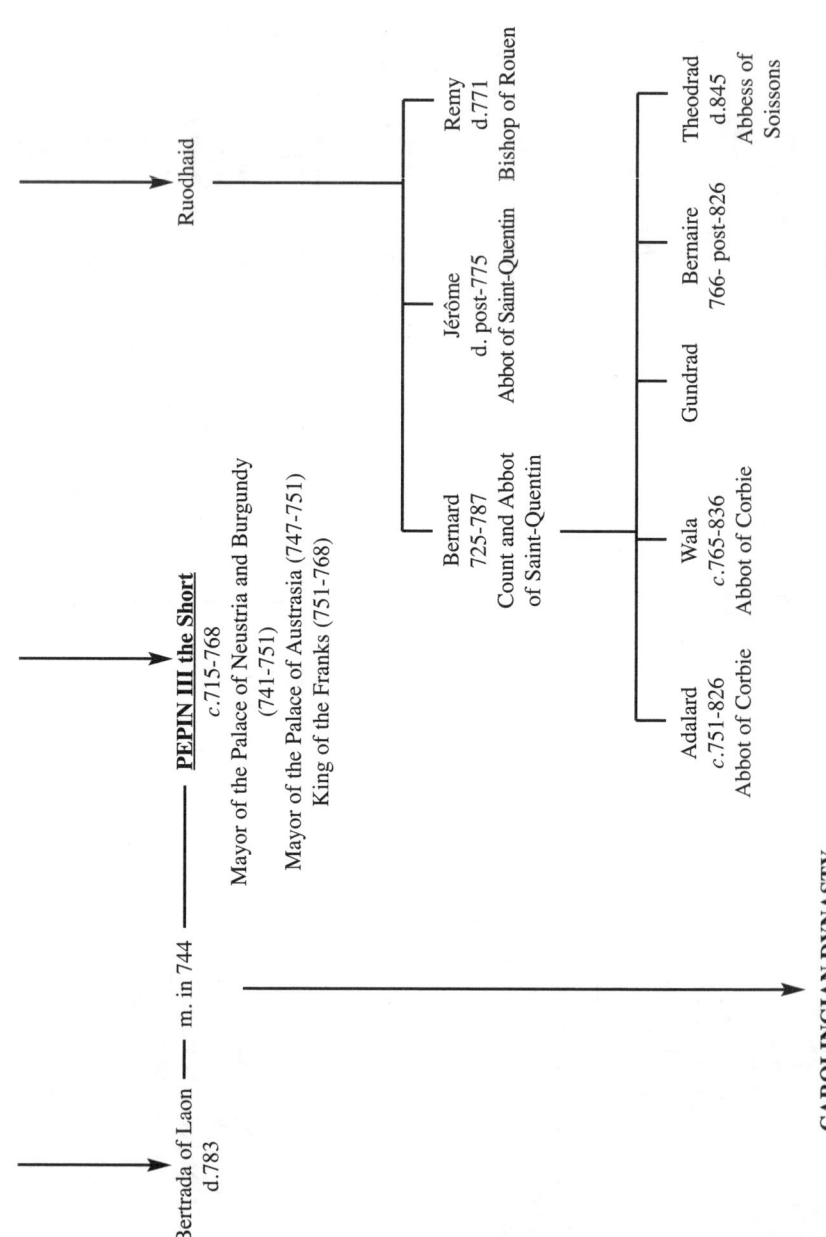

Bertrada of Laon —— m. in 744 ——
d.783

PEPIN III the Short
c.715-768
Mayor of the Palace of Neustria and Burgundy
(741-751)
Mayor of the Palace of Austrasia (747-751)
King of the Franks (751-768)

Ruodhaid

Bernard
725-787
Count and Abbot
of Saint-Quentin

Jérôme
d. post-775
Abbot of Saint-Quentin

Remy
d.771
Bishop of Rouen

Adalard
c.751-826
Abbot of Corbie

Wala
c.765-836
Abbot of Corbie

Gundrad

Bernaire
766- post-826

Theodrad
d.845
Abbess of
Soissons

CAROLINGIAN DYNASTY

Pepin the Short (c. 715-768). King of the Franks (751-768).

Pepin the Short was born in Jupille in Austrasia. He was the grandson of Pippin of Heristal and one of the sons of Charles Martel. Both his forebears were Mayors of the Palace of Austrasia under Merovingian kings. When his father died in 741 A.D, he shared power with his brother, Carloman, and became Mayor of the Palace of Neustria and Burgundy. In 742 A.D, the brothers set a Merovingian monarch back on the throne, Childeric III, thereby ending an interregnum that had lasted since 737 and, by the same occasion, putting an end to a revolt. After his brother Carloman's entry into holy orders in 747 A.D, Pepin the Short also became Mayor of the Palace of Austrasia. Having earlier obtained the support and approval of the Pope in return for his work in reorganising the Frankish Church (after a succession of Councils in 743-747 A.D.), Pepin had the last Merovingian king, Childeric III, shut away in an abbey. He then had himself elected king by the kingdom's leading noblemen. He was crowned by the bishops in 751 A.D. The coronation ceremony was repeated in Saint-Denis by Pope Stephen II in 754 A.D, giving the future Carolingian dynasty legitimacy and divine power. It also marked the alliance between the papacy and the Frankish monarchy. The new king, Pepin the Short, immediately strengthened the alliance by organising two expeditions in Italy against the Lombards who were posing a threat to the Pope (754 and 756 A.D). He took the Pentapole from them, as well as the exarchate of Ravenna which he gifted to the Holy See. These territories were to form the basis of the future Papal States. He also waged war against the Saxons, whom he defeated in 758 A.D, brought Bavaria to heel, won Septimania back from the Saracens in 759 A.D, and quelled the revolt in Aquitaine by launching several campaigns between 760 and 768. Pepin the Short died in 758 A.D. and his kingdom was divided between his two sons, Charlemagne and Carloman.

LESESTRE.

Charlemagne visiting a school

THE CAROLINGIANS

This dynasty of kings and emperors reigned over part of Western Europe from the middle of the 8th century to the 10th century. It gets its name from its most illustrious member, Charlemagne.

The founder of the dynasty was Pepin the Short who put an end to the Merovingian dynasty in 751 A.D. by removing Childeric III from the throne and having himself proclaimed King of the Franks.

His son, Charlemagne, continued to conquer territories and unified much of Western Europe before having himself crowned Holy Roman Emperor in 800 A.D. However, in 843 A.D, the empire was divided between Charlemagne's three grandsons and its western part produced the first French territory, *Francia occidentalis*. It was this country which was ruled by a succession of Carolingian kings from Charles the Bald to Louis V, over a period of 150 years.

The 10th century saw the weakening of the Carolingian monarchy which was incapable of combating the division of the kingdom of France into principalities and unable to fight off foreign invasions. On several occasions, the kingdom's leading noblemen elected a king from the Robertian family (888 to 898 A.D. and 922 to 936 A.D). The death of King Louis V the Lazy in 987 A.D. marked the end of the French branch of the Carolingian dynasty.

Charlemagne crowned Holy Roman Emperor (800)

THE CAROLINGIAN DYNASTY

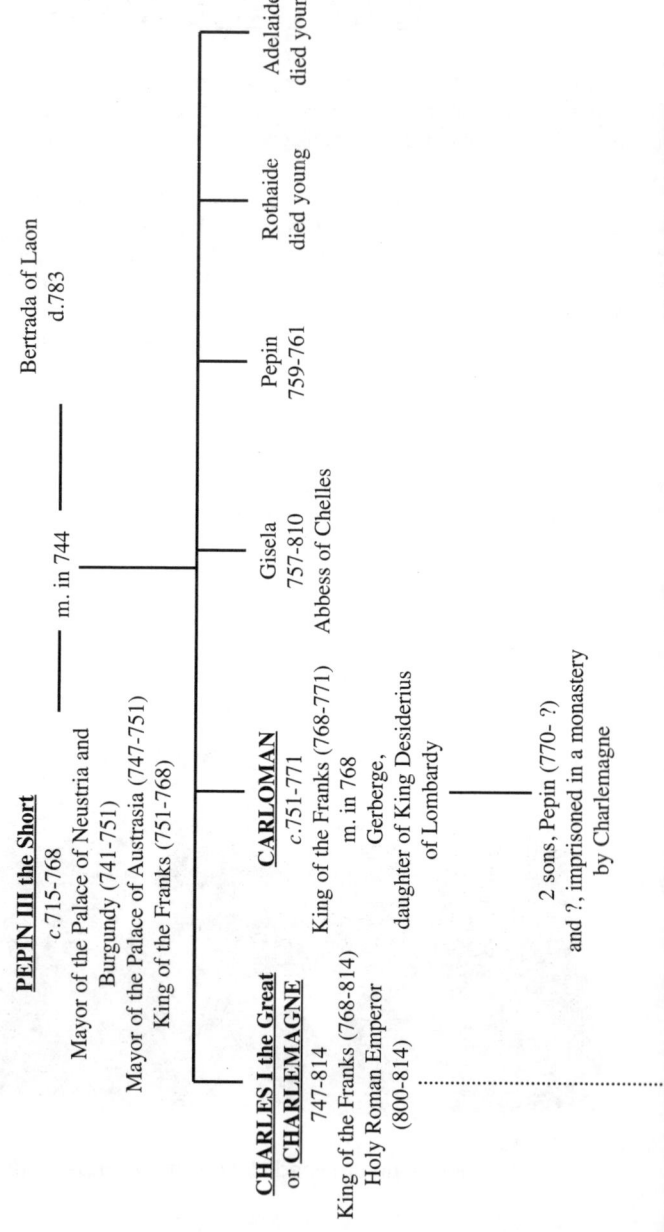

PEPIN III the Short
c.715-768
Mayor of the Palace of Neustria and
Burgundy (741-751)
Mayor of the Palace of Austrasia (747-751)
King of the Franks (751-768)

———— m. in 744 ————

Bertrada of Laon
d.783

CARLOMAN
c.751-771
King of the Franks (768-771)
m. in 768
Gerberge,
daughter of King Desiderius
of Lombardy

CHARLES I the Great
or **CHARLEMAGNE**
747-814
King of the Franks (768-814)
Holy Roman Emperor
(800-814)

Gisela
757-810
Abbess of Chelles

Pepin
759-761

Rothaide
died young

Adelaide
died young

2 sons, Pepin (770- ?)
and ?, imprisoned in a monastery
by Charlemagne

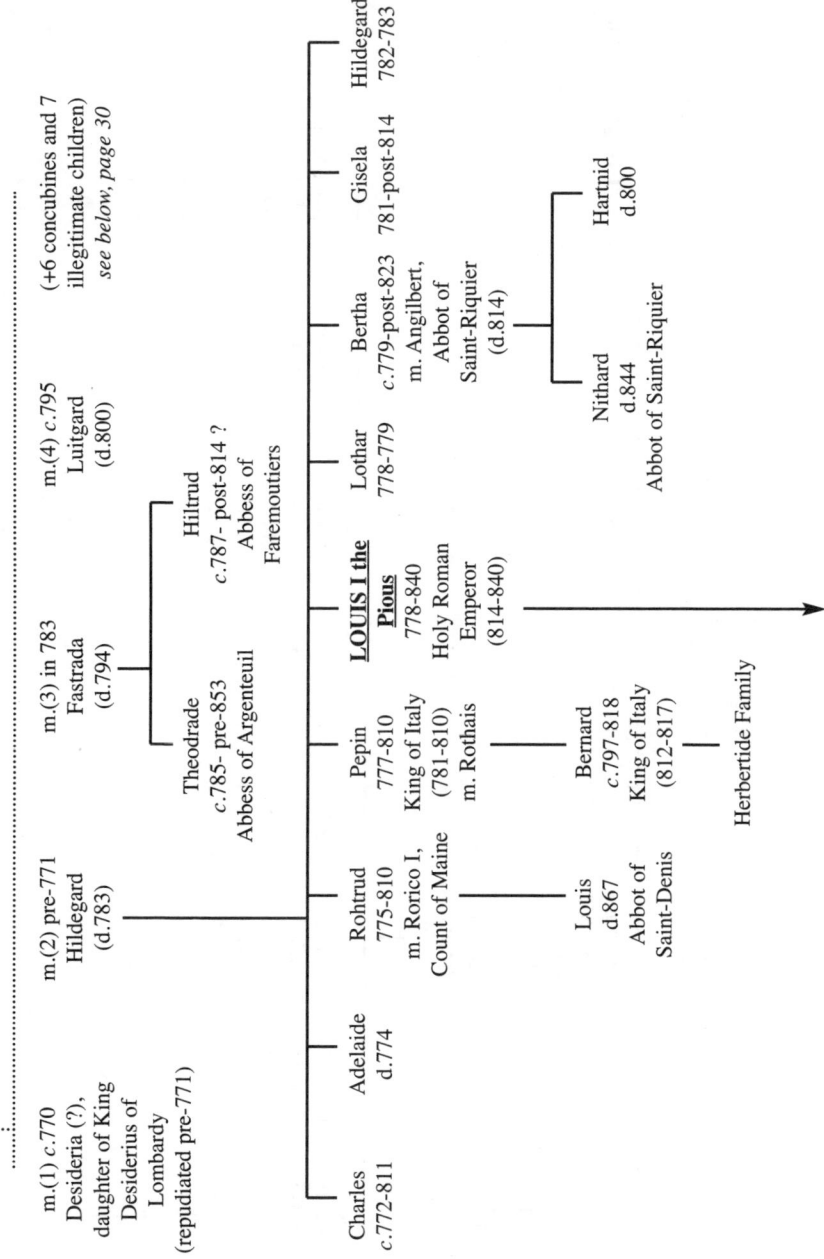

m.(1) c.770
Desideria (?),
daughter of King
Desiderius of
Lombardy
(repudiated pre-771)

m.(2) pre-771
Hildegard
(d.783)

m.(3) in 783
Fastrada
(d.794)

m.(4) c.795
Luitgard
(d.800)

(+6 concubines and 7
illegitimate children)
see below, page 30

Charles
c.772-811

Adelaide
d.774

Rohtrud
775-810
m. Rorico I,
Count of Maine

Theodrade
c.785- pre-853
Abbess of Argenteuil

Hiltrud
c.787- post-814 ?
Abbess of
Faremoutiers

Pepin
777-810
King of Italy
(781-810)
m. Rothais

LOUIS I the
Pious
778-840
Holy Roman
Emperor
(814-840)

Lothar
778-779

Bertha
c.779-post-823
m. Angilbert,
Abbot of
Saint-Riquier
(d.814)

Gisela
781-post-814

Hildegard
782-783

Louis
d.867
Abbot of
Saint-Denis

Bernard
c.797-818
King of Italy
(812-817)

Nithard
d.844
Abbot of Saint-Riquier

Hartnid
d.800

Herbertide Family

25

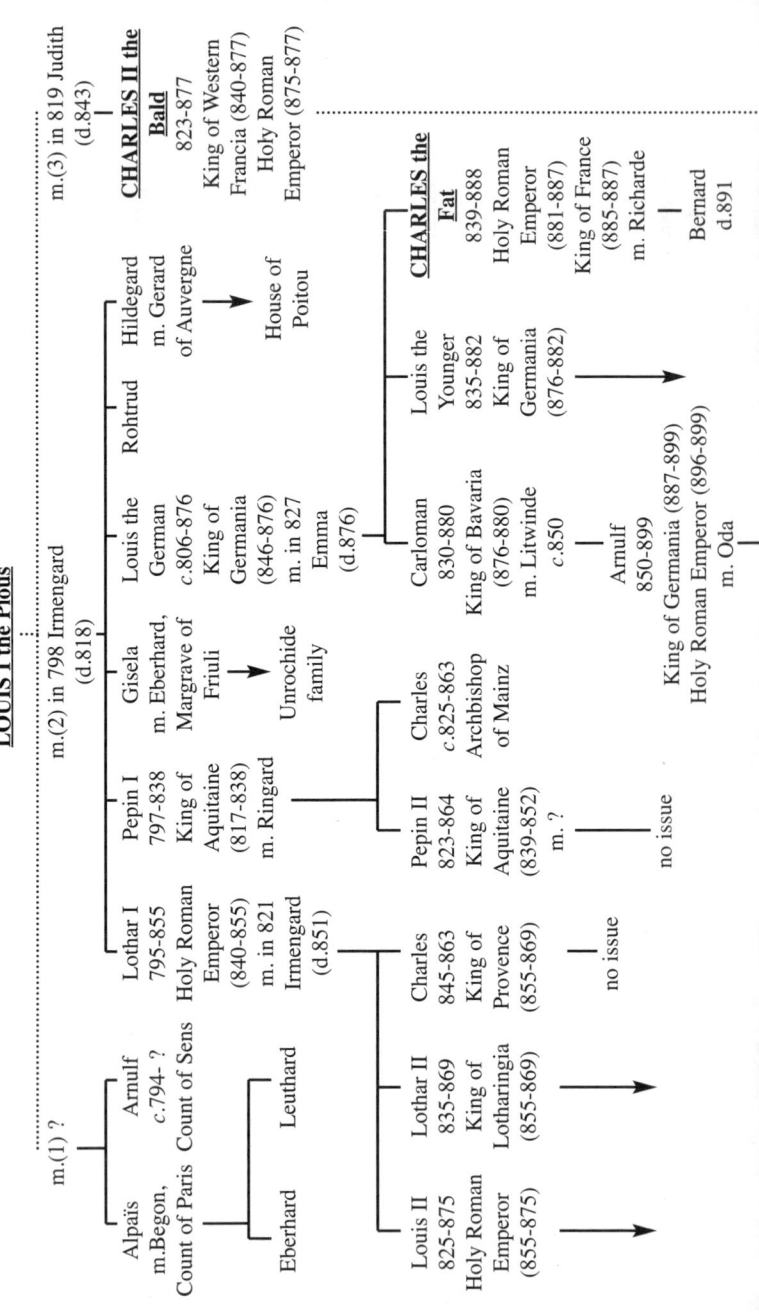

LOUIS I the Pious

m.(1) ?

Alpaïs
m. Begon,
Count of Paris

Arnulf
c.794- ?
Count of Sens

Eberhard

Leuthard

m.(2) in 798 Irmengard
(d.818)

Lothar I
795-855
Holy Roman
Emperor
(840-855)
m. in 821
Irmengard
(d.851)

Louis II
825-875
Holy Roman
Emperor
(855-875)

→

Lothar II
835-869
King of
Lotharingia
(855-869)

→

Charles
845-863
King of
Provence
(855-869)

no issue

Pepin I
797-838
King of
Aquitaine
(817-838)
m. Ringard

Pepin II
823-864
King of
Aquitaine
(839-852)
m. ?

no issue

Charles
c.825-863
Archbishop
of Mainz

Gisela
m. Eberhard,
Margrave of
Friuli

→ Unrochide
family

Louis the
German
c.806-876
King of
Germania
(846-876)
m. in 827
Emma
(d.876)

Carloman
830-880
King of Bavaria
(876-880)
m. Litwinde
c.850

Arnulf
850-899
King of Germania (887-899)
Holy Roman Emperor (896-899)
m. Oda

Louis the
Younger
835-882
King of
Germania
(876-882)

→

Rohtrud

Hildegard
m. Gerard
of Auvergne

→ House of
Poitou

**CHARLES the
Fat**
839-888
Holy Roman
Emperor
(881-887)
King of France
(885-887)
m. Richarde

Bernard
d.891

m.(3) in 819 Judith
(d.843)

**CHARLES II the
Bald**
823-877
King of Western
Francia (840-877)
Holy Roman
Emperor (875-877)

26

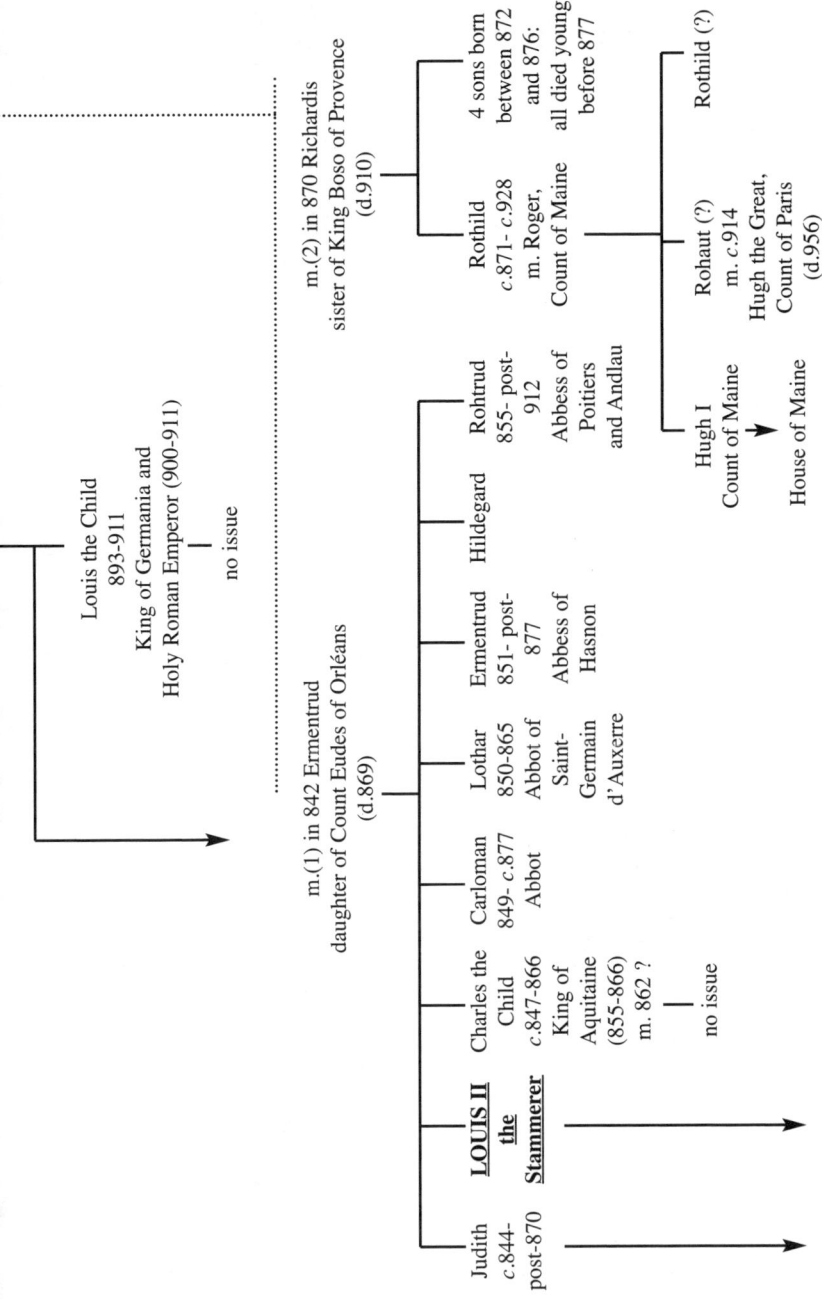

Louis the Child
893-911
King of Germania and
Holy Roman Emperor (900-911)

no issue

m.(2) in 870 Richardis
sister of King Boso of Provence
(d.910)

4 sons born
between 872
and 876:
all died young
before 877

Rothild
c.871- c.928
m. Roger,
Count of Maine

Rohaut (?)
m. c.914
Hugh the Great,
Count of Paris
(d.956)

Rothild (?)

m.(1) in 842 Ermentrud
daughter of Count Eudes of Orléans
(d.869)

Charles the
Child
c.847-866
King of
Aquitaine
(855-866)
m. 862 ?

no issue

Carloman
849- c.877
Abbot

Lothar
850-865
Abbot of
Saint-
Germain
d'Auxerre

Ermentrud
851- post-
877
Abbess of
Hasnon

Hildegard

Rohtrud
855- post-
912
Abbess of
Poitiers
and Andlau

Hugh I
Count of Maine → House of Maine

LOUIS II
the
Stammerer

Judith
c.844-
post-870

27

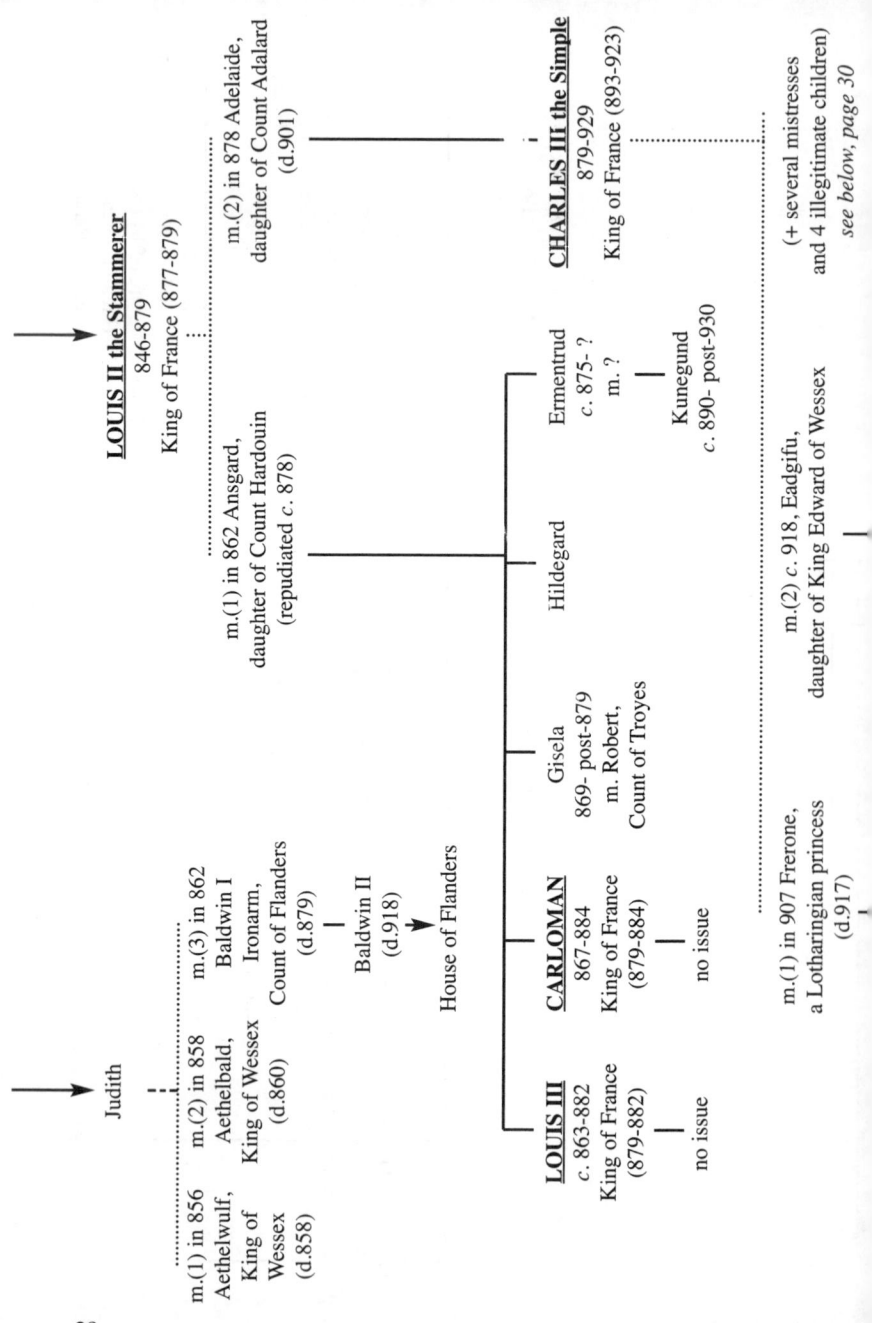

LOUIS II the Stammerer
846-879
King of France (877-879)

m.(1) in 862 Ansgard,
daughter of Count Hardouin
(repudiated c. 878)

m.(2) in 878 Adelaide,
daughter of Count Adalard
(d.901)

CHARLES III the Simple
879-929
King of France (893-923)

(+ several mistresses
and 4 illegitimate children)
see below, page 30

Judith

m.(1) in 856
Aethelwulf,
King of Wessex
(d.858)

m.(2) in 858
Aethelbald,
King of Wessex
(d.860)

m.(3) in 862
Baldwin I
Ironarm,
Count of Flanders
(d.879)

Baldwin II
(d.918)

House of Flanders

LOUIS III
c. 863-882
King of France
(879-882)

no issue

CARLOMAN
867-884
King of France
(879-884)

no issue

Gisela
869- post-879
m. Robert,
Count of Troyes

Hildegard

Ermentrud
c. 875- ?
m. ?

Kunegund
c. 890- post-930

m.(1) in 907 Frerone,
a Lotharingian princess
(d.917)

m.(2) c. 918, Eadgifu,
daughter of King Edward of Wessex

28

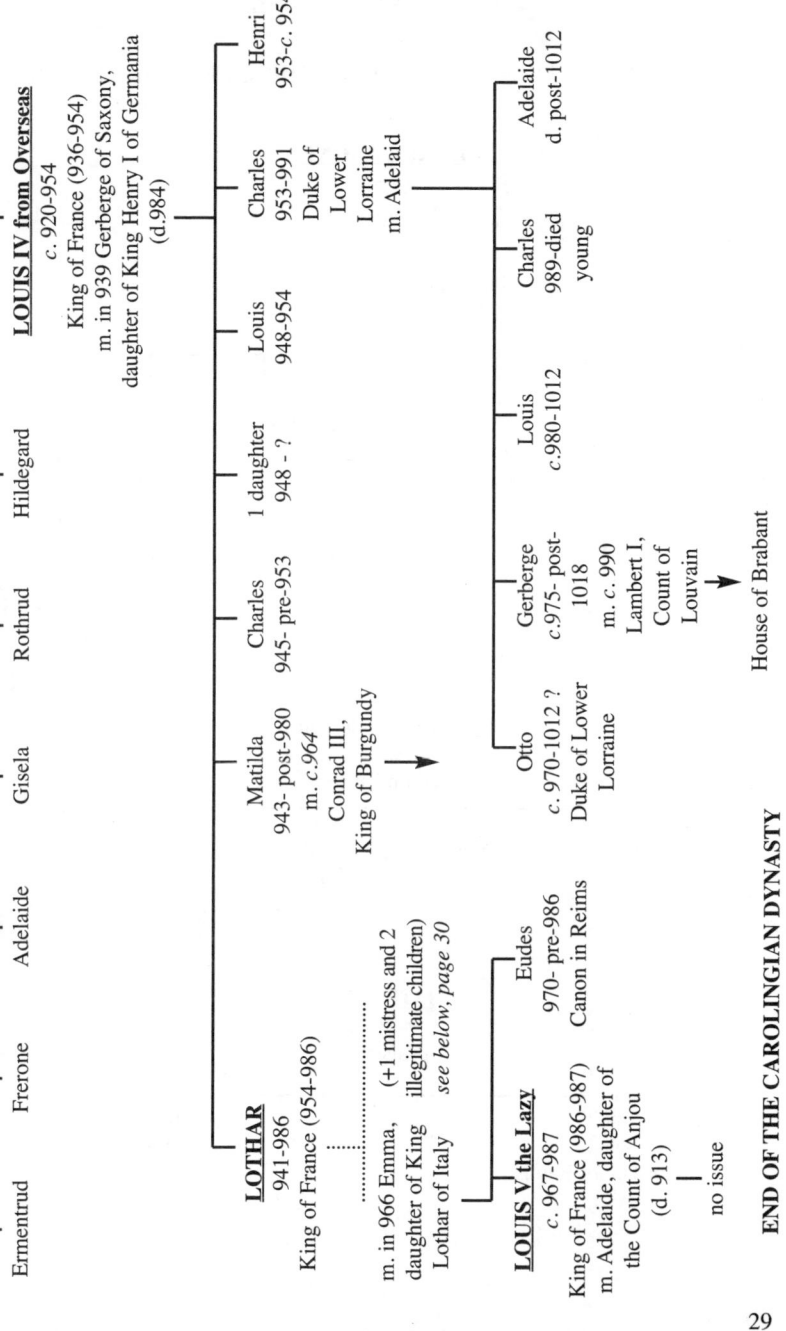

LOUIS IV from Overseas
c. 920-954
King of France (936-954)
m. in 939 Gerberge (936-954)
daughter of King Henry I of Germania
(d.984)

Ermentrud | Frerone | Adelaide | Gisela | Rothrud | Hildegard

LOTHAR
941-986
King of France (954-986)

(+1 mistress and 2
illegitimate children)
see below, page 30

m. in 966 Emma, daughter of King
Lothar of Italy

Matilda
943- post-980
m. *c.*964
Conrad III,
King of Burgundy →

1 daughter
948 - ?

Charles
945- pre-953

Louis
948-954

Charles
953-991
Duke of
Lower
Lorraine
m. Adelaid

Henri
953-*c.* 954

LOUIS V the Lazy
c. 967-987
King of France (986-987)
m. Adelaide, daughter of
the Count of Anjou
(d. 913)
|
no issue

Eudes
970- pre-986
Canon in Reims

Otto
c. 970-1012
Duke of Lower
Lorraine →

Gerberge
*c.*975- post-
1018
m. *c.* 990
Lambert I,
Count of
Louvain
↓
House of Brabant

Louis
*c.*980-1012

Adelaide
d. post-1012

Charles
989–died
young

END OF THE CAROLINGIAN DYNASTY

29

THE ILLEGITIMATE DESCENDENTS OF THE CAROLINGIAN LINE

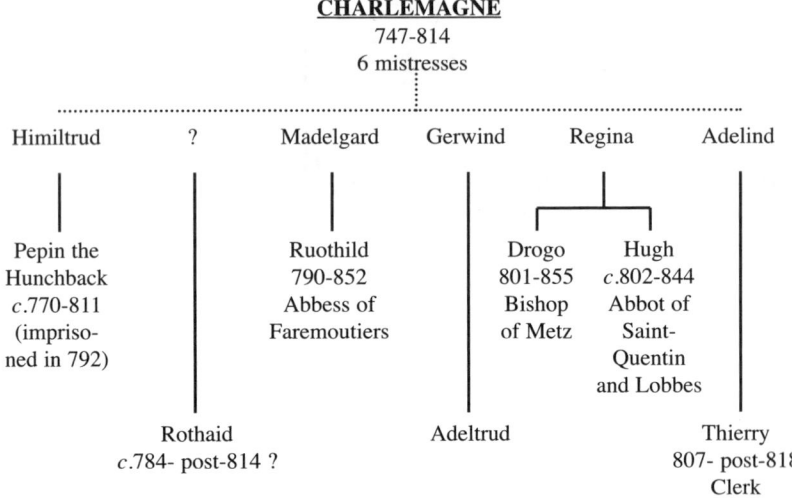

CHARLEMAGNE
747-814
6 mistresses

Himiltrud	?	Madelgard	Gerwind	Regina	Adelind

Pepin the
Hunchback
c.770-811
(impriso-
ned in 792)

Ruothild
790-852
Abbess of
Faremoutiers

Drogo
801-855
Bishop
of Metz

Hugh
c.802-844
Abbot of
Saint-
Quentin
and Lobbes

Rothaid
c.784- post-814 ?

Adeltrud

Thierry
807- post-818
Clerk

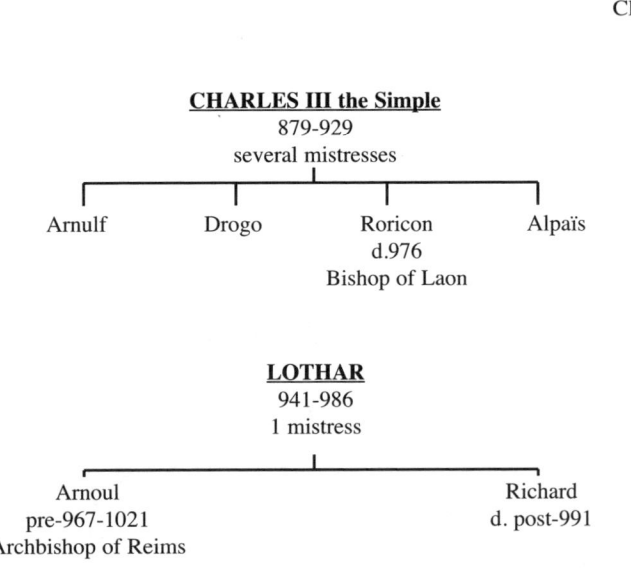

CHARLES III the Simple
879-929
several mistresses

Arnulf	Drogo	Roricon	Alpaïs

Roricon
d.976
Bishop of Laon

LOTHAR
941-986
1 mistress

Arnoul
pre-967-1021
Archbishop of Reims

Richard
d. post-991

Charles II the Bald

Charles I the Great or Charlemagne (747-814). King of the Franks (768-814), Holy Roman Emperor (800-814).

Charlemagne, the elder son of Pepin the Short and Bertha, became King of the Franks upon the death of his father in 768 A.D. but had to share the kingdom with his brother Carloman. When he, in turn, died in 771 A.D, Charlemagne became sole monarch of the Franks at the head of a kingdom that he was to extend considerably, making him one of the most powerful sovereigns of his day. He was a soldier and conqueror, spending most of his life at war. In 773 A.D, he travelled to Italy at the behest of Pope Adrian I who was under threat from King Desiderius of Lombardy. The king was defeated and exiled and Charlemagne mounted the Lombard throne. This action renewed the alliance between the kingdom of the Franks and the papacy. In 778 A.D, Charlemagne led his first expedition into Spain but it failed (the campaign was marked by the death of Roland at Roncesvalles). Not until twenty years later did he succeed in crushing the regions to the north of the Ebro. In 781 A.D, in acknowledgement of certain regional particularities, he appointed his son Pepin King of Italy and his son Louis King of Aquitaine. Charlemagne waged war one last time in 788 A.D. against the rebel Duke Tassilo III of Bavaria, deposing him and annexing his territory. However, the longest and most difficult war of his reign was the struggle against the Saxons, a pagan Germanic tribe that was posing a threat to Austrasia. The conflict lasted from 722 to 803 A.D. It involved countless expeditions and Charlemagne was forced to have recourse to brutal methods in order to overcome them once and for all. An uprising led by Widukind broke out in 782, followed by a revolt in 793 A.D. These uprisings forced the Franks to wage war yet again. Eventually, Charlemagne had to implement large-scale deportations of Saxons, replacing them by Frankish settlers. In order to protect this border of his kingdom, he waged war against the Friesians and Avars. All around the Empire, he created "marches", quasi-military governments whose leaders, the "margraves" were responsible for the defence of the territory. Through his conquests, Charlemagne became the master of an empire that covered much of Western Europe. No other sovereign had achieved such power since 476 A.D. In 800 A.D, Charlemagne travelled to Rome to set Leo III back on the papal throne after he had been removed by a revolt of noblemen. On 25th December that same year, Pope Leo III crowned him Emperor. This marked the restoration of an imperial title in Western Europe and gave Charlemagne even greater prestige. In domestic affairs, his reign was marked by an equally outstanding effort at administrative organisation. He divided the kingdom into counties (the "counts" were then at the tip of the pyramidal feudal system), instituted regular meetings with lay and ecclesiastical dignitaries, promulgated capitularies and sent *missi dominici* out into the provinces to monitor the counts' administration. As regards currency, he confirmed the royal monopoly on the minting of coinage. The sovereign was surrounded by a large number of civil servants and advisers who constituted, with their monarch, central government. The Court followed Charlemagne everywhere he went and it was not until 807 A.D. that he decided on

Aachen (Aix-la-Chapelle) as his capital. Finally, his reign was remarkable for its intellectual and artistic revival, with the opening of schools, the presence at Court of educated men such as Alcuin, Eginhard and Paul Diacre, and the construction of religious buildings. Charlemagne had four legally-recognised wives and at least six mistresses, and fathered eighteen children. In 806 A.D, again following the Frankish tradition, he provided for the division of his kingdom between his three sons but Pepin died in 810 A.D. and Charles in 811. On Charlemagne's death in 814 A.D, his grandson Bernard became King of Italy and his last surviving son, Louis, succeeded him at the head of the empire.

Carloman (c. 751-771). King of the Franks (768-771).

Carloman, the son of Pepin the Short and brother of Charlemagne, became King of the Franks jointly with Charlemagne upon the death of their father in 768 A.D. Carloman's early death in 771 A.D. left Charlemagne to rule the kingdom of the Franks on his own, while Carloman's wife, Gerberge, sought refuge with the King of Lombardy, Desiderius, and his two sons were shut up in a monastery by their uncle.

Louis I the Pious (778-840). Holy Roman Emperor (814-840).

Louis, the third son of Charlemagne and Hildegarde, became King of Aquitaine in 781 A.D. His father then involved him more closely in affairs of State in 813, after the death of his two brothers. He was, therefore, sole heir to the entire empire upon Charlemagne's death in 814 A.D. Like his father, he was crowned Emperor by the Pope, Stephen IV, in 816 in Reims and his reign was marked by the strong influence of ecclesiastical figures. In 817 A.D, Louis I wanted to settle the problem posed by his succession through the *Ordinatio imperii*. It defined the share to be granted to each of his three sons, Lothar (whom he brought into the empire), Pepin and Louis. The division cause a revolt led by Bernard, King of Italy, the nephew of Louis I and grandson of Charlemagne. He was defeated by the emperor and, in punishment, Louis ordered Bernard's eyes to be put out. Bernard died in 818 A.D. Louis I, however, was a staunch Christian and he undertook public penance in Attigny in 822 A.D. before the Empire's leading noblemen. This weakened his prestige. The difficulties of settling his succession became increasingly complex. He was a widower, since his first wife, Ermengard, had died in 818 but he remarried in 819 A.D. with Judith who bore him a fourth son, Charles, in 823 A.D. In order to give this son a share of the estate, he modified the 817 A.D. arrangements at a meeting in Worms in 829 A.D. As a result, his three elder sons revolted in 830 and again in 833 A.D. Louis I was defeated, brought to trial, sentenced and deposed at Lügenfeld. He was then imprisoned in a monastery. Disagreement between his sons enabled him to mount the throne again in 834 A.D. but he was unable to regain all his erstwhile authority. On the death of his second son, Pepin, in 838, Louis I divided the kingdom for the third time, to the benefit of Charles (839 A.D). His reign was marked, in the area of domestic policy, by a continuation of the Carolingian renaissance undertaken by his father, Charlemagne, in administrative, religious and intellectual matters. As for military action, Louis I completed Charlemagne's conquests, defeating the Bretons, Saxons and Slavs from Pannonia. Finally, it was during this period that the empire first fell under threat from Viking raids along the Atlantic coasts and incursions by the Saracen in Provence. Louis I died in 840 A.D. without any solution having been found to the problem of his succession. This eventually led to the division of the kingdom.

Charles II the Bald (823-877). King of Western Francia (840-877). Holy Roman Emperor (875-877).

Charles was the last son of Louis I the Pious and was the cause of the troubles that marked the end of his father's reign since Louis wanted to give him a major position in his projects for his succession. When Louis died, Charles II the Bald allied himself with his brother, Louis the German, against their other brother, Lothar, who had become emperor. Lothar was defeated at the Battle of Fontenoy-en-Puisaye in 841 A.D. Charles and Louis strengthened their alliance through oaths taken at Strasburg in 842 and forced Lothar to negotiate a peace. Eventually, through the Treaty of Verdun (843 A.D.) the three brothers shared the empire between themselves. Charles II the Bald received the territories to the west of the Scheldt, Meuse, Saône and Rhône, territories which constituted *Francia occidentalis*. He extended his territory slightly by obtaining part of Lotharingia in 870. He was forced to fight the Bretons who declared themselves to be politically independent in 846 A.D. He was also in conflict with his nephew, Pepin, until 864 A.D. regarding control of Aquitaine. The entire reign of Charles II the Bald was marked by the first major Viking invasions. The Normans pillaged Paris in 845, 858 and 861 A.D. and began to settle on a permanent basis in certain regions. On the death of Emperor Louis II, Pope John VIII offered Charles the imperial crown. Charles travelled to Rome where he was crowned emperor in 875 A.D. On the death of his brother, Louis the German, in 876 A.D, Charles II the Bald seized part of Louis' kingdom but was defeated by his nephew, Louis the Younger, at Andernach in 876. Charles was forced to retreat. In 877, he answered a call from the Pope who was under threat from the Saracen. He issued the Quierzy capitulary by which he entrusted the kingdom to his son, Louis, and to the leading noblemen. This marked a new development in the feudal system. He then set off for Italy. However, his campaign failed and he died on the return journey. His only surviving son, Louis II the Stammerer, succeeded him on the throne of France.

Louis II the Stammerer (846-879). King of France (877-879).

Louis, the elder son of Charles II the Bald, succeeded his father in 877 A.D. but found it difficult to impose his will on the kingdom's noblemen because of his sickly constitution and stutter. He confirmed the earlier division of

Lotharingia (870 A.D.) by signing the Treaty of Fouron in 878 A.D. with Louis the Younger, King of Germany. Louis II the Stammerer reigned for only two years and died in 879 A.D. His first marriage, with Ansgard, brought him two sons, Louis III and Carloman, who succeeded him jointly; from his second marriage, with Adelaide, he had a third son, Charles III the Simple, who reigned much later on.

Louis III (c. 863-882). King of France (879-882).

Louis, the eldest son of Louis II the Stammerer, succeeded him in 879 A.D, with his brother Carloman. The division of the kingdom between the two gave Louis III Francia and Neustria. With his brother, he was obliged to recognise the transfer of Lotharingia to Louis the Younger, King of Germany. He defeated the Vikings in Saucourt-en-Vimeu in 881 A.D. and died without an heir in 882 A.D, leaving his brother Carloman as sole monarch.

Carloman (867-884). King of France (879-884).

Carloman, Louis II the Stammerer's second son, initially shared the crown with his brother, Louis III, and received Aquitaine and Burgundy as his territory. He then reigned on his own after Louis' death in 882 A.D. He was forced to acknowledge Boson as King of Provence. He also fought the Vikings. He died at an early age as a result of a hunting accident in 884 A.D, without leaving an heir. The only claimant to the throne was the last son of Louis II the Stammerer, Charles, then aged five.

Charles the Fat (869-888). King of France (885-887).

Charles the Fat, who had been Holy Roman Emperor since 881 A.D, was the third son of Louis the German and the great-grandson of Charlemagne. In 885 A.D, after the death of King Carloman, leading noblemen in the kingdom of France asked him to act as Regent because of the young age of Louis II the Stammerer's last son, Charles, who was born in 879 A.D. He had to fight the Vikings who were besieging Paris, but his weakness and incompetence led the Diet of Tivoli to depose him in 887 A.D.

Charles III the Simple (879-929). King of France (893-923).

Charles was the posthumous son of Louis II the Stammerer. He was not crowned king in 884 A.D. on the death of his brother Carloman, since the kingdom's noblemen chose Emperor Charles the Fat in his place. He again failed to win the throne in 888 A.D. when the honour went to Count Eudes of Paris who had won distinction during the siege of Paris by the Vikings. Charles III the Simple was finally crowned king in 893 A.D. He then had to fight Eudes but eventually succeeded in signing an agreement with him. It stated that Charles would succeed Eudes after the latter's death, and this was complied with in 898 A.D. Charles III the Simple temporarily annexed Lotharingia to France but was required to grant the Caux area in feu to Rollo, the Viking chieftain, in 911 .A.D (Treaty of Saint-Clair-sur-Epte) in order to put an end to the Normans' pillaging. Charles III the Simple was faced with a revolt on the part of the kingdom's leading noblemen in 922 and with the election of Robert, Marquis of Neustria, to the throne of France. Despite his rival's death during the Battle of Soissons, Charles III the Simple was taken prisoner and deposed in 923 A.D. He died in 929 in Péronne where he was still being held prisoner.

Louis IV from Overseas (c. 920-954). King of France (936-954).

Louis, the son of Charles III the Simple and Eadgiva of Wessex, was taken to England by his mother when his father was deposed in 923 A.D. He was recalled in 936 A.D. by Hugh the Great, Duke of the Franks, and crowned king but he then had to spend much of his reign fighting Hugh. In 945 A.D, he was taken prisoner by the Vikings and was only freed, by Hugh, when he agreed to hand over the town of Laon. Louis IV sought assistance from King Otto of Germany and this gave him the upper hand. Hugh was forced to recognise his sovereignty in 950 and they signed a final peace treaty in 953 A.D. Louis IV died after a fall from a horse. He was succeeded by his son, Lothar.

Lothar (941-986). King of France (954-986).

Lothar, the eldest son of Louis IV from Overseas, succeeded his father in 954 A.D. During his reign, the Robertian clan acquired greater power and influence, through Hugh the Great to whom Lothar granted sovereignty over Aquitaine in 955 A.D. and through Hugh Capet who became King of the Francs in 960 A.D. In 978, Lothar waged war against King Otto II of Germany but this served only to facilitate Hugh Capet's rise to power. Lothar died in 986 and was succeeded by his son, Louis V.

Louis V the Lazy (c. 967-987). King of France (986-987).

Louis, Lothar's son, succeeded his father in 986 A.D. but reigned under the control of his mother, Emma. He was in conflict with Archbishop Adalberon of Reims, who was allied with Hugh Capet. He died in 987 A.D. as a result of a fall from a horse and had no heir. His death marked the end of the French branch of the Carolingian dynasty and he was succeeded on the throne of France by Hugh Capet.

THE ROBERTIANS

The Robertians, the ancestors of the Capetians, owed their name to Robert the Strong, who was Marquis of Neustria in the middle of the 9th century. They gave France several kings over the 9th and 10th centuries, alternating with members of the Carolingian dynasty.

The family gradually gained power and influence during this period by taking advantage of the increasing weakness of Charlemagne's descendents. The two sons of Count Robert the Strong, Eudes (888-898) and Robert I (922-923), became Kings of France and Robert's son-in-law, Rudolf (Raoul), also mounted the throne (923-936).

Although the Carolingians returned to the throne (936-987), the subsequent election of the Duke of the Franks, Hugh Capet, grandson of King Robert I, marked the end of the Carolingian dynasty and the final seizure of power by the Robertians. Since Hugh Capet founded a long line of monarchs, it was named after him and became the "Capetian" dynasty.

The election of the Duke of the Franks, Hugh Capet

THE ROBERTIAN DYNASTY

(ancestors of Hugh Capet)

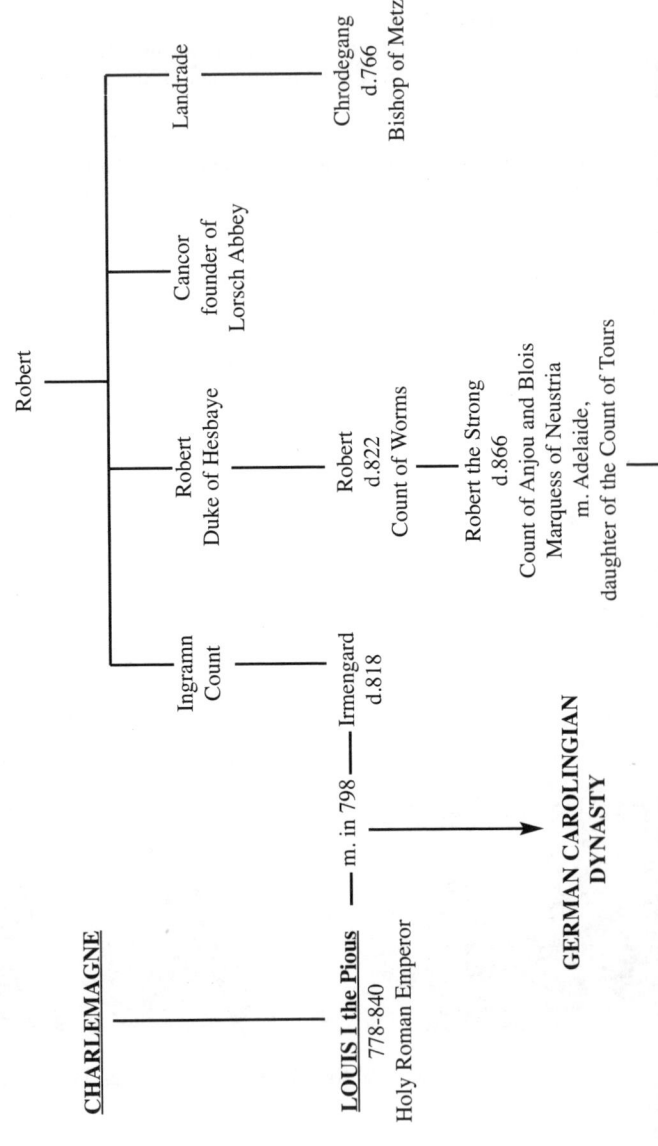

CHARLEMAGNE

LOUIS I the Pious
778-840
Holy Roman Emperor

— m. in 798 — Irmengard
d.818

Ingramn
Count

Robert

Robert
Duke of Hesbaye

Robert
d.822
Count of Worms

Robert the Strong
d.866
Count of Anjou and Blois
Marquess of Neustria
m. Adelaide,
daughter of the Count of Tours

Cancor
founder of
Lorsch Abbey

Landrade

Chrodegang
d.766
Bishop of Metz

GERMAN CAROLINGIAN
DYNASTY

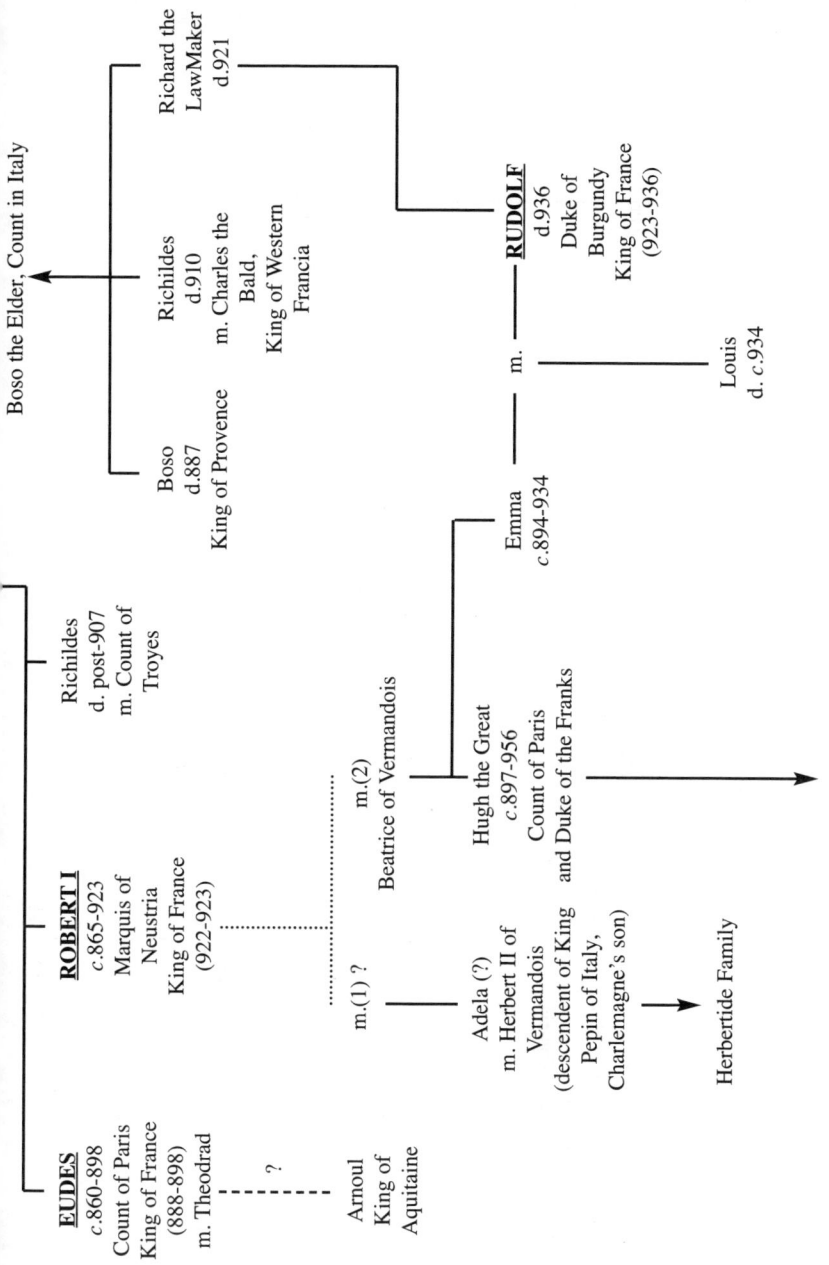

Boso the Elder, Count in Italy

EUDES
c.860-898
Count of Paris
King of France
(888-898)
m. Theodrad

Richildes
d. post-907
m. Count of Troyes

ROBERT I
c.865-923
Marquis of Neustria
King of France
(922-923)

Richildes
d.910
m. Charles the Bald,
King of Western Francia

Boso
d.887
King of Provence

Richard the LawMaker
d.921

RUDOLF
d.936
Duke of Burgundy
King of France
(923-936)

m.

Louis
d. c.934

Emma
c.894-934

m.(2)
Beatrice of Vermandois

Hugh the Great
c.897-956
Count of Paris
and Duke of the Franks

m.(1) ?

Adela (?)
m. Herbert II of Vermandois
(descendent of King Pepin of Italy,
Charlemagne's son)

Herbertide Family

?

Arnoul
King of Aquitaine

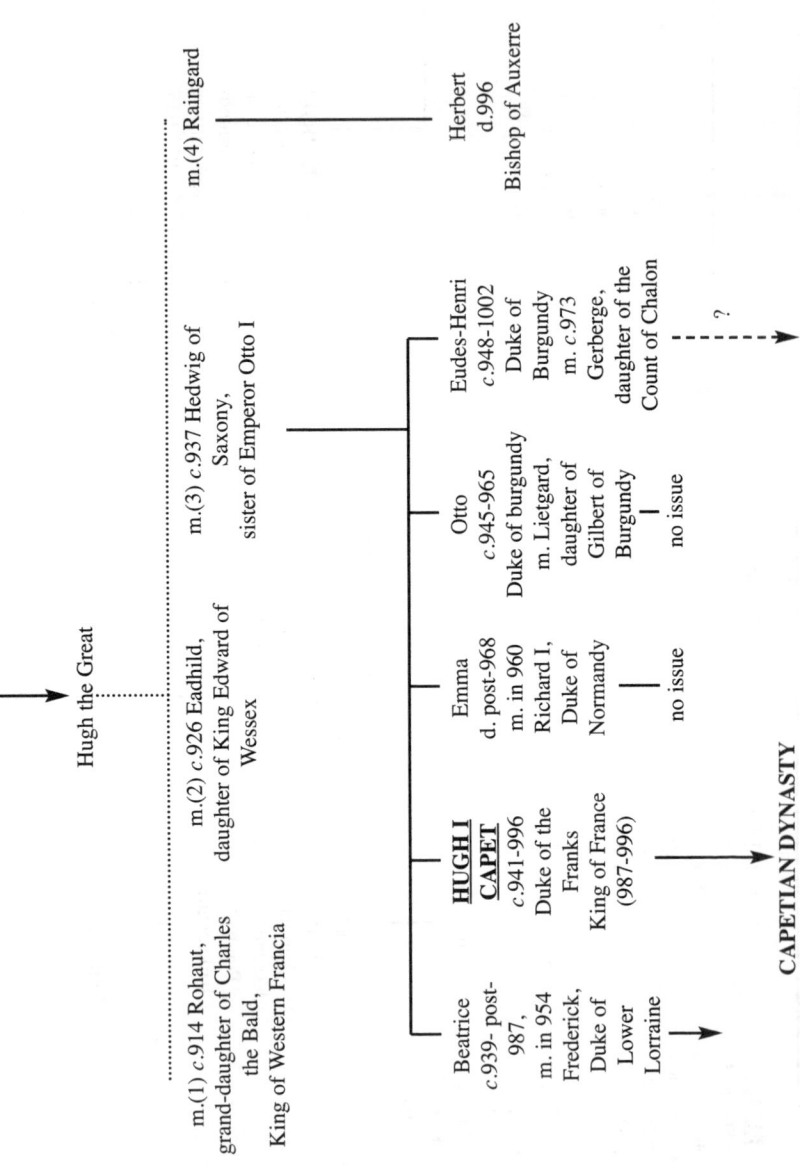

Hugh the Great

m.(1) c.914 Rohaut, grand-daughter of Charles the Bald, King of Western Francia

m.(2) c.926 Eadhild, daughter of King Edward of Wessex

m.(3) c.937 Hedwig of Saxony, sister of Emperor Otto I

m.(4) Raingard

Beatrice c.939- post-987, m. in 954 Frederick, Duke of Lower Lorraine

HUGH I CAPET c.941-996 Duke of the Franks King of France (987-996)

Emma d. post-968 m. in 960 Richard I, Duke of Normandy

no issue

Otto c.945-965 Duke of burgundy m. Lietgard, daughter of Gilbert of Burgundy

no issue

Eudes-Henri c.948-1002 Duke of Burgundy m. c.973 Gerberge, daughter of the Count of Chalon

?

Herbert d.996 Bishop of Auxerre

CAPETIAN DYNASTY

40

Eudes (c. 860-898). King of France (888-898).

Eudes, the eldest son of Robert the Strong, Marquis of Neustria, was given the title of Count of Paris *c*. 882 A.D. He rose to fame by defending the capital when it was besieged by the Vikings from 885 to 887 A.D, although he failed to force them to lift the siege and King Charles the Fat was eventually obliged to pay them to leave. When Charles was deposed in 887 A.D, Eudes was elected and crowned King of France in Compiègne (888 A.D.) in preference to Charles the Simple, the son of Louis II the Stammerer and the last member of the Carolingian line. Eudes was the first non-Carolingian monarch since Pepin the Short. His reign marked the beginning of the struggle between Carolingians and Robertians for the throne of France; it was to last until the end of the 10th century. Eudes continued to fight the Vikings, defeating them in Montfaucon-en-Argonne in 888 A.D. but losing to them in 891 A.D. He also had to defend his throne against the Carolingian claimant, Charles III the Simple, who had been crowned king in 893 A.D. After a struggle lasting three years, the two kings signed a peace treaty. Eudes gave Charles part of his kingdom and made him his heir (897 A.D). Eudes died in 898 A.D, leaving the French throne to the Carolingian.

Robert I (c. 865-923). King of France (922-923).

Robert, the second son of Robert the Strong and brother of King Eudes, became Marquis of Neustria in 888 A.D. when his brother mounted the throne of France. Robert was initially loyal to King Charles III the Simple and he won fame during the struggle against the Vikings who were defeated in 911 A.D. In 920, however, he rebelled against the king, fomenting a plot with leading noblemen of the kingdom, including Duke Rudolf of Burgundy. In 922 A.D, he was elected king and crowned. During the struggle opposing him to Charles III the Simple, Robert I was killed during a battle near Soissons in 923 A.D. However, his death did not mean victory for the Carolingian pretender. Instead, Robert's son-in-law, Rudolf of Burgundy, succeeded him and Charles III the Simple was imprisoned.

Rudolf (? - 936). King of France (923-936).

Rudolf, who became Duke of Burgundy upon the death of his father, Richard, in 921 A.D, was involved in the rebellion fomented by his father-in-law, Robert, Marquis of Neustria, against King Charles III the Simple in 922 A.D. When Robert I died in 923 A.D, Rudolf was elected King of France; Charles the Simple was deposed and imprisoned. During his reign, Rudolf had to fight Rollo then William Longsword, Dukes of Normandy. He also had to fight leading vassals in revolt such as Herbert de Vermandois. In 935 A.D, he acknowledged the loss of Lorraine which had again become a German possession. Finally, he had to repulse raids by Magyars in the east of his kingdom. Rudolf died in 936 A.D. without leaving an heir and was succeeded by the Carolingian, Louis IV from Overseas.

Philip V the Long

THE DIRECT CAPETIAN LINE

The election of Hugh Capet to the throne of France in 987 A.D. marked the birth of a long dynasty which reigned over France through direct or indirect succession for more than eight centuries, until 1848, with a short break between 1792 and 1814.

The direct Capetian line reigned from 987 A.D. to 1328, with fifteen kings in 341 years. Among the most outstanding figures were Philip II Augustus (1180-1223), St. Louis (1226-1270) or Philip IV the Fair (1285-1314). The idea of hereditary transmission of the crown based on male primogeniture gradually gained ground. From 987 A.D. to 1316, thirteen kings succeeded each other, with sons succeeding their fathers, from Hugh Capet down to John I the Posthumous. All of them worked along the same lines and gave the dynasty a solid foundation. Their aim was to impose their authority on leading feudal lords, extend the royal estates and combat foreign powers.

In 1316, the question of succession was posed for the first time, after the death of John I the Posthumous since the child-king died only a few days after he was born. It was his uncle, Philip V the Long, who mounted the throne. Again, in 1322, when he died without leaving a male heir, it was his brother, Charles IV the Fair, the last surviving son of Philip IV the Fair, who became king. Salic Law was applied, even if not formally expressed as such until later, excluding women from any succession to the throne.

In 1328, the death of Charles IV the Fair and the lack of a male heir marked the end of the direct Capetian dynasty and the crown passed to the Valois line.

THE DIRECT CAPETIAN LINE

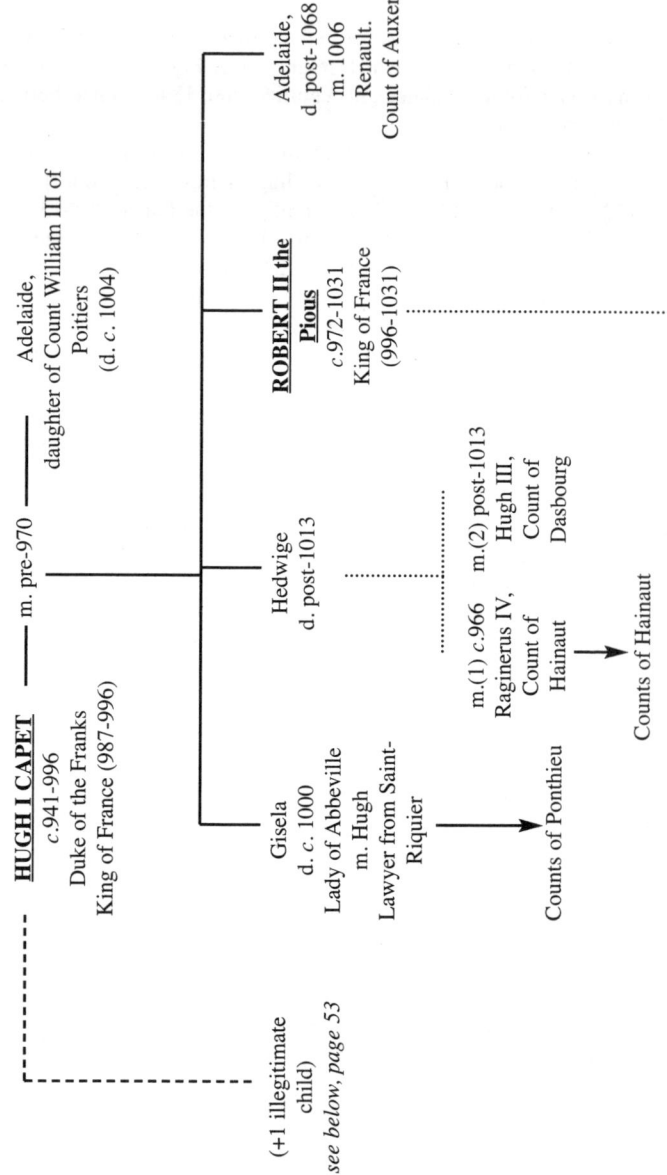

HUGH I CAPET ——— m. pre-970 ——— Adelaide,
c.941-996   daughter of Count William III of
Duke of the Franks   Poitiers
King of France (987-996)   (d. c. 1004)

(+1 illegitimate
child)
see below, page 53

Gisela
d. c. 1000
Lady of Abbeville
m. Hugh
Lawyer from Saint-
Riquier

Counts of Ponthieu

Hedwige
d. post-1013

m.(1) c.966
Raginerus IV,
Count of
Hainaut

m.(2) post-1013
Hugh III,
Count of
Dasbourg

Counts of Hainaut

**ROBERT II the
Pious**
c.972-1031
King of France
(996-1031)

Adelaide,
d. post-1068
m. 1006
Renault.
Count of Auxerre

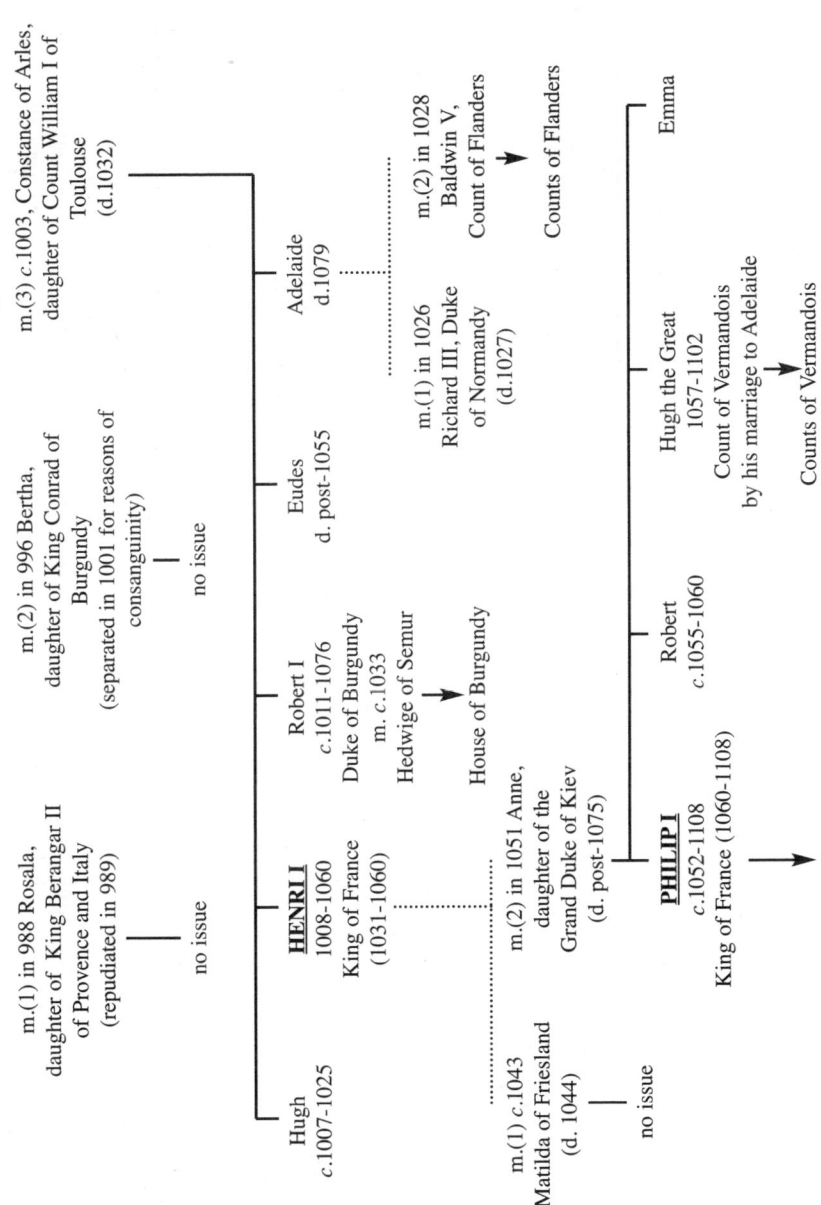

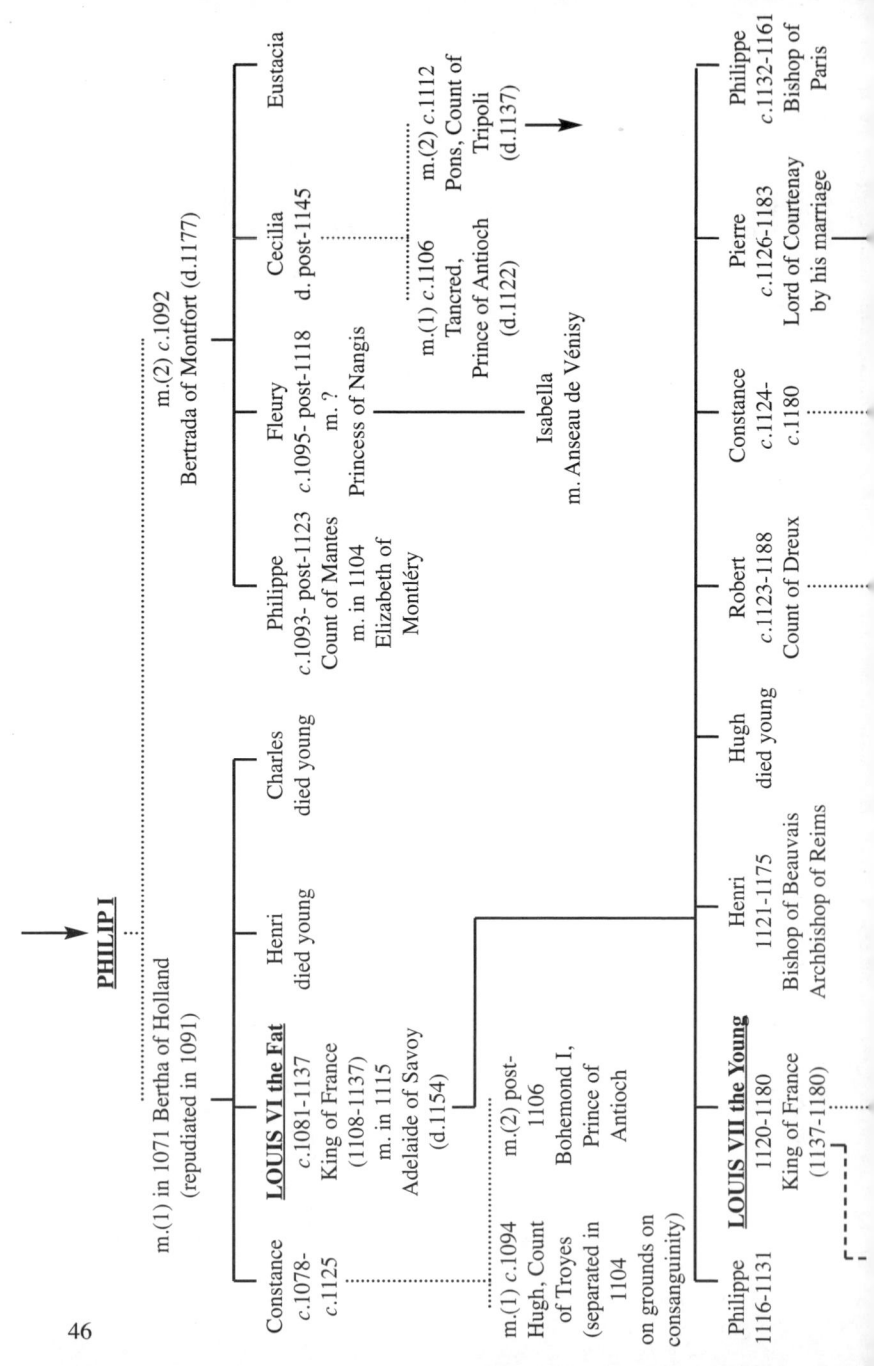

PHILIP I

m.(1) in 1071 Bertha of Holland
(repudiated in 1091)

m.(2) c.1092
Bertrada of Montfort (d.1177)

Constance
c.1078-
c.1125

m.(1) c.1094
Hugh, Count
of Troyes
(separated in
1104
on grounds on
consanguinity)

LOUIS VI the Fat
c.1081-1137
King of France
(1108-1137)
m. in 1115
Adelaide of Savoy
(d.1154)

m.(2) post-
1106
Bohemond I,
Prince of
Antioch

Henri
died young

Charles
died young

Philippe
c.1093- post-1123
Count of Mantes
m. in 1104
Elizabeth of
Montléry

Fleury
c.1095- post-1118
m. ?
Princess of Nangis

Cecilia
d. post-1145

m.(1) c.1106
Tancred,
Prince of Antioch
(d.1122)

m.(2) c.1112
Pons, Count of
Tripoli
(d.1137)

Eustacia

Isabella
m. Anseau de Vénisy

LOUIS VII the Young
1120-1180
King of France
(1137-1180)

Philippe
1116-1131

Henri
1121-1175
Bishop of Beauvais
Archbishop of Reims

Hugh
died young

Robert
c.1123-1188
Count of Dreux

Constance
c.1124-
c.1180

Pierre
c.1126-1183
Lord of Courtenay
by his marriage

Philippe
c.1132-1161
Bishop of Paris

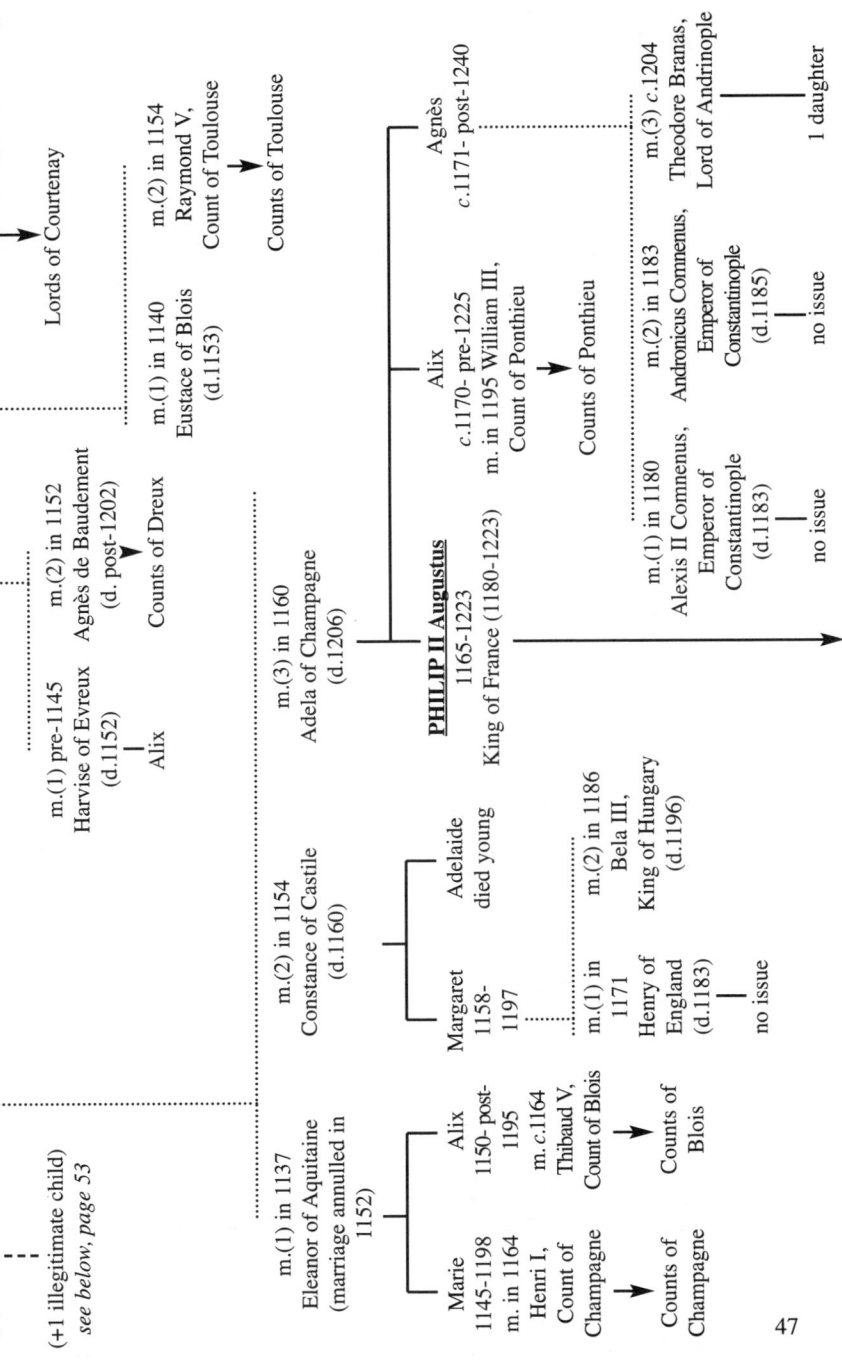

Lords of Courtenay

m.(2) in 1154
Raymond V,
Count of Toulouse
→ Counts of Toulouse

m.(1) in 1140
Eustace of Blois
(d.1153)

m.(2) in 1152
Agnès de Baudement
(d. post-1202)
→ Counts of Dreux

m.(1) pre-1145
Harvise of Evreux
(d.1152)
Alix

Agnès
c.1171- post-1240

m.(3) c.1204
Theodore Branas,
Lord of Andrinople
— 1 daughter

Alix
c.1170- pre-1225
m. in 1195 William III,
Count of Ponthieu
→ Counts of Ponthieu

m.(2) in 1183
Andronicus Comnenus,
Emperor of
Constantinople
(d.1185)
no issue

m.(1) in 1180
Alexis II Comnenus,
Emperor of
Constantinople
(d.1183)
no issue

m.(3) in 1160
Adela of Champagne
(d.1206)

PHILIP II Augustus
1165-1223
King of France (1180-1223)

(+1 illegitimate child)
see below, page 53

m.(1) in 1137
Eleanor of Aquitaine
(marriage annulled in
1152)

m.(2) in 1154
Constance of Castile
(d.1160)

Adelaide
died young

Margaret
1158-
1197

m.(2) in 1186
Bela III,
King of Hungary
(d.1196)

m.(1) in
1171
Henry of
England
(d.1183)
no issue

Marie
1145-1198
m. in 1164
Henri I,
Count of
Champagne
→ Counts of
Champagne

Alix
1150-post-
1195
m. c.1164
Thibaud V,
Count of Blois
→ Counts of Blois

47

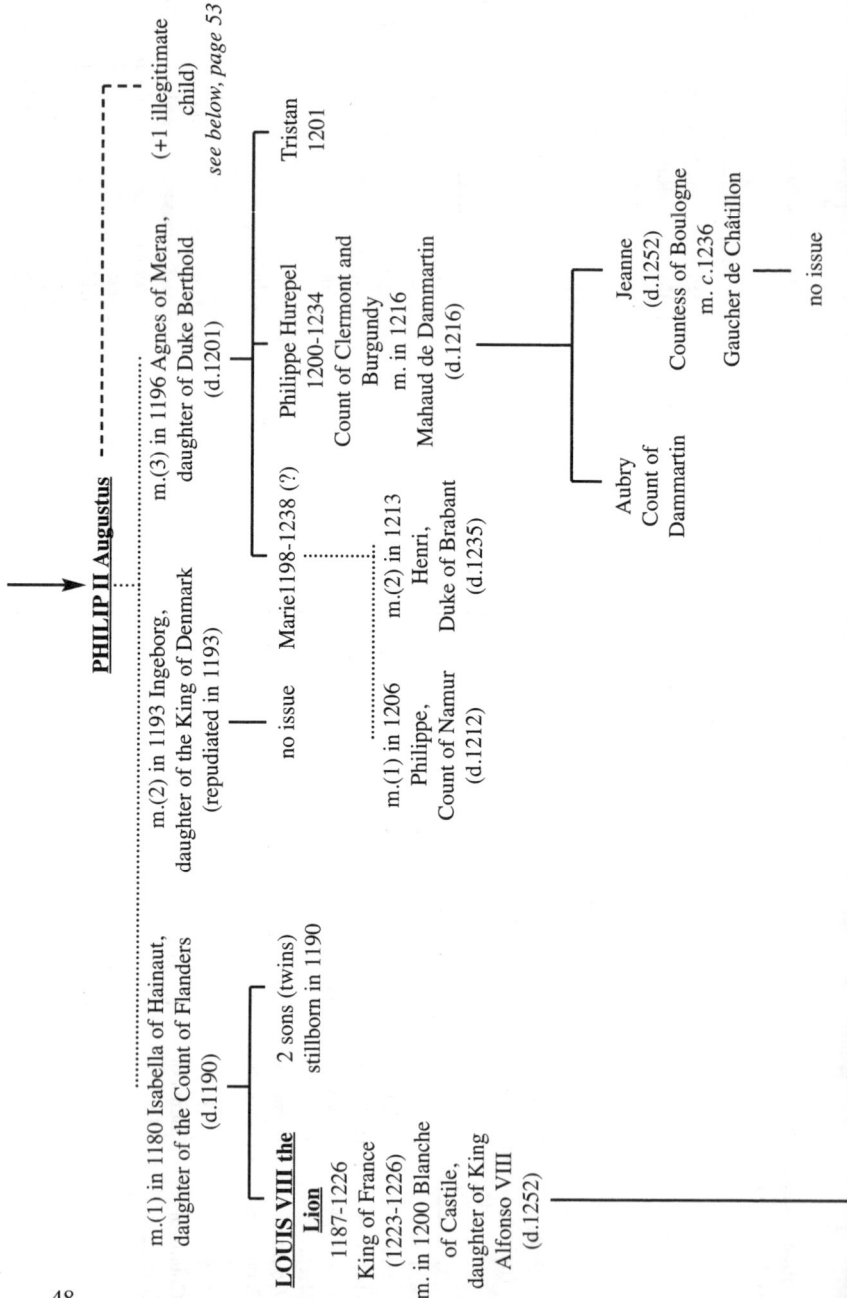

PHILIP II Augustus

m.(1) in 1180 Isabella of Hainaut, daughter of the Count of Flanders (d.1190)

m.(2) in 1193 Ingeborg, daughter of the King of Denmark (repudiated in 1193)

m.(3) in 1196 Agnes of Meran, daughter of Duke Berthold (d.1201)

(+1 illegitimate child) *see below, page 53*

no issue

LOUIS VIII the Lion
1187-1226
King of France (1223-1226)
m. in 1200 Blanche of Castile, daughter of King Alfonso VIII (d.1252)

2 sons (twins) stillborn in 1190

Marie 1198-1238 (?)

m.(1) in 1206 Philippe, Count of Namur (d.1212)

m.(2) in 1213 Henri, Duke of Brabant (d.1235)

Philippe Hurepel 1200-1234
Count of Clermont and Burgundy
m. in 1216 Mahaud de Dammartin (d.1216)

Tristan 1201

Aubry Count of Dammartin

Jeanne (d.1252)
Countess of Boulogne
m. c.1236 Gaucher de Châtillon

no issue

48

Top generation (children):

- **1 daughter** 1205
- **Philippe** 1209-1218
- **twins** stillborn in 1213
- **LOUIS IX (ST. LOUIS)** 1214-1270 — King of France (1226-1270), m. in 1234 Margaret of Provence, daughter of Raymond-Berangar V (d.1295)
- **Robert I** 1216-1250 — Count of Artois, m. in 1237 Mahaud of Brabant → Counts of Artois
- **Jean** 1219-1228
- **Alphonse** 1220-1271 — Count of Poitiers and Toulouse, m. in 1241 Jeanne, daughter of Count Raymond VII of Toulouse (d.1271) — no issue
- **Philippe-Dagobert** 1221-1232
- **Isabelle** 1225-1270 — Abbess of Longchamp
- **Etienne** d.1225
- **Charles I** 1227-1285 — Count of Maine and Anjou, Count of Provence, King of Sicily, King of Naples, King of Jerusalem
  - m.(1) in 1246 Beatrice of Provence, daughter of Raymond-Berangar V (d.1267) → Counts of Anjou
  - m.(2) c.1268 Margaret of Burgundy, Countess de Tonnerre — no issue

Children of LOUIS IX (ST. LOUIS):

- **Blanche** 1240-1243
- **Isabella** 1242-1271 — m. in 1258 Thibaud II, King of Navarre (d.1270) — no issue
- **Louis** 1244-1260
- **PHILIP III the Bold** →
- **Jean** d.1248
- **Jean-Tristan** 1250-1270 — Count de Valois, m. in 1266 Yolande of Burgundy (d.1280) — no issue
- **Pierre** →
- **Blanche** 1253-1320 — m. in 1269 Ferdinand de la Cerda, son of King Alfonso X of Castile (d.1275) →
- **Margaret** 1254-1271 — m. c. 1270 John I, Duke of Brabant (d.1294)
- **Robert** →
- **Agnes** 1260-1327 — m. in 1279 Robert II, Duke of Burgundy (d.1305) → Dukes of Burgundy

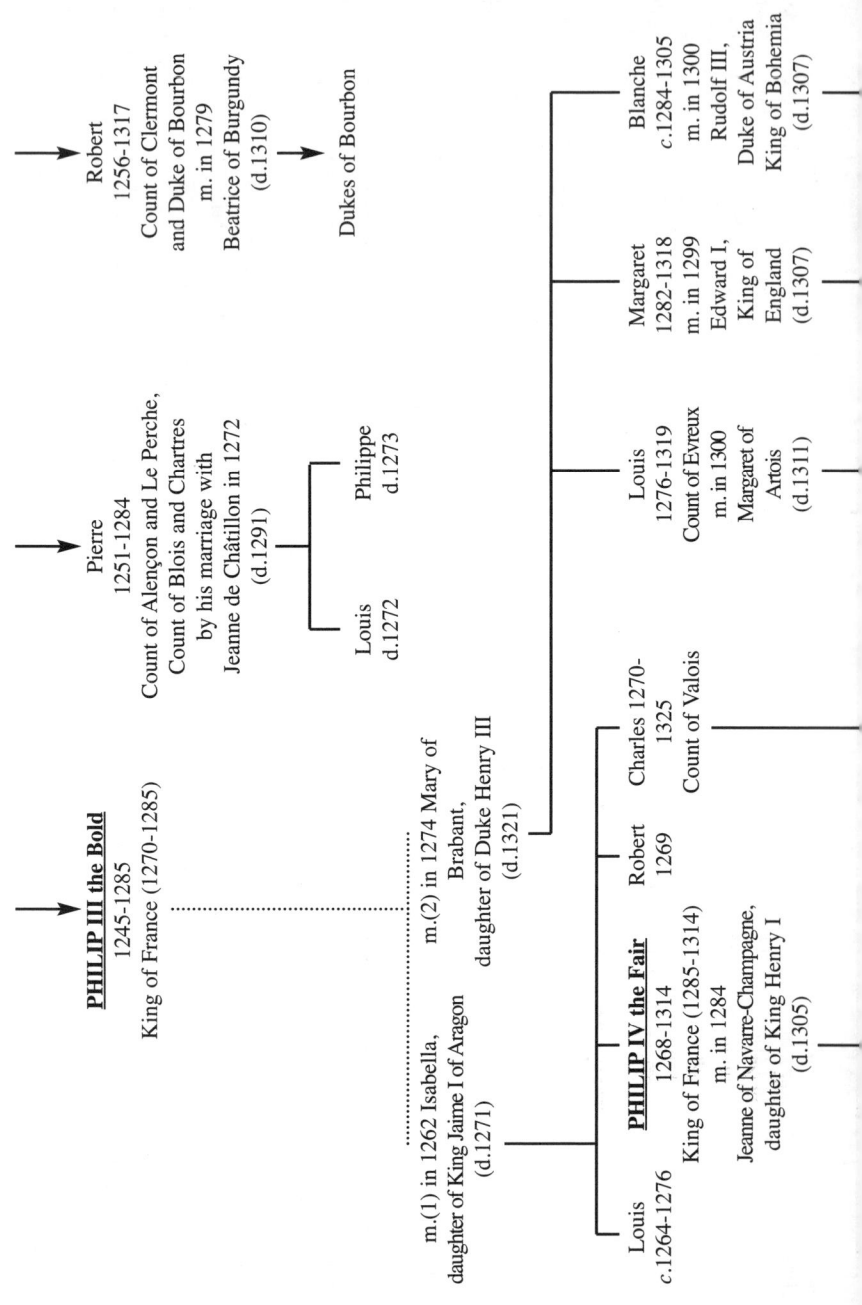

PHILIP III the Bold
1245-1285
King of France (1270-1285)

m.(1) in 1262 Isabella,
daughter of King Jaime I of Aragon
(d.1271)

m.(2) in 1274 Mary of
Brabant,
daughter of Duke Henry III
(d.1321)

Louis
c.1264-1276

PHILIP IV the Fair
1268-1314
King of France (1285-1314)
m. in 1284
Jeanne of Navarre-Champagne,
daughter of King Henry I
(d.1305)

Robert
1269

Charles 1270-
1325
Count of Valois

Pierre
1251-1284
Count of Alençon and Le Perche,
Count of Blois and Chartres
by his marriage with
Jeanne de Châtillon in 1272
(d.1291)

Louis
d.1272

Philippe
d.1273

Robert
1256-1317
Count of Clermont
and Duke of Bourbon
m. in 1279
Beatrice of Burgundy
(d.1310)

Dukes of Bourbon

Louis
1276-1319
Count of Evreux
m. in 1300
Margaret of
Artois
(d.1311)

Margaret
1282-1318
m. in 1299
Edward I,
King of
England
(d.1307)

Blanche
c.1284-1305
m. in 1300
Rudolf III,
Duke of Austria
King of Bohemia
(d.1307)

no issue

THE VALOIS DYNASTY

Counts of Evreux
and kings of Navarre

Marguerite
died young

**LOUIS X the
Stubborn**
1289-1316
King of France
(1314-1316)

(+1 illegitimate child)
see below, page 53

Blanche
died young

m.(2) in 1315
Clemence of Hungary,
daughter of
King Charles Martel
(d.1328)

JOHN I the Posthumous
1316
King of France (1316)

m.(1) in 1305
Margaret of Burgundy,
daughter of Duke
Robert II
(d.1315)

Jeanne II
1311-1349
Queen of Navarre
m. in 1329 Philip III,
Count of Evreux and King of Navarre

Counts of Evreux and kings of Navarre

Isabella
c.1292-1358
m. in 1308
Edward II
King of
England
(d.1327)

Edward III
1312-1377
King of England

**PHILIP V
the Long**
c.1293-1322
King of France
(1316-1322)

**CHARLES IV
the Fair**
1294-1328
King of France
(1322-1328)

Robert
c.1297-1308

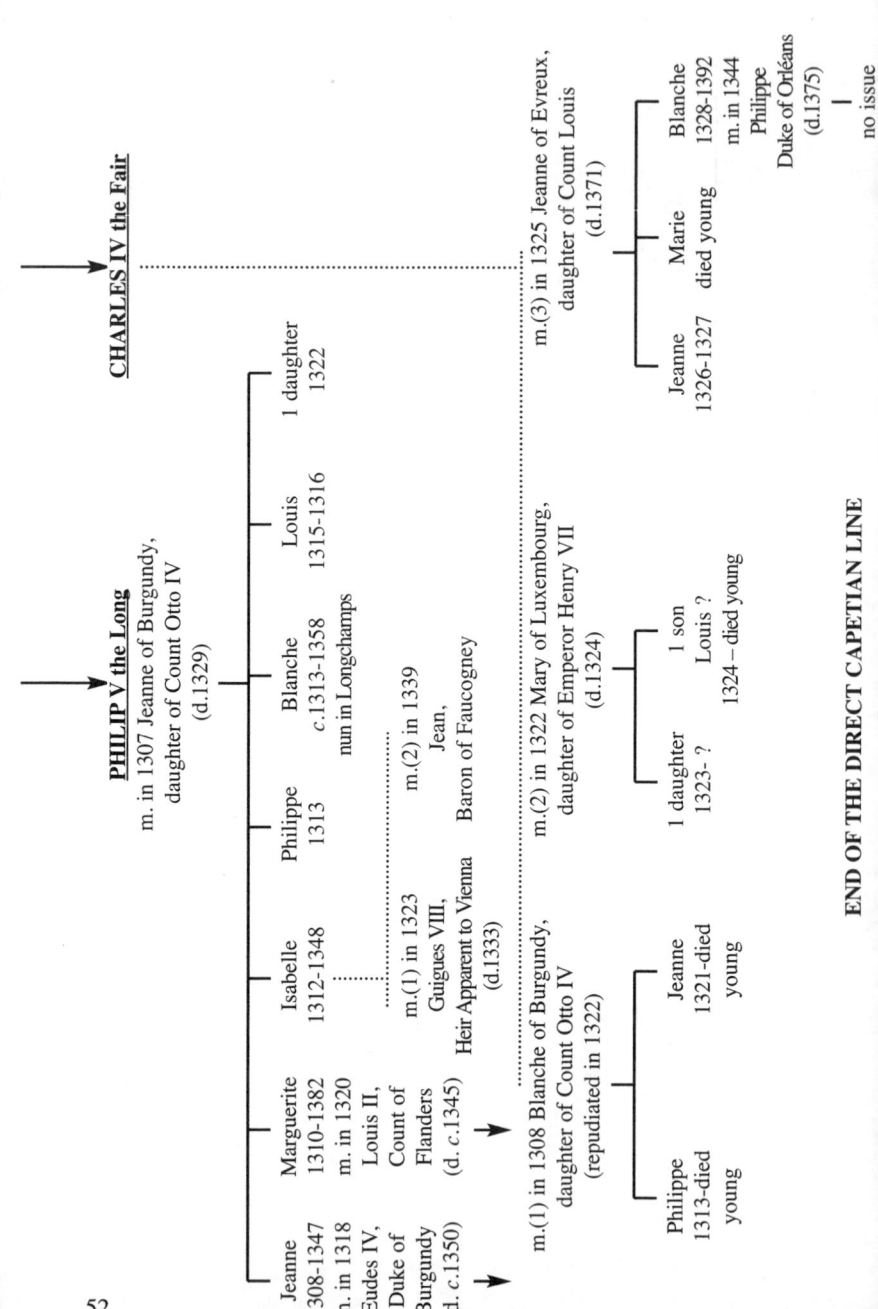

CHARLES IV the Fair

m.(3) in 1325 Jeanne of Evreux, daughter of Count Louis (d.1371)

| Jeanne 1326-1327 | Marie died young | Blanche 1328-1392 m. in 1344 Philippe Duke of Orléans (d.1375) — no issue |

PHILIP V the Long

m. in 1307 Jeanne of Burgundy, daughter of Count Otto IV (d.1329)

Jeanne 1308-1347 m. in 1318 Eudes IV, Duke of Burgundy (d. c.1350)

Marguerite 1310-1382 m. in 1320 Louis II, Count of Flanders (d. c.1345)

Isabelle 1312-1348 m.(1) in 1323 Guigues VIII, Heir Apparent to Vienna (d.1333)

Philippe 1313 m.(2) in 1339 Jean, Baron of Faucogney

Blanche c.1313-1358 nun in Longchamps

Louis 1315-1316

1 daughter 1322

m.(1) in 1308 Blanche of Burgundy, daughter of Count Otto IV (repudiated in 1322)

| Philippe 1313-died young | Jeanne 1321-died young |

m.(2) in 1322 Mary of Luxembourg, daughter of Emperor Henry VII (d.1324)

| 1 daughter 1323- ? | 1 son Louis ? 1324 – died young |

END OF THE DIRECT CAPETIAN LINE

52

THE ILLEGITIMATE DESCENDENTS OF THE DIRECT CAPETIAN LINE

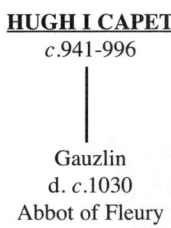

HUGH I CAPET
c.941-996

Gauzlin
d. *c*.1030
Abbot of Fleury

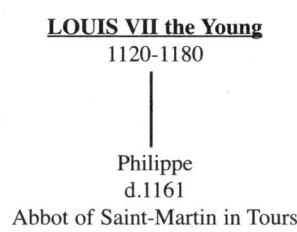

LOUIS VII the Young
1120-1180

Philippe
d.1161
Abbot of Saint-Martin in Tours

PHILIPPE II Augustus
1165-1223
to an unknown bourgeois woman from
Arras

Pierre Charlot
c.1205-1249
Bishop of Noyon

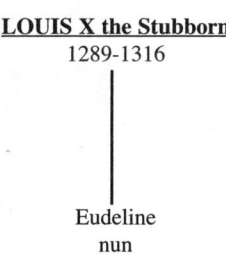

LOUIS X the Stubborn
1289-1316

Eudeline
nun

Philip II Augustus

Hugh I Capet (c. 941-996). King of France (987-996).

Hugh Capet was the grandson of Robert I and the son of Hugh the Great whom he succeeded as Duke of the Franks in 960 A.D. The rise to power of his family, the Robertians, was somewhat slowed by the recovery of the Carolingian dynasty under Kings Lothar and Louis V the Lazy. Before 970 A.D, Hugh married Adelaide, daughter of William III, Count of Poitiers. When Louis V died without leaving an heir, in 987 A.D, Hugh I Capet was elected King of France by the country's leading noblemen, thanks to the support of the Roman Catholic Church and, in particular, Archbishop Adalberon of Reims. This assembly chose Hugh in preference to Duke Charles of Lower Lorraine, brother of King Lothar and heir of the Carolingian dynasty. Hugh Capet had his son Robert crowned in 987 A.D, thereby ensuring the continuity of his line and marking the beginning of the Capetian reign. However, he owned only a very small territory in the Paris Basin and he struggled to impose his will on leading feudal lords, especially Charles of Lorraine, his Carolingian rival who had been proclaimed king by his supporters. Eventually, Charles was handed over and imprisoned, in 991 A.D. During Hugh Capet's reign, a succession of councils of bishops decreed the Peace of God in an attempt to counteract the devastation caused by feudal warfare. When Hugh Capet died in 996 A.D, he was succeeded by his son, Robert II the Pious.

Robert II the Pious (*c*. 972-1031). King of France (996-1031).

Robert, Hugh Capet's son, was crowned in 987 A.D. and involved in affairs of State from then on. He succeeded his father in 996. The beginning of his reign was marked by serious conflict with the papacy. Robert II the Pious married Rosala of Provence in 988 A.D. but repudiated her in the following year. He then remarried, with Bertha of Burgundy, in 996 A.D. Pope Gregory V excommunicated him on grounds of consanguinity and the king, despite strong resistance that lasted for four years, was eventually forced to submit to papal will. He left Bertha of Burgundy in 1001 and married Constance of Arles *c*. 1003 after his first wife had become a nun. During his reign, Robert the Pious was forced, like his father, to combat the feudal lords. From 1002 to 1016, he fought to enforce his claims to the duchy of Burgundy after the Duke's death. He also brought the counties of Paris and Melun under the authority of the Crown. A succession of meetings proclaimed the Peace of God, but in vain. In 1017, King Robert involved his eldest son, Hugh, in affairs of State then, after Hugh's death in 1025, brought his second son, Henri, closer to the throne, having him crowned in 1027. The end of Robert II the Pious' reign was marked by a revolt on the part of his two sons. He died in 1031 and was succeeded by his son, Henri I.

Henri I (1008-1060). King of France (1031-1060).

Henri, the second son of Robert II the Pious and Constance of Arles, was involved in affairs of State by his father in 1027 and succeeded him in 1031. He was faced with hostility on the part of his brother, Robert, who also laid claim to the

Crown with the support of his mother and leading noblemen. Henri I won the struggle but was forced to give Robert the Duchy of Burgundy. He spent his reign warring against the feudal lords. Having initially supported the Duke of Normandy, William the Bastard, he waged war on him and suffered two defeats, in Mortemer (1054) and Varaville (1058). It was during Henri I's reign that the Truce of God was introduced, at the Council of Provence in 1041. The intention of the Roman Catholic Church was to limit feudal wars, while at the same time instigating the Peace of God. In 1051, Henri I took Anne of Kiev as his second wife, thereby developing relations with Russia. In 1059, he involved his elder son, Philip, in affairs of State. Henri died in the following year.

Philip I (c. 1052-1108). King of France (1060-1108).

Philip, the elder son of Henri I and Anne of Kiev, was involved in affairs of State in 1059 and became king in 1060 at the age of eight. His uncle, Beaudouin V, Count of Flanders, acted as Regent. During his reign, he was involved in the struggles between leading feudal lords. After the Count's death, Philip I launched an expedition to ensure the Flemish succession but was defeated at Kassel in 1071 by Robert the Frisian. In 1087, Philip supported Robert Shorthose against his father, William the Conqueror, Duke of Normandy and King of England, but in vain. He extended the Crown estates by acquiring the Gâtinais, Vexin, Corbie and Bourges areas and, during his reign, royal authority began to make its mark. In 1071, Philip I married Bertha of Holland but he repudiated her in 1091 in order to marry Bertrade of Montfort, the wife of Fulk of Anjou, after kidnapping her. He was excommunicated for his actions by Pope Urban II (1094) and the kingdom was struck by a papal interdict (1100). However, Philip ignored the excommunications and continued a life more given to pleasure than to official functions. Eventually, in 1105, he submitted to papal will. Because of his problems with the Pope, Philip I did not take part in the First Crusade (1096-1099) organised in order to reconquer places in the Holy Land. He died in 1108, having paved the way for his succession by having his son, Louis, crowned in 1100.

Louis VI the Fat (c. 1081-1137). King of France (1108-1137).

Louis VI the Fat was the elder son of Philip I and Bertha of Holland and he was involved in affairs of State by his father in 1100. He succeeded his father in 1108. His reign marked a decisive stage in the strengthening of the Capetian monarchy, in particular as regards its relationship with leading noblemen. Louis VI worked initially to strengthen his authority over the royal estate by combating pillaging lords who were rampaging through the Paris Basin. In this struggle, he received the support of the Church (Abbot Suger was his adviser) and of the people. He was the first Capetian to begin to intervene outside his own lands and become involved in the affairs of certain feudal estates, in particular in the Bourbonnais area (1109), Auvergne (1122, 1126) and Flanders (1128). His longest struggle, however, was against the most fearsome of all his vassals, Henry I Beauclerk, Duke of

Normandy and King of England. He waged war on Henry three times between 1109 and 1124 but without any real success (he was defeated in Brémule in 1119). Intervention on the part of Emperor Henry V in 1123 enabled Louis VI to summon his vassals and repulse danger; this increased his personal prestige. His reign was also marked by a move to release towns from the control of local lords. The king encouraged such action when it was in his interest to do so. In 1129, he began preparing his succession and had his elder son, Philip, crowned. On Philip's death in 1131, he had his second son, Louis, crowned in his place. Louis VI's reign ended with the marriage of his son and heir, Louis, to Eleanor of Aquitaine (1137). This extended the royal estates to the Pyrenees.

Louis VII the Younger (1120-1180). King of France (1137-1180).

Louis VII, the second son of King Louis VI the Fat, was crowned in 1131 and succeeded his father in 1137. A few days before the latter's death, Louis VII married Eleanor of Aquitaine. She brought as her dowry the entire south-west of France. From the beginning of his reign, Louis VII the Younger was faced with a serious crisis involving the Pope and Thibaud IV of Champagne, concerning the appointment of the Archbishop of Bourges (1142-1144). Eventually, the King of France was forced into submission by the Treaty of Vitry. In order to expiate his faults, Louis VII announced his intention to become a crusader. He took part in the Second Crusade in the Holy Land, preached by Bernard of Clairvaux, with Emperor Conrad III, leaving his kingdom under the control of Abbot Suger who acted as Regent for two years (1147-1149). The crusade however, was a total failure. Louis VIII lost his army and the episode also revealed the beginnings of discord between the royal spouses. After the death of Suger in 1151, the king finally had his marriage to Eleanor of Aquitaine annuled by the Council of Beaugency (1152). The queen, who had given Louis no heir, immediately remarried, with Henry II Plantagenet, Count of Anjou, Duke of Normandy and future King of England (1154). The marriage represented a serious threat for Louis VII since Henry then had control of almost the whole of the western half of France and was, therefore, more powerful than the French monarch. This marked the beginning of a long struggle between Capetians and Plantagenets, a struggle that was to last for three centuries. Louis VII supported his enemies in order to combat the King of England, first Thomas Becket, Archbishop of Canterbury (1164-1170) then the English monarch's rebel sons (1173-1174) but the French sovereign was unable to shake his enemy's power. The Treaty of Gisors (1180) marked the end of this series of wars between France and England. Louis VII's reign also highlighted a continued strengthening of royal authority over the provinces. In particular, he was the first king to publish ordinances, such as the one in 1155 which declared a ten-year peace in the kingdom. Louis VII only had an heir when he took a third wife, Adela of Champagne, and after a reign lasting 28 years. His heir was Philip Augustus, born in 1165 and crowned in 1179.

Philip II Augustus (1165-1223). King of France (1180-1223).

Philip, the only male child among the seven offspring that Louis VII had with his three wives, represented the heir that had been awaited for so long in order to ensure the continuation of the dynasty and he was only fifteen years old when his father died in 1180. From the outset, Philip II Augustus was confronted by a coalition of leading feudal lords from Flanders, Champagne and Burgundy but he succeeded in defeating them and, by the Treaty of Boves (1185) he obtained the Artois and Vermandois areas as well as Amiens. He then took up the struggle against Henry II of England again, providing support for the rebel son, Richard the Lionheart (1187-1189). He set off with Richard on the Third Crusade in 1190 but quickly returned on his own (late 1191) and took advantage of Richard's arrest, on his return, by the Duke of Austria who handed him over to Emperor Henry VI (1194). Philip invaded Normandy but was defeated at Fréteval (1194) then in Courcelles (1198). After the death of Richard the Lionheart in 1199, Phiip Augustus continued the fight, against the new King of England, John Lackland. Taking a feudal conflict as his excuse, he confiscated John's lands in France and invaded Normandy in 1202. Between 1204 and 1208, Philip Augustus took Normandy, Touraine, Anjou and the Poitiers area. John then set up a coalition with the Counts of Flanders and Boulogne and Emperor Otto of Brunswick whom Philip Augustus succeeded in defeating at Bouvines in 1214. Despite an attempt on the part of the King of France to invade England, the conflict ended, temporarily, in 1217. Thanks to major territorial gains from England, added to the new lands acquired at the beginning of his reign, Philip Augustus considerably extended the royal estates. His reign was also marked by increased control of the kingdom through the appointment of bailiffs or seneschals. The Cathar Crusade preached by the Pope and instigated by Simon de Montfort in 1209 gave the monarchy a foothold in southern France. The king was faced with serious conflict with the papacy. After the death of his first wife, Isabella of Hainaut, in 1190, he married Ingeborg of Denmark in 1193 but repudiated her immediately and remarried in 1196, this time with Agnès de Méranie. He was condemned by Pope Innocent III and the kingdom was struck by an interdict (1199). After the death of Agnès de Méranie in 1201, Philip Augustus agreed, in 1213, to bring back Queen Ingeborg. It was during his reign that Paris became the capital of the kingdom. The king had a wall built round it and commissioned the building of the first Louvre Palace. Philip II Augustus was succeeded by his eldest son, Louis VIII.

Louis VIII the Lion (1187-1226). King of France (1223-1226).

Prince Louis, Philip II Augustus' elder son, took part in the battles against the English early in his father's reign (1214-1217). He succeeded his father in 1223 and continued the struggle to recapture English possessions in France (the Poitou and Saintonge areas). Louis VIII then engaged in a crusade against the Cathars (Albigensians) and took control of Languedoc (1226) but fell ill and died on the return journey. In 1225, he granted land to his sons in appanage. Robert received the Artois area, Alphonse the Poitou region and Jean the Anjou and Maine areas (which were later granted to Charles). His eldest son, Louis, whom he had had with Blanche of Castile, succeeded him on the throne.

Louis IX or St. Louis (1214-1270). King of France (1226-1270).

Louis IX, son of, and successor to, Louis VIII the Lion, mounted the throne of France at the age of twelve. Initially, he reigned under the control of his mother, Blanche of Castile, who was confronted by a coalition of major vassals led by Peter Mauclerc, Count of Brittany. She succeeded in defeating him in 1234 after several campaigns while Louis IX himself put down a revolt on the part of noblemen supported by King Henry III of England in 1230. Under the terms of the Treaty of Meaux (1229), the regent ended that war against the Albigensians and prepared for the annexation of the County of Toulouse to the Crown (through the marriage of her other son, Alphonse, with the heiress to the County of Toulouse in 1241). Louis IX was proclaimed to have reached the age of majority in 1234 but he left his mother to continue governing the country and, that same year, she married him to Margaret of Provence. A further revolt by a leading vassal, Hugh of Lusiganan, in 1241 re-opened hostilities between France and England. Henry III landed on the continent in 1242 but was defeated by Louis IX in Taillebourg and Saintes. A five-year truce was agreed the following year. First and foremost, however, the King of France sought a fair, long-lasting peace with England. He signed the Treaty of Paris with Henry III in 1258. Under it, the monarchs made reciprocal territorial concessions (the King of England waived his claims to the lands lost since the reign of Philip Augustus and the King of France gave him the Limousin, Quercy and Périgord regions). In the same vein, Louis IX signed the Treaty of Corbeil with Jaime I of Aragon during the same year. As far as domestic policy was concerned, Louis IX's reign was marked by his desire for order and justice (private warfare and duelling were prohibited, royal investigators were sent out to monitor the affairs of bailiffs, there were numerous ordinances aimed at reforming the kingdom, a parliament was set up and monetary reform was undertaken). France then became highly influential throughout Europe on an ethical, intellectual and artistic level. All these measures underlined a strengthening of royal power. The monarchy was to be at the service of all since it was often the people's only effective safeguard against the disorders of the feudal system. Louis IX was a sovereign with a fervent Christian faith and, after a serious illness, he made a promise to take part in a crusade. He participated in the last two crusades to the Holy Land. During the first one, he was absent from his kingdom for six years, from 1248 to 1254, leaving his mother and, later, his brothers, to govern. It was, though, a failure. He was even held prisoner in Egypt in 1250 before spending several years in Syria organising the fortification of French strongholds. During the second crusade, in 1270, Louis IX did not lead the expeditionary forces very far – he died of plague during an epidemic off Tunis. He was canonised in 1297. He was succeeded by his son, Philip III the Bold, since his elder son, Louis, had died in 1260.

Philip III the Bold (1245-1285). King of France (1270-1285).

Louis IX's second son succeeded his father in 1270 and was proclaimed king in Tunis, having accompanied his father on the crusade. In 1271, when his uncle, Alphonse of Poitiers, died, Philip III annexed the Poitou area and County of Toulouse to the Crown. He also inherited from his brother, Pierre, the Perche area and County of Alençon, in 1284. However, he gave the Comtat Venaissin to the Pope in 1274. His first wife, Isabella of Aragon, gave him four sons, including the future Philip the Fair. He became a widower and married again in 1274, to Mary of Brabant. With England and its new king, Edward I, Philip III the Bold continued the policy of peace instigated by his father and signed the Treaty of Amiens in 1279. This confirmed the Treaty of Paris signed in 1258. After the "Sicilian Vespers" (1282), during which the French were chased out of Sicily by King Peter III of Aragon, Pope Martin IV excommunicated the monarch of Aragon and attributed his kingdom to Charles of Valois, the King of France's son. Philip III then organised an expedition to conquer Aragon but it soon failed. The French fleet was destroyed and the King of France died during an epidemic in Perpignan (1285) to which he had retreated with his army. He was succeeded by his second son, Philip IV the Fair.

Philip IV the Fair (1268-1314). King of France (1285-1314).

Philip IV the Fair, second son of Philip III the Bold and Isabella of Aragon, mounted the throne in 1285 on the death of his father. In 1284, he married Jeanne of Navarre-Champagne, bringing these two provinces to the Crown. Philip the Fair began by signing the Treaty of Tarascon (1291) in order to end the Aragon crusade. He then turned his attention to Flanders and England. In 1294, he confiscated Edward I's lands in France. War was waged in Guyenne, in south-western France, which the French monarch's army conquered in 1296; it ended with the signature of the Treaty of Montreuil in 1299, paving the way for the marriage of Philip the Fair's sister with Edward I and the wedding of the King of France's daughter with the heir to the throne of England. Under the terms of the Treaty of Paris, signed in 1303, Philip the Fair returned to Edward I the territories conquered between 1294 and 1297. However, the alliance between England and Flanders moved the fighting to the north of France. After the French victory in Furnes in 1297, the French army occupied Flanders in 1300 but a revolt forced the French out of Bruges and Philip the Fair was defeated in Courtrai in 1302. The King of France took his revenge over the Flemings in Mons-en-Pévèle in 1304. The Peace of Athis, signed the following year, enabled him to annex Flanders. During his reign, he also took over the Bar and Lyon areas. In order to finance the wars, and overcome a difficult financial situation, Philip the Fair implemented a series of devaluations between 1290 and 1309. He sought further funding by confiscating property belonging to the Lombards and Jews in 1292 then levied the first indirect tax. However, the monarch's main preoccupation was the levying of exceptional taxes on the clergy; this led him into serious conflict with the Pope from 1296 onwards. When, in 1301, Philip the Fair ordered the arrest of Bernard Saisset, Bishop of Pamiers and papal legate, on charges of treason, Pope Boniface VIII convened a council of the Church of France in Rome. The king countered with a meeting of the three orders of the kingdom (April 1302), a forerunner of the future States General. The meeting gave him its support. In the papal bull entitled *Unam sanctam*, the Pope repeated his theory of papal superiority over soveriegns (1302). The struggle ended with the terrorist attack in Anagni in 1303, an attempt at intimidation but which, in fact , cost the Pope his life. Reconciliation did not occur until the election of the French Pope, Clement V, in 1305. He transferred the Holy See to Avignon in 1309. Financial difficulties led Philip the Fair into conflict with the Order of the Temple, which was abolished. Its members were arrested, sentenced and put to death; among them was the Grand Master, Jacques de Molay (1307-1314). The king's domestic policies were aimed at a strengthening of royal prerogatives, aided by his legal advisers (Pierre Flote, Enguerrand de Marigny and Guilllaume de Nogaret). This frequently led him to convene meetings of the three orders in order to seek approval for his ideas. The last months of Philip the Fair's reign were marred by the scandal surrounding his sons' wives who were condemned for adultery. The monarch was also faced with a revolt on the part of the nobility, discontented with the levying of further taxation. The king died in 1314 and was succeeded by his eldest son, Louis X the Stubborn.

Louis X the Stubborn (1289-1316). King of France (1314-1316).

Philip IV the Fair's eldest son, who became King of Navarre on his mother's death in 1305, succeeded his father on the throne of France in 1314. Louis the Stubborn's short reign (it lasted only eighteen months) was marked by strong feudal reaction to his father's policies and revolt against the advisers who had served him. Louis X was married to Margaret of Burgundy in 1305 but he repudiated her in 1314 because of her misbehaviour. He had her imprisoned and strangled in 1315. The king's untimely death, leaving his second wife, Clemenza of Hungary pregnant, posed the problem of the royal succession for the first time since the days of Hugh Capet. Until such time as the child was born, the regency was provided by the dead king's brother, Philip.

John I the Posthumous (1316). King of France (1316).

John I was the posthumous son of Louis X the Stubborn, who died leaving his wife Clemenza of Hungary pregnant. John was the long-awaited heir but he lived only a few days and may have been murdered at his uncle's instigation. For the first time since 987 A.D and the accession of the Capetian dynasty, there was no direct male descendent. The Crown therefore passed to Philip V the Long, second son of Philip the Fair.

Philip V the Long (*c*. 1293-1322). King of France (1316-1322).

Philip the Fair's second son was proclaimed regent upon the death of his brother, Louis X the Stubborn, in 1316 leaving the queen pregnant. The birth then death of a posthumous heir in the person of John I, took Philip V to the throne in preference to Jeanne, Louis X's daughter, since he had the States General declare women to be incapable of mounting the throne (1317). He put an end to the simmering revolt by leading vassals and to a new rebellion in Flanders. His reign was also marred by a countrymen's revolt in the south of France. He continued his father's domestic policy by issuing a large number of ordinances. He reorganised the Privy Council (1318) and gave the Chamber of Accounts its definitive status (1320). Through his marriage with Jeanne of Burgundy, he acquired Franche-Comté. He died in 1322 leaving only daughters, and the crown passed to his brother, Charles, the last surviving son of Philip the Fair.

Charles IV the Fair (1294-1328). King of France (1322-1328).

Charles IV, the third and last surviving son of Philip the Fair, succeeded his brother, Philip V the Long, who had died without leaving a male heir. He was faced with a new rebellion in Flanders in 1323; it ended with the Treaty of Arques (1326). The situation with England again became tense and Charles IV confiscated Guyenne which his uncle, Charles de Valois, conquered in 1324. After the death of Edward II of England in 1327, part of the territory was handed back to his successor, Edward III. In domestic policies, the king continued to reorganise the justice system and finances. His reign was also marked by the problem of his succession. After repudiating his first wife, Blanche of Burgundy, who had been accused of adultery, he married a second time, with Mary of Luxembourg (1322) who died in childbirth in 1324 without leaving him any living child. His third wife, Jeanne of Evreux, gave him only daughters. Charles IV's early death in 1328 left the throne with no direct heir for the first time since the days of Hugh Capet. He was, therefore, the last member of the direct Capetian line and the crown passed to his cousin, Philip VI de Valois.

Philip IV the Fair

Louis IX

THE DIRECT VALOIS LINE

This branch of the Capetian dynasty mounted the throne of France in 1328 through Philip VI, son of Charles de Valois and nephew of Philip IV the Fair, since the latter's three sons had all died without leaving a male heir. The new king was chosen by leading noblemen in the kingdom in preference to King Edward III of England, despite the fact that he was Philip IV the Fair's grandson through his mother, Isabella.

The Valois dynasty ruled France from 1328 to 1589. Three lines resulted from the dynasty. The direct Valois line (1328-1498) gave France seven kings from Philip VI to Charles VIII, was another 170-year period of succession from father to son.

This was a very difficult time, marked by the Hundred Years' War, the imprisonment of King John II the Good, the insanity of King Charles VI and the civil war between Armagnacs and Burgundians. However, the second half of the 15th century brought a strengthening of royal authority with King Charles VII (1422-1461) and King Louis XI (1461-1483).

In 1498, Charles VIII died without a male heir and the crown passed to the nearest living prince of the blood, his cousin, the Duke d'Orléans who became King Louis XII.

Philip VI de Valois

THE DIRECT VALOIS LINE

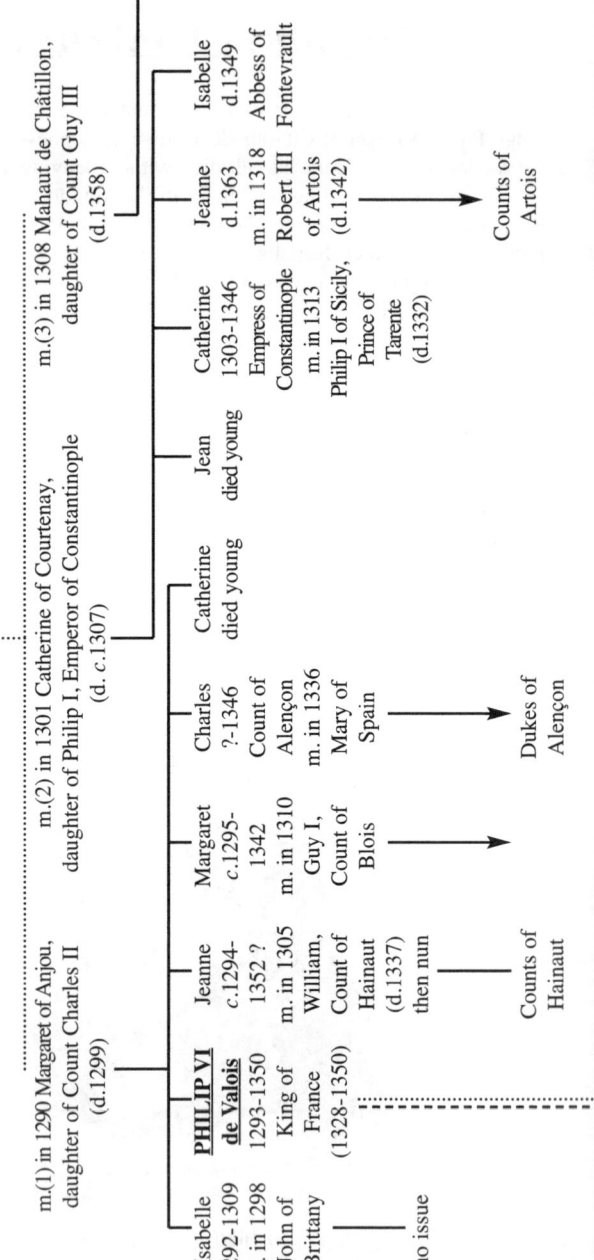

Charles
1270-1325
Count of Valois
Brother of Philip IV the Fair

m.(1) in 1290 Margaret of Anjou, daughter of Count Charles II (d.1299)

m.(2) in 1301 Catherine of Courtenay, daughter of Philip I, Emperor of Constantinople (d. c.1307)

m.(3) in 1308 Mahaut de Châtillon, daughter of Count Guy III (d.1358)

Isabelle
1292-1309
m. in 1298
John of Brittany

no issue

PHILIP VI de Valois
1293-1350
King of France
(1328-1350)

Jeanne
c.1294-1352 ?
m. in 1305
William, Count of Hainaut (d.1337)
then nun

Counts of Hainaut

Margaret
c.1295-1342
m. in 1310
Guy I, Count of Blois

Charles
?-1346
Count of Alençon
m. in 1336
Mary of Spain

Dukes of Alençon

Catherine
died young

Jean
died young

Catherine
1303-1346
Empress of Constantinople
m. in 1313
Philip I of Sicily, Prince of Tarente (d.1332)

Jeanne
d.1363
m. in 1318
Robert III of Artois (d.1342)

Counts of Artois

Isabelle
d.1349
Abbess of Fontevrault

64

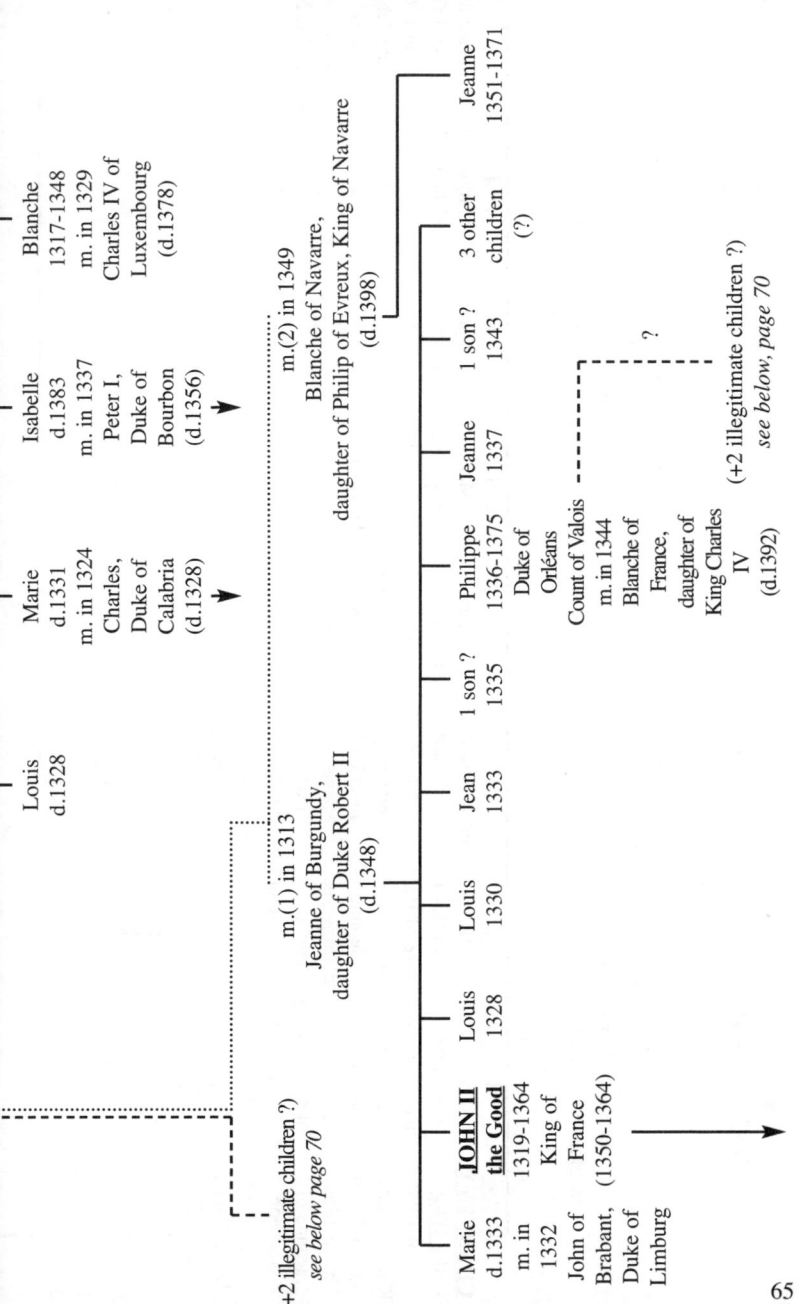

Marie
d.1333
m. in
1332
John of
Brabant,
Duke of
Limburg

**JOHN II
the Good**
1319-1364
King of
France
(1350-1364)

Louis
1328

Louis
1330

Jean
1333

m.(1) in 1313
Jeanne of Burgundy,
daughter of Duke Robert II
(d.1348)

1 son ?
1335

Philippe
1336-1375
Duke of
Orléans
m. in 1344
Blanche of
France,
daughter of
King Charles
IV
(d.1392)

Count of Valois

Jeanne
1337

1 son ?
1343

m.(2) in 1349
Blanche of Navarre,
daughter of Philip of Evreux, King of Navarre
(d.1398)

3 other
children
(?)

Louis
d.1328

Marie
d.1331
m. in 1324
Charles,
Duke of
Calabria
(d.1328)

Isabelle
d.1383
m. in 1337
Peter I,
Duke of
Bourbon
(d.1356)

Blanche
1317-1348
m. in 1329
Charles IV of
Luxembourg
(d.1378)

Jeanne
1351-1371

(+2 illegitimate children ?
see below page 70

(+2 illegitimate children ?
see below, page 70

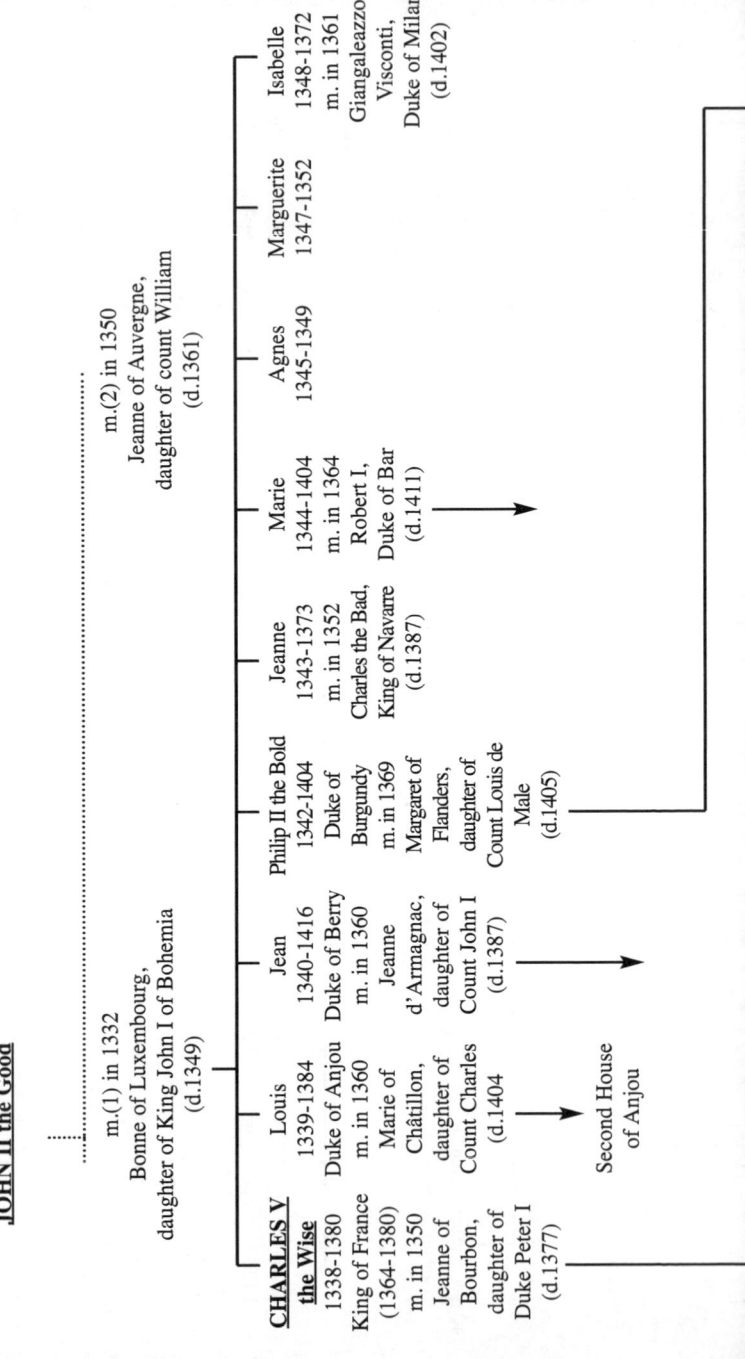

66

JOHN II the Good

m.(1) in 1332
Bonne of Luxembourg,
daughter of King John I of Bohemia
(d.1349)

m.(2) in 1350
Jeanne of Auvergne,
daughter of count William
(d.1361)

CHARLES V the Wise
1338-1380
King of France
(1364-1380)
m. in 1350
Jeanne of Bourbon,
daughter of Duke Peter I
(d.1377)

Louis
1339-1384
Duke of Anjou
m. in 1360
Marie of Châtillon,
daughter of Count Charles
(d.1404)

Second House
of Anjou

Jean
1340-1416
Duke of Berry
m. in 1360
Jeanne d'Armagnac,
daughter of Count John I
(d.1387)

Philip II the Bold
1342-1404
Duke of Burgundy
m. in 1369
Margaret of Flanders,
daughter of Count Louis de Male
(d.1405)

Jeanne
1343-1373
m. in 1352
Charles the Bad,
King of Navarre
(d.1387)

Marie
1344-1404
m. in 1364
Robert I,
Duke of Bar
(d.1411)

Agnes
1345-1349

Marguerite
1347-1352

Isabelle
1348-1372
m. in 1361
Giangaleazzo Visconti,
Duke of Milan
(d.1402)

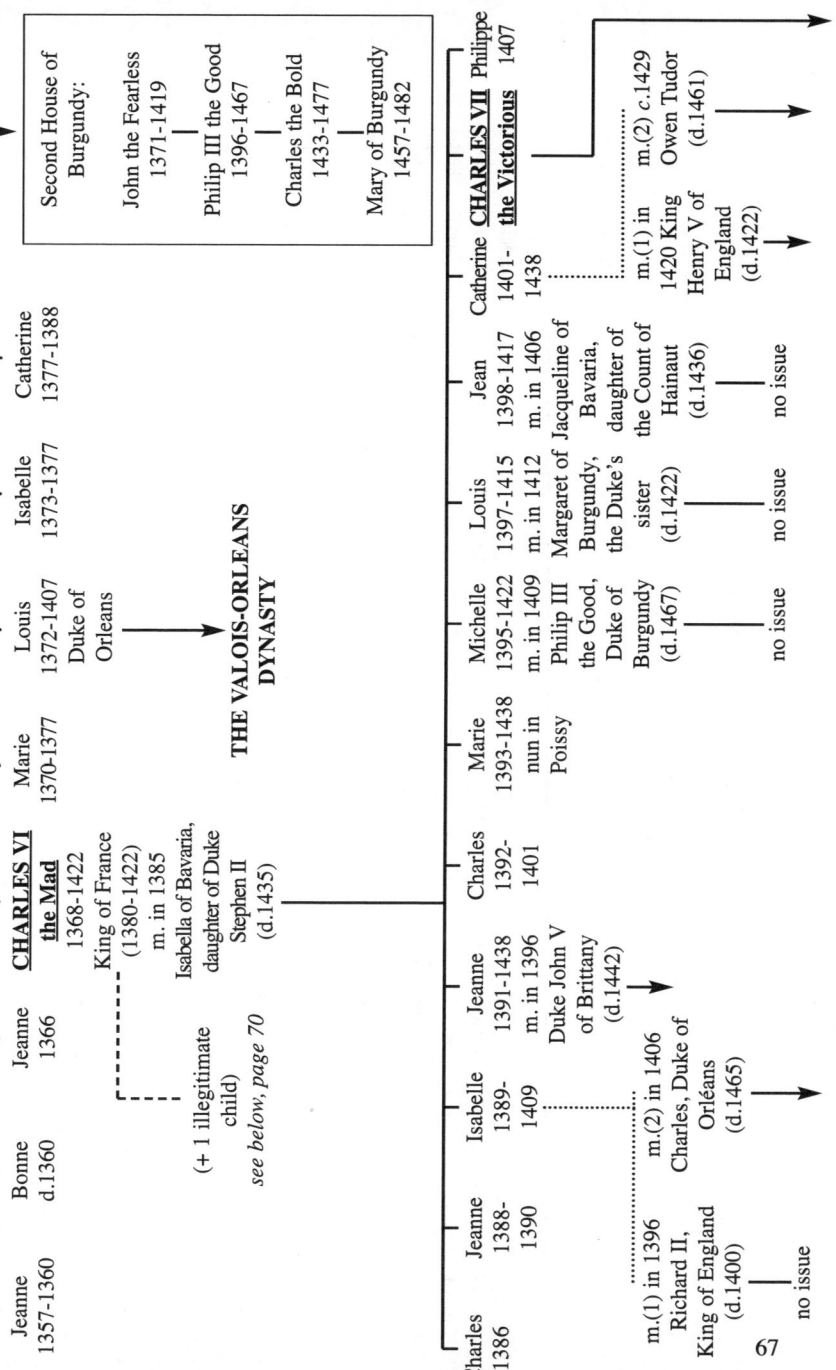

Second House of Burgundy:

John the Fearless
1371-1419
│
Philip III the Good
1396-1467
│
Charles the Bold
1433-1477
│
Mary of Burgundy
1457-1482

Jeanne
1357-1360

Bonne
d.1360

Jeanne
1366

Marie
1370-1377

Louis
1372-1407
Duke of
Orleans →

**THE VALOIS-ORLEANS
DYNASTY**

Isabelle
1373-1377

Catherine
1377-1388

**CHARLES VI
the Mad**
1368-1422
King of France
(1380-1422)
m. in 1385
Isabella of Bavaria,
daughter of Duke
Stephen II
(d.1435)

(+ 1 illegitimate
child)
see below, page 70

Charles
1386

Jeanne
1388-
1390

Isabelle
1389-
1409

Jeanne
1391-1438
m. in 1396
Duke John V
of Brittany
(d.1442) →

Charles
1392-
1401

Marie
1393-1438
nun in
Poissy

Michelle
1395-1422
m. in 1409
Philip III
the Good,
Duke of
Burgundy
(d.1467)

no issue

Louis
1397-1415
m. in 1412
Margaret of
Burgundy,
the Duke's
sister
(d.1422)

no issue

Jean
1398-1417
m. in 1406
Jacqueline of
Bavaria,
daughter of
the Count of
Hainaut
(d.1436)

no issue

Catherine
1401-
1438

**CHARLES VII
the Victorious**

Philippe
1407

m.(1) in 1396
Richard II,
King of England
(d.1400)

m.(2) in 1406
Charles, Duke of
Orléans
(d.1465) →

no issue

m.(1) in 1420 King
Henry V of
England
(d.1422) →

m.(2) c.1429
Owen Tudor
(d.1461) →

67

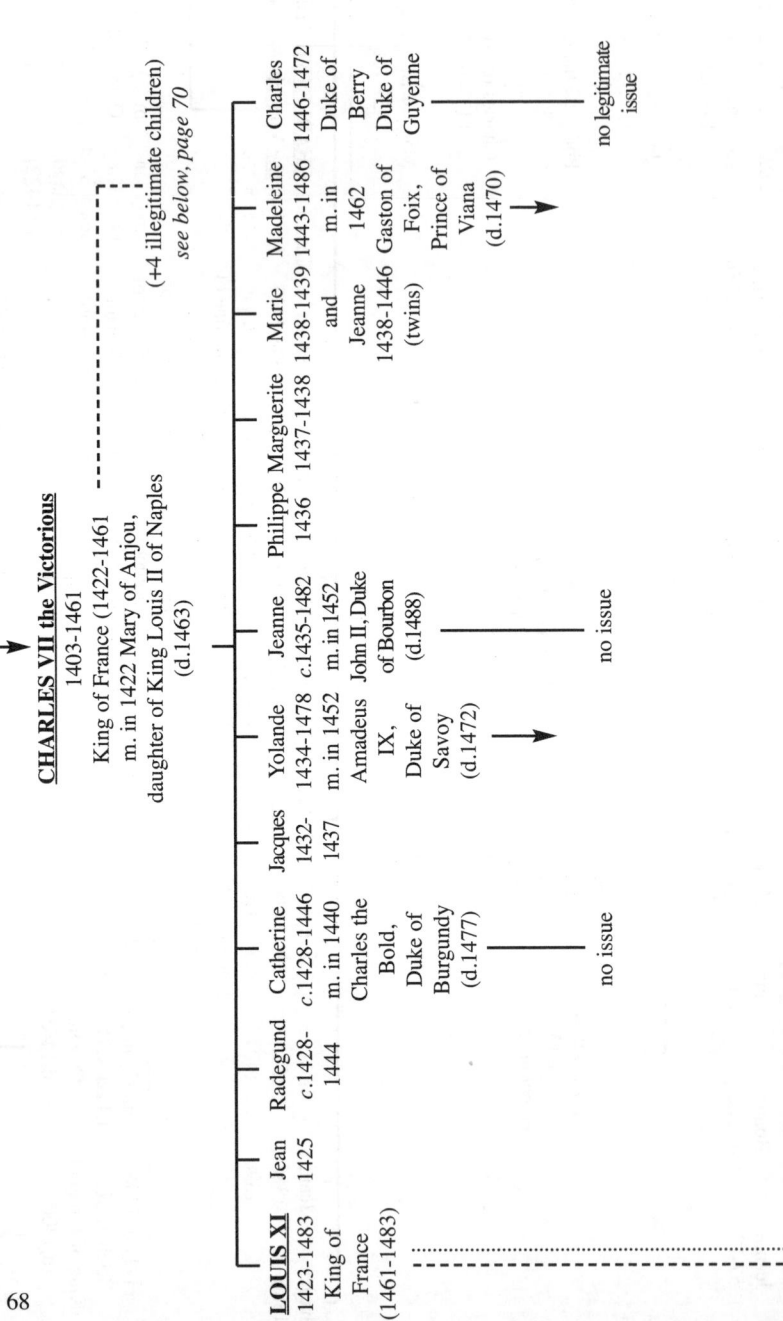

CHARLES VII the Victorious
1403-1461
King of France (1422-1461)
m. in 1422 Mary of Anjou,
daughter of King Louis II of Naples
(d.1463)

(+4 illegitimate children)
see below, page 70

LOUIS XI
1423-1483
King of
France
(1461-1483)

Jean
1425

Radegund
c.1428-
1444

Catherine
c.1428-1446
m. in 1440
Charles the
Bold,
Duke of
Burgundy
(d.1477)

no issue

Jacques
1432-
1437

Yolande
1434-1478
m. in 1452
Amadeus
IX,
Duke of
Savoy
(d.1472)

Jeanne
c.1435-1482
m. in 1452
John II, Duke
of Bourbon
(d.1488)

no issue

Philippe
1436

Marguerite
1437-1438

Marie
1438-1439
and
Jeanne
1438-1446
(twins)

Madeleine
1443-1486
m. in
1462
Gaston of
Foix,
Prince of
Viana
(d.1470)

Charles
1446-1472
Duke of
Berry
Duke of
Guyenne

no legitimate
issue

68

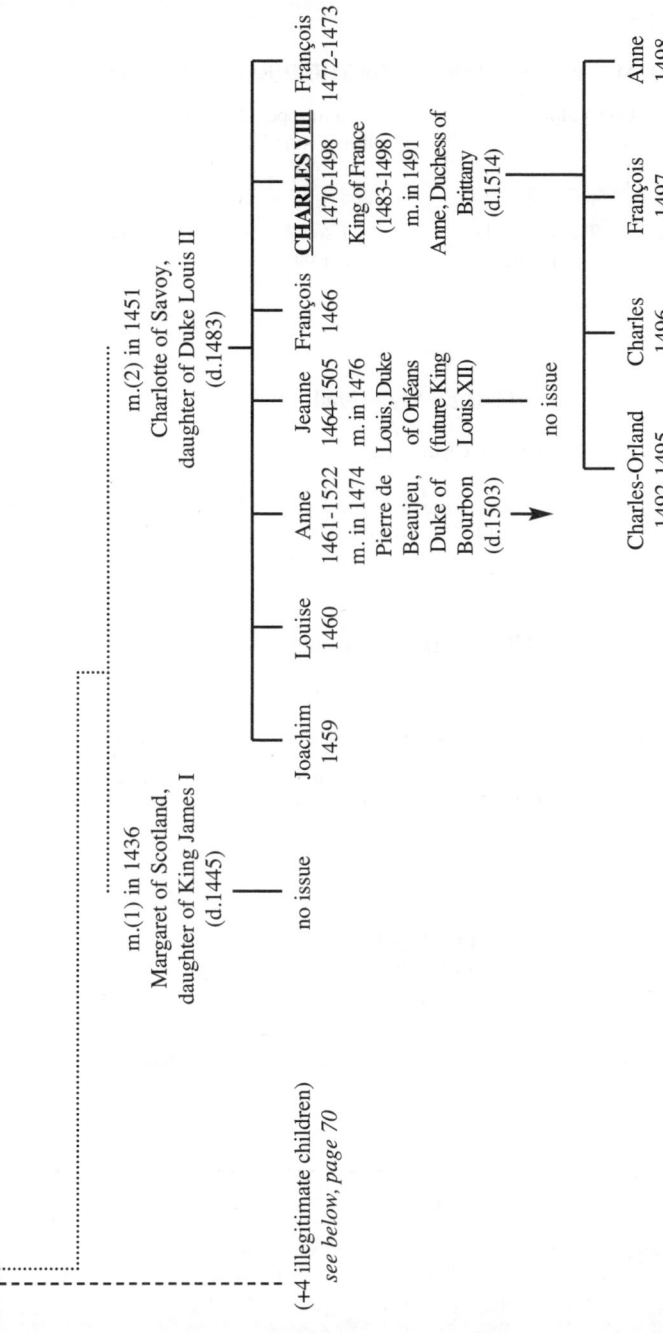

m.(1) in 1436
Margaret of Scotland,
daughter of King James I
(d.1445)

no issue

m.(2) in 1451
Charlotte of Savoy,
daughter of Duke Louis II
(d.1483)

Joachim 1459

Louise 1460

Anne 1461-1522
m. in 1474
Pierre de Beaujeu,
Duke of Bourbon
(d.1503)

Jeanne 1464-1505
m. in 1476
Louis, Duke of Orléans
(future King Louis XII)

no issue

François 1466

CHARLES VIII
1470-1498
King of France
(1483-1498)
m. in 1491
Anne, Duchess of Brittany
(d.1514)

François 1472-1473

Charles-Orland 1492-1495

Charles 1496

François 1497

Anne 1498

END OF THE DIRECT VALOIS LINE

(+4 illegitimate children)
see below, page 70

69

THE ILLEGITIMATE DESCENDENTS OF THE DIRECT VALOIS LINE

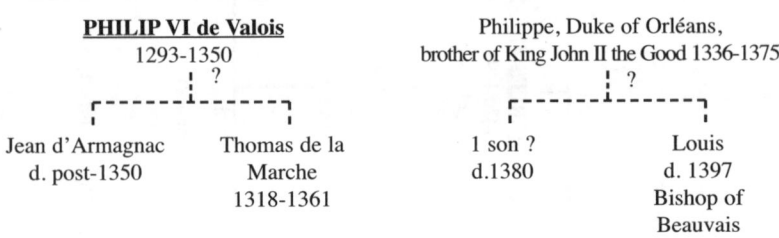

PHILIP VI de Valois
1293-1350
?

Jean d'Armagnac
d. post-1350

Thomas de la
Marche
1318-1361

Philippe, Duke of Orléans,
brother of King John II the Good 1336-1375
?

1 son ?
d.1380

Louis
d. 1397
Bishop of
Beauvais

CHARLES VI the Mad
1368-1422
with Odette de Champdivers (d. *c.*1424)

Marguerite de Valois
1407- pre-1458

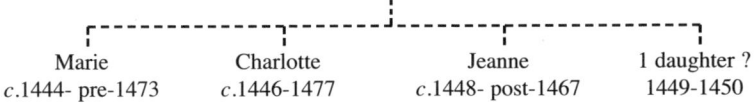

CHARLES VII the Victorious
1403-1461
with Agnès Sorel (d.1450)

Marie
*c.*1444- pre-1473

Charlotte
*c.*1446-1477

Jeanne
*c.*1448- post-1467

1 daughter ?
1449-1450

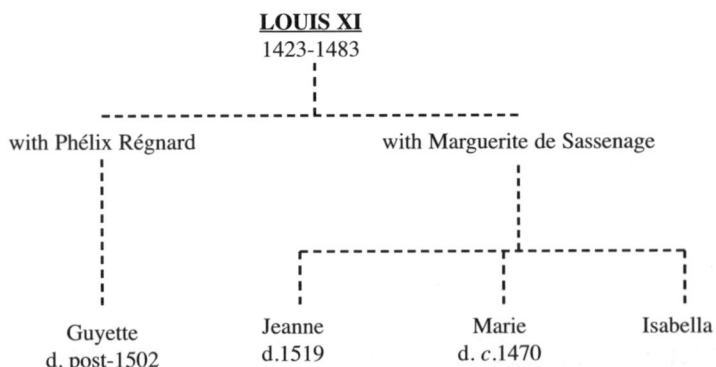

LOUIS XI
1423-1483

with Phélix Régnard

with Marguerite de Sassenage

Guyette
d. post-1502

Jeanne
d.1519

Marie
d. *c.*1470

Isabella

Philip VI de Valois (1293-1350). King of France (1328-1350).

Philip VI, the son of Charles de Valois and Margaret of Anjou and nephew of Philip the Fair, became Regent then, on the death of Charles IV in 1328 without a male heir, he mounted the throne, setting aside the claims of Philippe of Evreux and Edward III of England. He was the founder of the Valois dynasty which was to give France its monarchs until 1589. Philip VI began by launching a campaign in Flanders which was again in the grip of rebellion. He won the Battle of Kassel in 1328. However, his reign was more particularly marked by the beginning of the Hundred Years' War. King Edward III of England agreed to pay homage to Philip VI for his lands in France in 1329 but Philippe's claims to Guyenne and Flanders swiftly led to an outbreak of hostilities. In 1337, the King of France announced the seizure of Guyenne. Edward III claimed the throne of France and allied himself with Flanders then with Brittany; he even proclaimed himself king in 1340. The war began badly for the French who were defeated at sea at the Battle of Sluis in 1340 and on land at Crécy in 1346. The English took Calais in the following year. The terrifying plague epidemic that then swept through Western Europe led to the signature of a truce in 1348, thanks to mediation from the Pope. Philip VI died before war broke out again. In addition to the lands he had held in appanage consisting of the Valois, Anjou and Maine areas, he acquired Champagne, Brie, Dauphiné and Montpellier for the Crown. His reign was marked by a strengthening of royal taxation to fund the war, by repeated meetings of the States General and by the definition of the role of the Parliament. When Philip VI de Valois died in 1350, he was succeeded by his eldest son, John II the Good.

John II the Good (1319-1364). King of France (1350-1364).

John II the Good was the eldest son of Philip VI de Valois and Jeanne of Burgundy; he succeeded his father in 1350. He was a man of limited intelligence, a good horseman but a mediocre politician who was poorly counselled and his reign remains a fairly disastrous period for France. The disorder resulting from the king's struggle against Charles the Bad, King of Navarre, led to another outbreak of war against the English in 1355. The Black Prince swept through Guyenne and Languedoc, spreading terror in his wake. King John II the Good lacked funds for the war so he convened the States General in order to obtain more. The States General, however, agreed to supply funds only if they had control over the way in which it was spent. In 1356, the French army was routed by the English at Poitiers and the King of France was taken prisoner. He was taken to London. During his four years in detention, John the Good lived a carefree life of luxury, leaving his son, Charles, to cope with the most serious crisis the French monarchy had ever known. The States General tried to impose on the Regent, Charles, extensive reform of the system of government including a supervisory role for them. This was the Grand Ordinance of 1357 and it would have meant a parliamentary monarchy. In 1358, Charles was also faced with a rebellion in Paris led by Etienne Marcel, Provost of Merchants, and with a peasant revolt called the "*Jacquerie*". He succeeded in quelling both uprisings. The two treaties signed in London in 1358 and 1359 led to the liberation of King John II the Good, who returned to France in July 1360, but under draconian conditions. The entire Atlantic seaboard of the kingdom was given to Edward III of England, a huge ransom was demanded, and hostages were taken, including two of the king's sons. They were to be released only in return for full and final settlement of the ransom. Since the conditions were refused by the States General, war broke out again until the signature of the Treaty of Calais in 1360. In 1361, the Duke of Burgundy died without leaving an heir and John the Good annexed the duchy to the Crown then granted it, in appanage, to his youngest son, Philip the Bold. In 1363, one of the hostages handed over to the English in return for the release of King John the Good succeeded in escaping. It was the monarch's own son, the Duke of Anjou. The King, oblivious to all but his own code of chivalry and the laws of honour, returned to London and gave himself up in place of his son at the beginning of 1364. He died there a few months later and was succeeded by his eldest son, Charles V.

Charles V the Wise (1338-1380). King of France (1364-1380).

Charles, the eldest son of John II the Good and Bonne of Luxembourg, was faced, at the age of eighteen, with his father's imprisonment in England (1356-1360) and found himself faced with the worst possible difficulties while acting as Regent. The States General were attempting to gain control of the monarchy, Etienne Marcel had fomented rebellion in Paris, there were threats from the King of Navarre, Charles the Bad, who coveted the crown and there was a peasants' revolt in the Beauvais area (the "*Jacquerie*" revolt). Having succeeded in overcoming domestic problems in 1358, Charles then had to withstand a new invasion by the English, to which he put an end by signing the Treaty of Calais in 1360. This laid down the conditions under which his father would be released. John the Good's return to London and subsequent death in 1364 took Charles V to the throne of France. With the assistance of a great warlord, Du Guesclin, he defeated Charles the Bad in Cocherel (1364), put an end to the war of succession in Brittany through the Treaty of Guérande (1365) and partly rid his kingdom of the groups of armed bandits who were pillaging it (1366). In 1369, war against the English broke out again after the confiscation of Guyenne by King Charles V. It was a war waged without any major battles, a conflict designed to wear down the other side, and one by one the King of France succeeded in reconquering each of the English-held territories (Rouergue, Quercy and Périgord in 1369, Limousin and Poitou in 1372, Aunis and Saintonge in 1373). By 1375, the only English possessions remaining in France were Guyenne and Calais. The accession of a new king to the throne of England in 1377, in the person of Richard II, led to a further outbreak of hostilities in 1379-1380. Charles V's domestic policy aimed at re-establishing royal authority which had suffered badly during his father's reign. In particular, he reorganised the army, forming it into "companies" (ordinances of 1373-1374), and the financial system, obtaining the funding he required for war by means of extraordinary taxes which, later, became permanent. Finally, he was a well-educated, literate king who enjoyed the company of educated men and a king-builder who commissioned work on the Louvre, Bastille, Hôtel Saint-Pol and the new town walls in Paris. When he died in 1380, his son, Charles VI, succeeded him.

Charles VI the Mad (1368-1422). King of France (1380-1422).

Charles VI was only 12 years old when he succeeded his father. A regency was therefore established under his uncles, the Dukes of Bourbon, Anjou, Berry and Burgundy, all of them engaged in a power struggle. The beginning of his reign was marked by numerous anti-tax revolts in various regions (the uprisings were known as "*Les Maillotins*" in Paris, "*La Hérelle*" in Rouen and "*Les Tuchins*" in Languedoc) and by uprisings in Flemish towns under the leadership of Philippe Van Artevelde who was killed at the Battle of Rosebeke in 1382. Charles VI signed several truces with England, maintaining peace until 1404. In 1388, the king decided to reign personally and dismissed his uncles, replacing them with his father's erstwhile advisers. This was the period of government by "old men". From 1392 onwards, however, Charles VI suffered fits of insanity, a source of major misfortune for France. He dismissed the old men and government was again placed in the hands of the Dukes, with Orléans and Burgundy struggling for power over a king who was lucid only intermittently. The assassination of Duke Louis of Orléans, the king's brother, in 1407, led to civil war between the Armagnacs who supported Duke Charles d'Orléans and the Burgundians who supported John the Fearless, Duke of Burgundy. Each of the factions took control of Paris in turn and wielded power. England then took advantage of the situation and recommenced the war. Henry IV signed an alliance with the Armagnacs in 1412 then landed in France. His successor, Henry V, laid claim to the crown of France, arrived on the continent in 1415 and inflicted the disastrous defeat of Azincourt on the French army. From 1417 to 1419, he took over Normandy. After the murder of John the Fearless, Duke of Burgundy, who was succeeded by Philip the Good, the King of England allied himself with the Burgundian faction (1419). The treachery of Queen Isabella of Bavaria and the Duke of Burgundy led to the signature, with England, of the terrible Treaty of Troyes (1420). Under the terms of the treaty, the heir apparent, Charles, lost his right to the crown of France and Henry V of England was acknowledged as Charles VI's heir. He then married Charles' daughter, Catherine. The death of Henry V followed by that of Charles VI in 1422 left the crown prince, Charles, with a catastrophic situation to settle, especially as Henry VI of England was then proclaimed King of France.

Charles VII the Victorious (1403-1461). King of France (1422-1461).

Charles was the fifth son of Charles VI and Isabella of Bavaria. He became heir apparent (or "*dauphin*") in 1417, on the death of his elder brothers. In 1418, he had to flee Paris which was occupied by the Burgundians; he sought refuge in

Bourges. Disinherited by his father under the terms of the Treaty of Troyes (1420) in favour of King Henry V of England, the death of Charles VI in 1422 made him a monarch whose legitimacy was controversial and whose authority was limited to an area south of the Loire River. He was known as the "King of Bourges". His main task was to reconquer his kingdom. The early years were difficult. The royal army was defeated at Cravant in 1423 then in Verneuil-sur-Avre in 1424 by the English and Burgundians who went on to besiege Orléans in 1428. Gradually, though, a feeling of national resistance began to grow, embodied by Joan of Arc from 1429 onwards. Having obtained English agreement to lift the Siege of Orléans, she took King Charles VII to Reims where he was crowned in July 1429. This gave him the legitimacy that he had previously lacked. Joan of Arc's capture in Compiègne in 1430 followed by her trial and death in 1431 did not prevent the situation turning in favour of Charles VII who then enjoyed support from courageous warriors such as La Hire, Xaintrailles or the Constable de Richemont. In 1435, he put an end to the Anglo-Burgundian alliance by signing the Peace of Arras with the Duke of Burgundy; this enabled him to retake Paris and officially enter the town in 1437. Despite rebellion against royal authority on the part of princes in 1440 (the "*Praguerie*"), he continued to reconquer his kingdom, taking land back from the English. In 1444, the English agreed to the signature of a five-year truce which Charles VII put to effect by reorganising the army (ordinances of 1445 and 1448 creating ordinance and archery companies). He also reorganised royal finances (since 1439, the tithe had been a permanent tax). A further outbreak of war in 1449 marked the final stages of Charles VII's reconquest of the kingdom. The English lost Normandy in 1450 after their defeat in Formigny and Guyenne after the French victory at Castillon-la-Bataille. Bordeaux was retaken in 1453. The Hundred Years' War was at an end and the only English possession left in France was Calais. The French monarchy emerged from these struggles in a stronger position thanks to the institutions set up by Charles VII. Of all the leading vassals, only one retained his power and influence – the Duke of Burgundy. The king had also shown his authority over the Church by the Pragmatic Sanction of Bourges (1438) which limited papal power over French bishops. The end of his reign was a period of revival, a foretaste of the "fine 16th century". On his death in 1461, he was succeeded by his eldest son, Louis XI.

Louis XI (1423-1483). King of France (1461-1483).

Louis, the eldest son of Charles VII and Mary of Anjou, spent his father's reign plotting against him (in 1440 during the "Praguerie" and again in 1456 when he was forced to seek refuge at the Duke of Burgundy's court). In 1447, Charles VII granted him the government of Dauphiné. Once he became king, on his father's death in 1461, he was able to take advantage of the order brought to the kingdom and he continued his father's work in the financial and legal spheres. By doing so, he was able to continue the territorial reconstruction of France, the main achievement of his reign, by fighting the last great noblemen, in particular the Duke of

Burgundy. In 1465, Louis XI was faced with a revolt on the part of the princes who had joined forces in the League of the Public Weal. After the indecisive Battle of Montlhéry, he signed the Treaties of Conflans and Saint-Maur-des-Fossés. A further feudal revolt led by Charles the Bold, who had been Duke of Burgundy since 1467, led to the meeting in Péronne at which Louis XI, believing he could outwit his adversary, was taken prisoner by Charles and only released under humiliating conditions (1468). From then on, Charles the Bold was the monarch's main enemy throughout his reign, an enemy whose power had to removed. The struggle between the two men lasted until 1477. Louis XI gradually isolated him, giving his own brother, Charles, the Duchy of Guyenne in 1469 then signing the Treaty of Picquigny with Edward IV of England in 1475. Charles the Bold's claims led to a rebellion on the part of the Swiss and Alsatians. Charles was defeated in Grandson and Morat (1476) and killed at the Siege of Nancy in 1477. Burgundy and Picardy were annexed to the crown; the remainder of the Burgundian possessions passed to the House of Austria (Treaty of Arras in 1482 signed with Maximilian of Austria). Louis XI then acquired Anjou, Maine and Provence in 1480-1481 when the House of Anjou died out. He encouraged an economic boom through tax exemptions, improvements to the transport system and incentives for the creation of fairs. He was succeeded by his only living son, Charles, in 1483.

Charles VIII (1470-1498). King of France (1483-1498).

Charles VIII was Louis XI's only living male heir and he became king at the age of 13 when his father died, in 1483. Initially, he reigned under the control of his sister, Anne, and her husband, Pierre de Beaujeu. They were faced with the "insane war", a revolt on the part of Breton noblemen and the Duke d'Orléans. It was ended by the victory of the royal troops at Saint-Aubin-du-Cormier and the signature of the Treaty of Le Verger in 1488. The question of Breton succession turned to the King of France's advantage when he married Anne, the heiress to the Duchy, in 1491. This paved the way for the region's future annexation to the crown of France (however, it had required negotiations with England leading to the signature of the Treaty of Etaples in 1492, then with Maximilian of Austria to whom Anne had been betrothed and the signature of the Treaty of Senlis in 1493). Charles VIII put an end to the regency in 1491 and decided to govern on his own. The main event in his reign was the beginning of the Italian Campaign. He sent a favourable response to the Pope in the latter's struggle against the King of Naples and, claiming that he held rights inherited from the House of Anjou, launched an expedition in 1494. It began victoriously with a rapid sweep through the peninsula and the capture of Naples in February 1495. The conquest then led to an uprising and the setting up of an anti-French league. Charles VIII abandoned the kingdom of Naples and found it difficult to make his way back to France although he was victorious at the Battle of Fornova in July 1495. His failure marked the end of the King of France's Italian dream. Charles VIII died in 1498 while preparing to take revenge. He left no living heir, since the three sons he had had by Anne of

Brittany all died young, and the crown passed to his cousin, the Duke d'Orléans, who reigned under the title Louis XII. Thus 1498 marked the end of the direct Valois line and the accession of the Valois-Orléans dynasty.

Louis XI

Charles VIII

THE VALOIS-ORLÉANS DYNASTY
THE VALOIS-ANGOULEME LINE

The Valois-Orléans line (1498-1515) had only one representative on the throne of France in the person of Louis XII. The line descended from Louis, Duke of Orléans, brother of Charles VI the Insane.

Louis XII died without leaving a male heir in 1515 and the crown passed to his son-in-law, François I, who was also a descendent of Louis, Duke of Orléans, through his father, Charles of Angoulême.

The Valois-Angoulême dynasty reigned over France from 1515 to 1589, giving the country five kings from François I to Henri III.

After the reigns of François I (1515-1547) and his son, Henri II (1547-1559), which marked the "fine 16th century", the monarchy became weaker and had to deal with the Wars of Religion. Henri II's three sons succeeded each other on the throne of France but were unable to put a halt to the civil war. Moreover, they all died without a male heir.

In 1589, the death of Henri III gave the crown to the King of Navarre, Henri, the closest heir to the throne. He founded the Bourbon dynasty.

Louis XII

THE VALOIS-ORLEANS
and VALOIS-ANGOULEME DYNASTIES

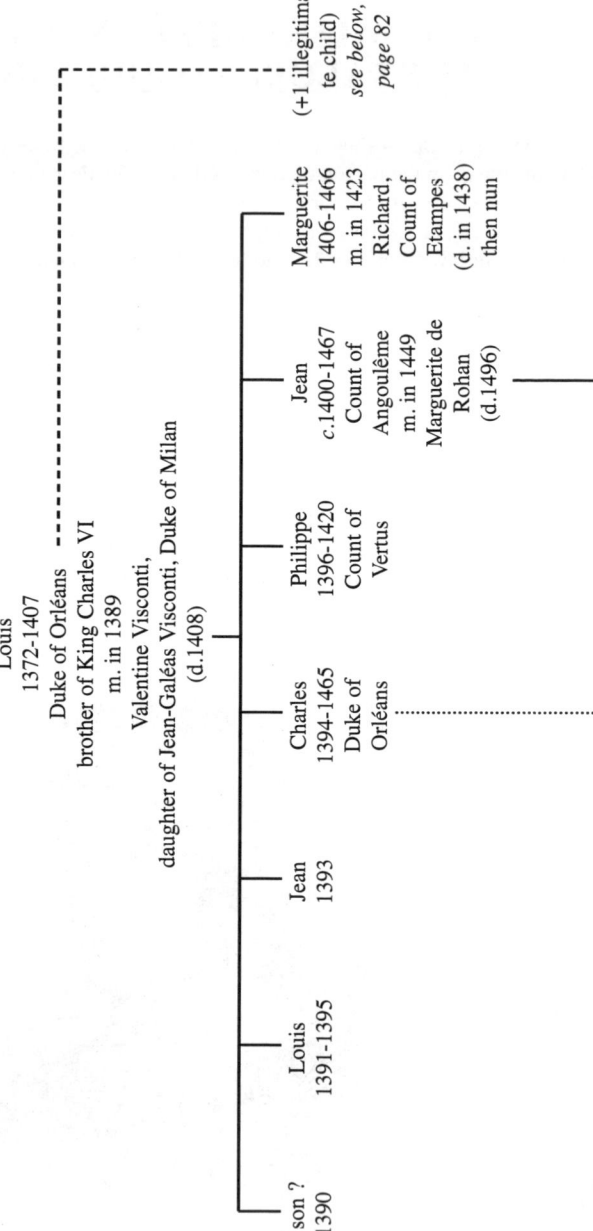

Louis
1372-1407
Duke of Orléans
brother of King Charles VI
m. in 1389
Valentine Visconti,
daughter of Jean-Galéas Visconti, Duke of Milan
(d.1408)

(+1 illegitima-te child)
see below, page 82

1 son ?
1390

Louis
1391-1395

Jean
1393

Charles
1394-1465
Duke of
Orléans

Philippe
1396-1420
Count of
Vertus

Jean
c.1400-1467
Count of
Angoulême
m. in 1449
Marguerite de
Rohan
(d.1496)

Marguerite
1406-1466
m. in 1423
Richard,
Count of
Etampes
(d. in 1438)
then nun

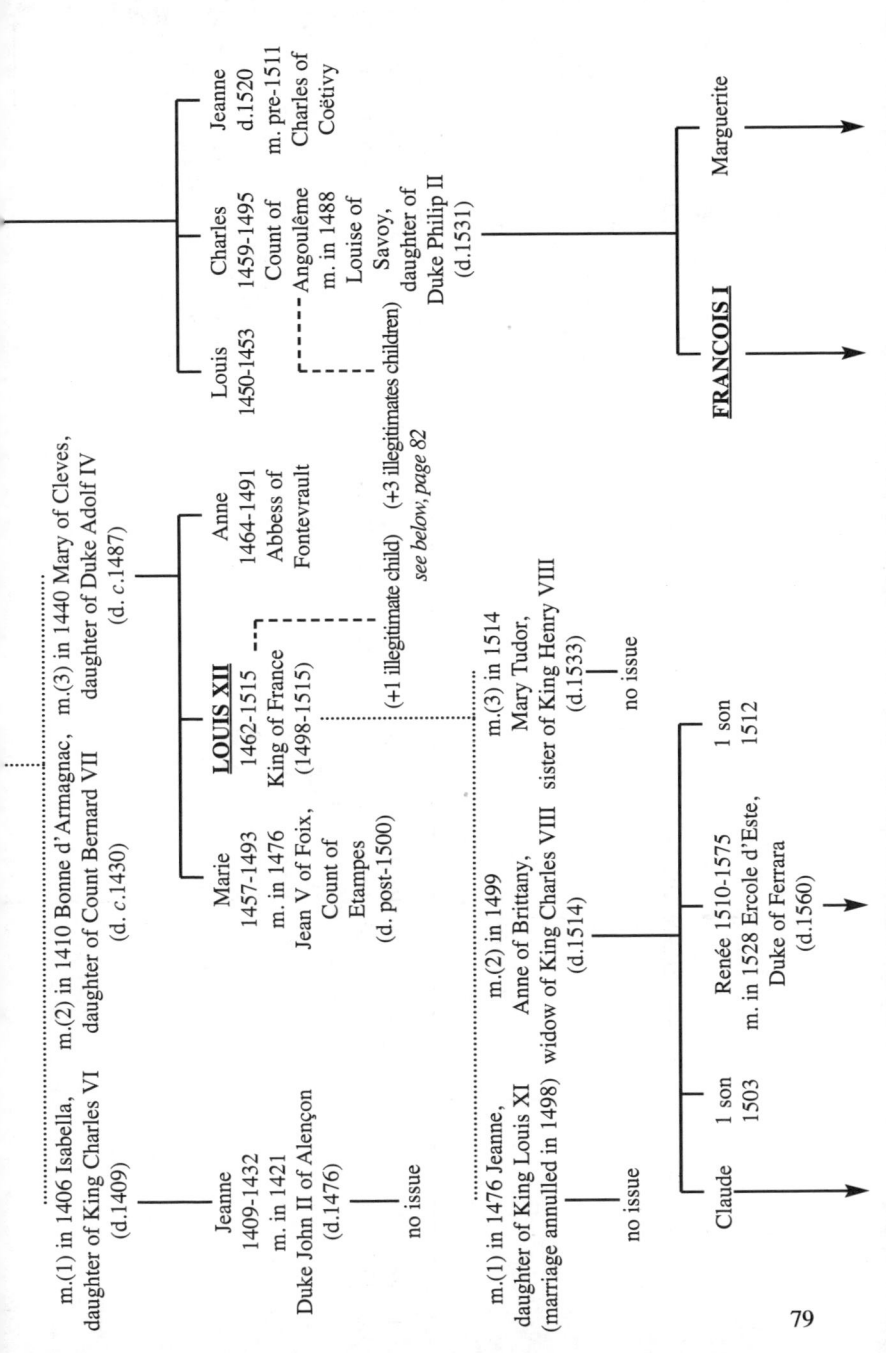

m.(1) in 1406 Isabella, daughter of King Charles VI (d.1409)

m.(2) in 1410 Bonne d'Armagnac, daughter of Count Bernard VII (d. c.1430)

m.(3) in 1440 Mary of Cleves, daughter of Duke Adolf IV (d. c.1487)

Jeanne 1409-1432 m. in 1421 Duke John II of Alençon (d.1476) — no issue

Marie 1457-1493 m. in 1476 Jean V of Foix, Count of Etampes (d. post-1500)

LOUIS XII 1462-1515 King of France (1498-1515)

Anne 1464-1491 Abbess of Fontevrault

(+1 illegitimate child)   (+3 illegitimates children)
see below, page 82

Louis 1450-1453

Charles 1459-1495 Count of Angoulême m. in 1488 Louise of Savoy, daughter of Duke Philip II (d.1531)

Jeanne d.1520 m. Charles of Coëtivy d.pre-1511

m.(1) in 1476 Jeanne, daughter of King Louis XI (marriage annulled in 1498) — no issue

m.(2) in 1499 Anne of Brittany, widow of King Charles VIII (d.1514)

m.(3) in 1514 Mary Tudor, sister of King Henry VIII (d.1533) — no issue

Claude

1 son 1503

Renée 1510-1575 m. in 1528 Ercole d'Este, Duke of Ferrara (d.1560)

1 son 1512

Marguerite

FRANCOIS I

79

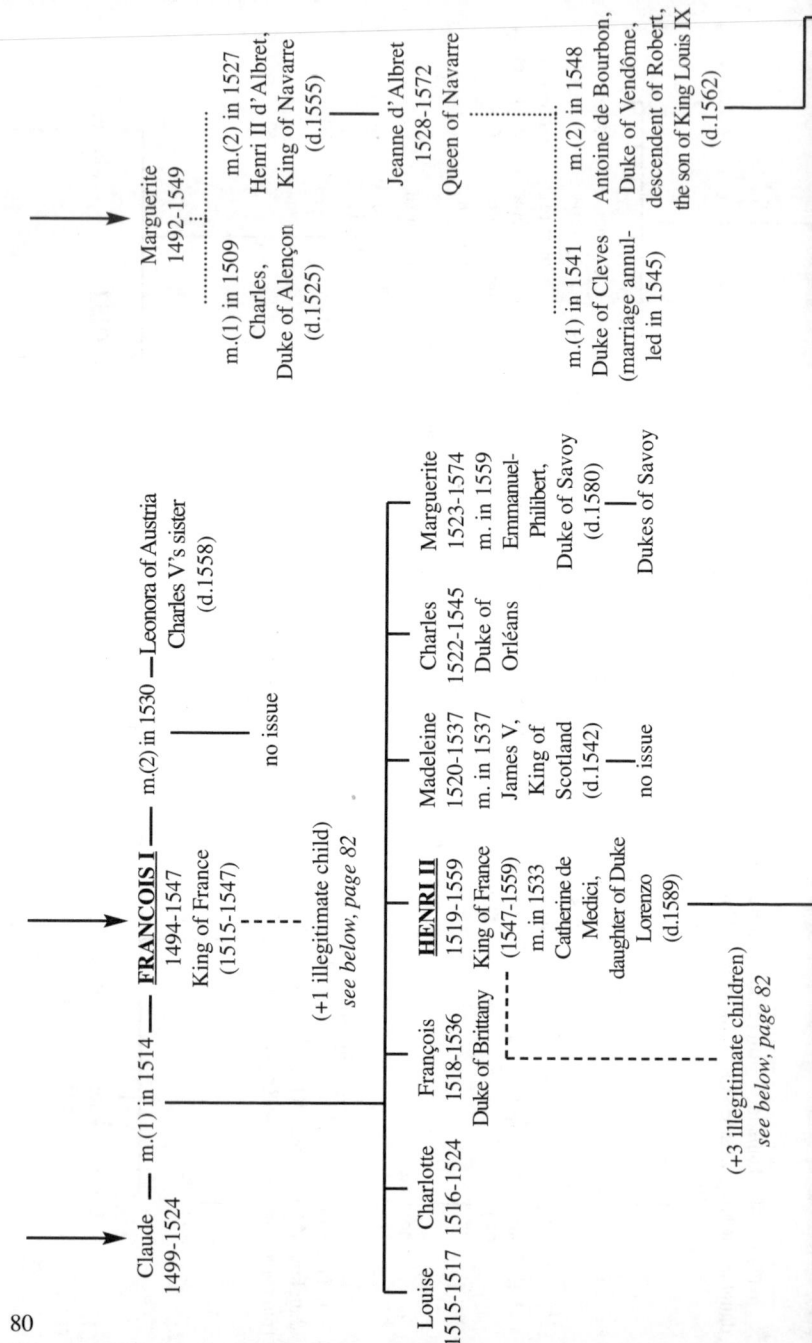

Louise
1515-1517

Charlotte
1516-1524

Claude — m.(1) in 1514 — FRANCOIS I — m.(2) in 1530 — Leonora of Austria
1499-1524

FRANCOIS I
1494-1547
King of France (1515-1547)

(+1 illegitimate child)
see below, page 82

Leonora of Austria
Charles V's sister
(d.1558)

no issue

François
1518-1536
Duke of Brittany

HENRI II
1519-1559
King of France
(1547-1559)
m. in 1533
Catherine de
Medici,
daughter of Duke
Lorenzo
(d.1589)

(+3 illegitimate children)
see below, page 82

Madeleine
1520-1537
m. in 1537
James V,
King of
Scotland
(d.1542)

no issue

Charles
1522-1545
Duke of
Orléans

Marguerite
1523-1574
m. in 1559
Emmanuel-
Philibert,
Duke of Savoy
(d.1580)

Dukes of Savoy

Marguerite
1492-1549

m.(1) in 1509
Charles,
Duke of Alençon
(d.1525)

m.(2) in 1527
Henri II d'Albret,
King of Navarre
(d.1555)

Jeanne d'Albret
1528-1572
Queen of Navarre

m.(1) in 1541
Duke of Cleves
(marriage annul-
led in 1545)

m.(2) in 1548
Antoine de Bourbon,
Duke of Vendôme,
descendent of Robert,
the son of King Louis IX
(d.1562)

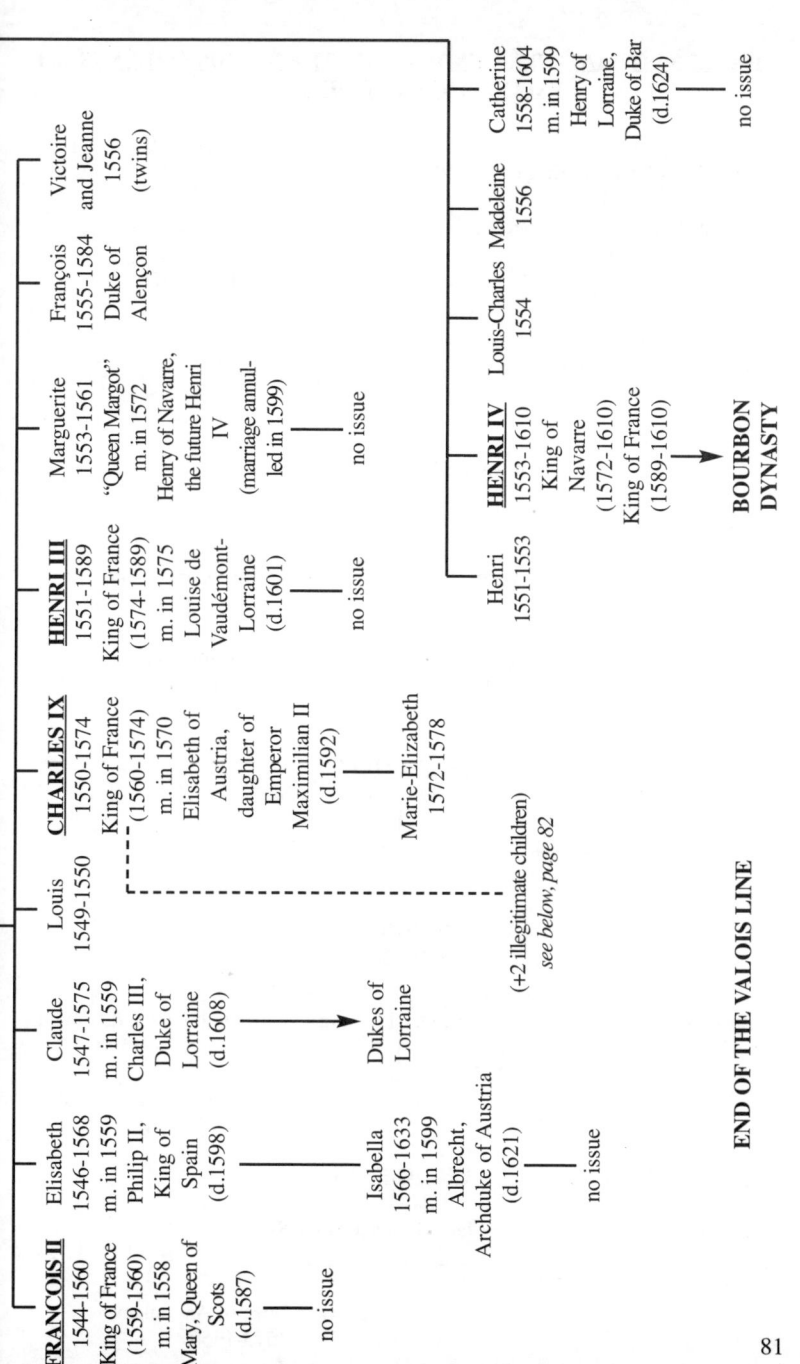

FRANÇOIS II
1544-1560
King of France
(1559-1560)
m. in 1558
Mary, Queen of
Scots
(d.1587)

no issue

Elisabeth
1546-1568
m. in 1559
Philip II,
King of
Spain
(d.1598)

Isabella
1566-1633
m. in 1599
Albrecht,
Archduke of
Austria
(d.1621)

no issue

Claude
1547-1575
m. in 1559
Charles III,
Duke of
Lorraine
(d.1608)

→ Dukes of
Lorraine

Louis
1549-1550

(+2 illegitimate children)
see below, page 82

CHARLES IX
1550-1574
King of France
(1560-1574)
m. in 1570
Elisabeth of
Austria,
daughter of
Emperor
Maximilian II
(d.1592)

Marie-Elizabeth
1572-1578

HENRI III
1551-1589
King of France
(1574-1589)
m. in 1575
Louise de
Vaudémont-
Lorraine
(d.1601)

no issue

Henri
1551-1553

Marguerite
1553-1561
"Queen Margot"
m. in 1572
Henry of Navarre,
the future Henri
IV
(marriage annul-
led in 1599)

no issue

HENRI IV
1553-1610
King of
Navarre
(1572-1610)
King of France
(1589-1610)

→ **BOURBON
DYNASTY**

François
1555-1584
Duke of
Alençon

Louis-Charles
1554

Madeleine
1556

Victoire
and Jeanne
1556
(twins)

Catherine
1558-1604
m. in 1599
Henry of
Lorraine,
Duke of Bar
(d.1624)

no issue

END OF THE VALOIS LINE

81

THE ILLEGITIMATE DESCENDENTS OF THE VALOIS-ORLEANS and VALOIS-ANGOULEME LINES

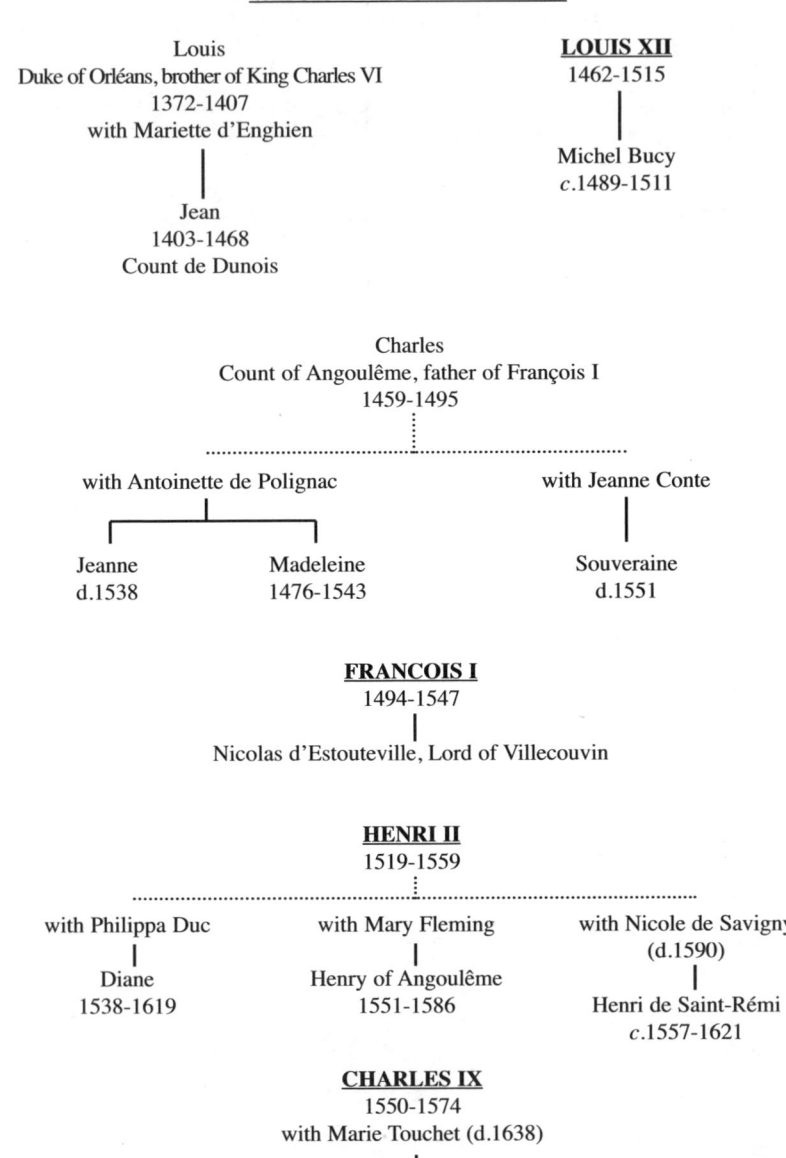

Louis
Duke of Orléans, brother of King Charles VI
1372-1407
with Mariette d'Enghien
|
Jean
1403-1468
Count de Dunois

LOUIS XII
1462-1515
|
Michel Bucy
c.1489-1511

Charles
Count of Angoulême, father of François I
1459-1495

with Antoinette de Polignac .... with Jeanne Conte

Jeanne	Madeleine	Souveraine
d.1538	1476-1543	d.1551

FRANCOIS I
1494-1547
|
Nicolas d'Estouteville, Lord of Villecouvin

HENRI II
1519-1559

with Philippa Duc | with Mary Fleming | with Nicole de Savigny (d.1590)
Diane | Henry of Angoulême | Henri de Saint-Rémi
1538-1619 | 1551-1586 | *c*.1557-1621

CHARLES IX
1550-1574
with Marie Touchet (d.1638)

1 son ?   Charles, Duke of Angoulême
1573-1650

Louis XII (14662-1515). King of France (1498-1515).

Louis, who became Duke of Orléans following the death of his father Charles, in 1465, married Jeanne of France, daughter of Louis XI, in 1476. He was one of the leaders of the "insane war" against the government of the Beaujeu couple who acted as regents until Charles VIII came of age. He was taken prisoner in 1488 and spent three years in detention before reconciling his differences with the king. He led a French army during the first Italian campaign in 1494-1495. When Charles VIII died without leaving an heir in 1498, he became King of France under the title of Louis XII. His first act was to annul his marriage with Jeanne of France and, in 1499, to marry Anne of Brittany, the widow of the previous monarch. He also launched an Italian campaign, following in his predecessor's footsteps and laying claim to the Milan area on the grounds that he was the grandson of Valentine Visconti. In 1499-1500, he seized the duchy then allied himself with Aragon in order to conquer the kingdom of Naples. However, following his success in the venture in 1501, a dispute broke out between the French and the Spaniards. The French were defeated and chased out of the area three years later. Under the terms of the Treaty of Blois (1504), Louis XII sought an alliance with Austria by promising his daughter, Claude, to the future Charles V. However, in the following year, the king changed his mind, annulled the intended marriage and promised his daughter to his cousin, François of Angoulême. A further expedition launched by Louis XII against Italy led to the capture of Genoa in 1507 and France joined the Cambrai League against Venice. After French victory at Agnadello (May 1509), the Pope turned against the French and set up the Holy League (1511) between Spain, Switzerland and England. The French army was victorious in Ravenna in 1512 but defeated in Novare in 1513 and Louis XII again lost the Milan area. At the same time, the monarch had to contend with an English landing in the north of France and his army was defeated in Guinegatte (1513). Eventually, in 1514, Louis XII made peace with England and negotiated his remarriage (Anne of Brittany having died) with Mary of England, the sister of King Henry VIII, hoping for the heir that he still did not have. Despite this final failure, the wars had no ill effects on the kingdom's prosperity; indeed, the French gained a great deal of wealth from Italy. Louis XII brought calm and peace back to the kingdom. He also ensured that government bodies operated efficiently by restructuring the Grand Council (1498), promulgating the Grand Ordinance of Blois (1499) and ensuring better management of taxation (1508 ordinance). He died without an heir in 1515 and was succeeded by his cousin and son-in-law, François of Angoulême.

François I (1494-1547). King of France (1515-1547).

François I, the son of Charles of Angoulême and Louise of Savoy, succeeded Louis XII, his cousin and father-in-law, in 1515. François I was the archetypal Renaissance knight. As soon as he acceded to the throne, he set off for Italy and began his reign with a resounding victory over the Swiss at the Battle of Marignano and the conquest of the Milan area (1515). He then put his name to a perpetual peace with the Swiss cantons and signed the Concordat of Bologna with the Pope (1516). However, the most outstanding feature of François I's reign was his long rivalry with Charles V, King of Spain in 1516 and Emperor of Germany in 1519. His territories, which then encircled France, were seen as a threat. François I initially sought an alliance with the English but the meeting with King Henry VIII at the Field of the Cloth of Cloth in 1520 was a diplomatic failure. Thereafter, war between Charles V and the king of France became inevitable and it lasted throughout François I's reign. The first conflict, from 1521 onwards, led to the abandonment of the Milan area by the French after defeat at the Battle of Bicocca (1522), and an attempted invasion of France by the English and the imperial army. The treachery of Constable de Bourbon in 1523 and the death of Bayard at the Battle of Sesia in 1524 did not prevent François I from again waging war in Italy but he was defeated and taken prisoner at Pavia (1525). He was taken to Spain as a captive and was held until he had signed the disastrous Treaty of Madrid (1526) by which he agreed to grant Burgundy to Charles V and waive all claims in Italy. However, once he had been freed, he refused to apply the treaty and reopened hostilities by forming the League of Cognac against the emperor. When a further expedition into Italy proved fruitless, peace was signed in 1529. François I waived his claims to Italy and married Charles V's sister in 1530 while the emperor left Burgundy to France. The King of France had not, however, given up his ideas of conquering the Milan area and he contacted the Sultan of the Turks, Suliman (1535). War broke out again but without any result and a truce was signed in 1538. A final period of warfare began in 1542 and the French won the Battle of Cerisole (1544). Under the terms of the Treaty of Crépy-en-Laonnais, François I was nevertheless obliged to waive his claims to Artois and Flanders and give the Milan area to his enemy. This marked the end of his dispute with Charles V. Although his entire reign focussed on external affairs, it was nevertheless marked by a profound change in domestic politics, namely the introduction of an absolute monarchy. From then on, the king's authority broached no resistance. The Duke of Bourbon's treachery eliminated the last great feudal lord and the aristocracy then became courtiers, receiving graces and favours from the king. François I continued the administrative unification of the kingdom by the Ordinance of Villers-Cotterêts (1539). In the religious field, Protestantism, which had long been tolerated by the king, began to be subjected to persecution, especially after the "Placards Affair" in 1534, and persecution worsened after the Edict of Fontainebleau (1540). During François I's reign, life at court underwent huge development, symbolising the luxury of the Renaissance period. Arts and letters enjoyed royal patronage. Indeed, François I was a great patron of the arts, founding the College of Royal Readers (1530) and the Royal Printing Works (1539). He protected artists and attracted famous Italians to his court (Leonardo da Vinci), thereby paving the way for the introduction of the Italian Renaissance in France. Finally, François I commissioned the building of many châteaux and palaces (Chambord, Fontainebleau, Saint-Germain-en-Laye) and began the reconstruction of the Louvre. He died in 1547 and was succeeded by his second son, Henri II.

Henri II (1519-1559). King of France (1547-1559).

Henri II, the second son of François I and Claude of France, became heir to the throne after the death of his elder brother in 1536. In 1533, he married Catherine de Medici. In 1547, he succeeded his father and continued the latter's policies which aimed to counter the House of Austria. Having negotiated with England to buy back Boulogne (1550), Henri II then contacted the Lutheran German princes, strengthened his alliance with Turkey and waged war against Charles V in 1552 by occupying the three bishoprics of Metz, Toul and Verdun. The imperial army besieged Metz in 1552 but failed to take the town. It also failed in its attempt to take over the Artois area in 1554. The French, for their part, capitulated in Sienna in Italy in 1555 and, eventually, a truce was signed in Vaucelles in 1556. It was to be short-lived for Henri II began to wage war again in the following year, against the son and successor of Charles V, Philip II. The latter was allied with England, having married Queen Mary Tudor. The war began badly for France, which was defeated in Saint-Quentin in 1557 and launched an expedition against Naples that proved to be a total failure. In 1558, however, François de Guise took Calais from the English. The two monarchs, tired of war and worried about the spread of Protestantism in their two countries, entered negotiations which led to the Treaty of Cateau-Cambrésis (1559). Henri II retained Calais and the three bishoprics but waived his claims to the Milan area, and this marked the end of the Italian Campaign. The King of France could then devote himself to the struggle against Protestantism. At the very beginning of his reign, influenced by his mistress, Diane of Poitiers, he promulgated the Edict of Châteaubriant which instigated sweeping repression. The Edict of Ecouen (1559) was even more stringent. Henri II's reign was also marked by the introduction of the "*présidial*", an intermediate Court, and of Secretaries of State. This was an indication of the strengthening of royal power. The financial situation, however, worsened and the government had to live on contingencies. Henri II died in 1559 after being wounded in the eye during a tournament arranged to celebrate the marriage of his daughter, Elisabeth, with Philip II of Spain. He was succeeded by his eldest son, François II.

François II (1544-1560). King of France (1559-1560).

François II, the eldest son of Henri II and Catherine de Medici, succeeded his father in 1559 at the age of fifteen; his mother acted as Regent. In the previous year, François II had married Mary, Queen of Scots. He left power in the hands of his wife's uncles, the de Guises, and they supported a repressive policy against the Protestants who were quick to react. In March 1560, in an attempt to remove François II from the de Guises' influence, the Protestants tried to kidnap him. This was known as the Amboise Conspiracy. It failed and its leaders were executed. The young king then died suddenly, without children, and the crown passed to his brother, Charles IX.

Charles IX (1550-1574). King of France (1560-1574).

The third son of Henri II and Catherine de Medici succeeded his brother, François II, in 1560 at the age of 10. His mother remained Regent until 1563 but was highly influential throughout his reign. With the Chancellor, Michel de L'Hospital, she instigated a policy of appeasement between Catholics and Protestants. However, the massacre of Protestants at Wassy by the Duc de Guise' followers in March 1562 led to the heart-rending Wars of Religion that were to spread bloodshed throughout France for 36 years. The first war was marked by a number of military campaigns, the alliance between the French Protestants and England (1562) and the assassination of Duc François de Guise (1563). It ended with the Peace of Amboise signed in March 1563. Once peace returned, Catherine de Medici set off with King Charles IX on a tour of France that lasted more than two years. Its aim was to unite the kingdom around the king. It was also at this time that the Grand Ordinance of Moulins was promulgated with a view to reforming the justice system and extending the monarch's powers (1566). An attempt by the Protestants to kidnap Charles IX in September 1567 re-opened hostilities. The Catholics won the Battle of Saint-Denis and a peace treaty was signed in Longjumeau in March 1568. The dismissal of Michel de L'Hospital in May 1568 resulted in a third wave of warfare. The Protestants were defeated in Jarnac and Moncontour (1569) and the war ended with the Peace of Saint-Germain (1570), an attempt at reconciliation on the part of the king who planned to marry his sister, Marguerite, to Henri of Navarre. Their marriage in August 1572 was one of the causes of the massacre of Protestants on St. Bartholomew's Day which Charles IX was unable to prevent and to which he grudgingly agreed to please his mother. This event re-ignited the war and the Catholics tried, in vain, to capture La Rochelle. The Edict of Boulogne put an end to this fourth war (July 1573). Charles IX died in 1574 just as fighting was about to break out again. His marriage with Elisabeth of Austria had produced only one daughter and the crown therefore passed to his brother, Henri III, the third son of Henri II.

Henri III (1551-1589). King of France (1574-1589).

Henri III, the fourth son of Henri II and Catherine de Medici, was initially Duke of Anjou before becoming King of Poland in 1573 thanks to his mother's intrigues. He mounted the throne of France in the following year, after the death of his brother, Charles IX, without a male heir. He took over a kingdom that had been torn between Catholics and Protestants for twelve years. After the St. Bartholomew's Day's massacre, royal authority no longer had the resources to ensure that it was respected. Henri III was not the right man for the job. Even though he wanted to preserve the unity of his kingdom, he was too indecisive and easily influenced. His mother still played a leading role and his favourites had too great a hold on him. He led a luxurious life at court, with little awareness of the ravages being caused by the fighting. The war broke out again at the beginning of his reign. The Catholics won the Battle of Dormans (October 1575) but, by signing the Peace of

Beaulieu (May 1576), the king granted advantages to the Protestants and this led to the setting up of the Roman Catholic League. The king became its leader in order to ensure greater control over it but the States General held in Blois forced him to take up the struggle against the Protestants again. The sixth war broke out in 1577. The Catholics were victorious at La Charité-sur-Loire and Issoire and the Treaty of Bergerac restricted Protestant worship. The League was dissolved. However, the Protestants did not uphold the new truce and a seventh war broke out in 1580 in Languedoc where Henri of Navarre captured Cahors. It ended with the Peace of Fleix which confirmed the Treaty of Bergerac. Henri III had no children from his marriage with Louise de Vaudémont in 1575 and his brother, François, was Heir Presumptive. The latter's death in 1584, however, led to a serious crisis since the pretender to the throne was thereafter Henri of Navarre. The possibility of Henri's mounting the throne was unacceptable to Catholics and led to the final war. The Catholics formed a new league and allied themselves with Philip II of Spain. They put pressure on Henri III who repealed all the concessions he had granted to the Protestants (July 1585). The "War of the Three Henry's" brought confusion for the monarch. Henri of Navarre won the Battle of Coutras (1587); Henri de Guise defeated the Swiss and German Protestant reinforcements and entered Paris where he met with significant popular support. Three days later, riots caused the king to flee (May 1588). Henri III was again forced to capitulate. He summoned the States General, which were dominated by the League, and held a meeting in Blois but then regained a measure of self-control and had Henri de Guise murdered (December 1588). The Leaguers controlled Paris and declared the destitution of the monarch. The only way in which Henri III could regain power was by allying himself with Henri of Navarre. The two men then laid siege to Paris (July 1589). However, a few days later, Henri III was assassinated by a fanatical monk named Jacques Clément. His reign, although troubled on the domestic front, was nevertheless marked by progress in royal administration. He ordered specialisation for the King's Councils (1578) and promulgated the Grand Ordinance of Blois (1579). When Henri III died without an heir, this marked the end of the Valois dynasty. He was succeeded by Henri IV.

François I

Henri IV

Louis XIII

Louis XIII.

THE BOURBONS

The Bourbon kings came from one line of the Capetian dynasty. They first acceded to the throne of France in 1589 through Henri IV, King of Navarre, who had a claim to the throne through his father, Antoine de Bourbon, an eighth-generation descendent of Robert, the son of St. Louis.

The Bourbons reigned from 1589 to 1792 and again from 1814 to 1830, giving France seven of its kings. Louis XIII and Louis XIV set up a system of government based on absolute monarchy but this was swept away by the French Revolution in 1789 during which Louis XVI was overthrown and sent to the guillotine.

Yet the dynasty survived through the brothers of the deceased monarch and, during the Restoration of the monarchy in 1814 (after the Revolutionary and Napoleonic periods), Louis XVIII and Charles X reigned in their turns.

After the 1830 Revolution and the abdication of Charles X, the crown passed to the Orléans line. The French Bourbon line died out in 1883 with the death of the Comte de Chambord, grandson of the last king, Charles X. However the Bourbon dynasty had many branches and has continued to exist in other countries e.g. Spain where its descendents still form the royal family.

Louis XV

THE BOURBON DYNASTY

Louis XIV

HENRI IV
1553-1610
King of Navarre (1572-1610)
King of France (1589-1610)

m.(1) in 1572 Marguerite, daughter of King Henri II of France (marriage annulled in 1599)

no issue

m.(2) in 1600 Marie de Medici, daughter of Grand-Duke Francesco of Tuscany (d.1642)

(+9 illegitimate children) *see below, page 96*

LOUIS XIII the Just
1601-1643
King of France (1610-1643)
m. in 1615 Anne of Austria, daughter of King Philip III of Spain

Elisabeth
1602-1644
m. in 1615 Philip IV, King of Spain (d.1665)

Christine
1606-1663
m. in 1619 Victor-Amadeus I, Duke of Savoy (d.1637)

Nicolas
1607-1611

Gaston
1608-1660
Duke of Orléans

Henrietta
1609-1669
m. in 1625 Charles I, King of England (d.1649)

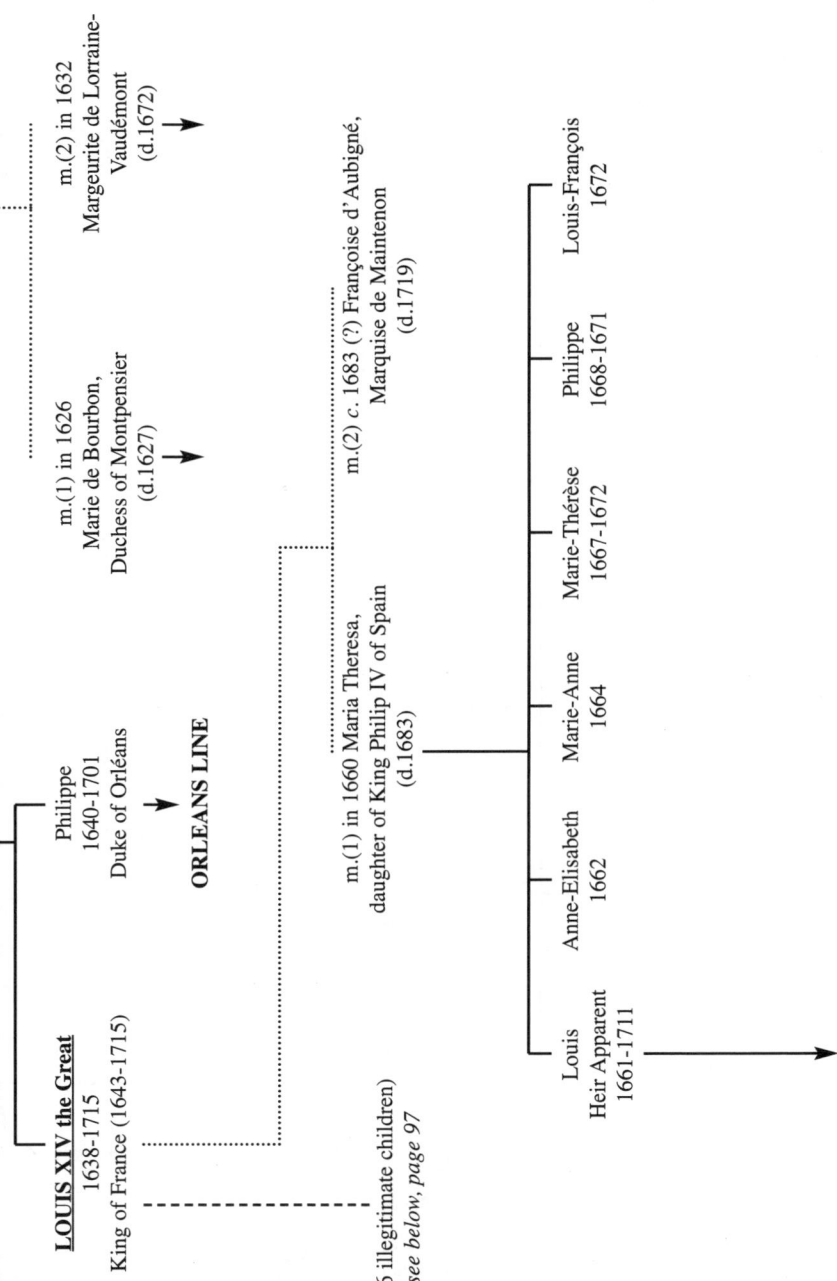

LOUIS XIV the Great
1638-1715
King of France (1643-1715)

Philippe
1640-1701
Duke of Orléans

ORLEANS LINE

(+16 illegitimate children)
see below, page 97

m.(1) in 1626
Marie de Bourbon,
Duchess of Montpensier
(d.1627)

m.(2) in 1632
Margeurite de Lorraine-
Vaudémont
(d.1672)

m.(1) in 1660 Maria Theresa,
daughter of King Philip IV of Spain
(d.1683)

m.(2) *c.* 1683 (?) Françoise d'Aubigné,
Marquise de Maintenon
(d.1719)

Louis
Heir Apparent
1661-1711

Anne-Elisabeth
1662

Marie-Anne
1664

Marie-Thérèse
1667-1672

Philippe
1668-1671

Louis-François
1672

91

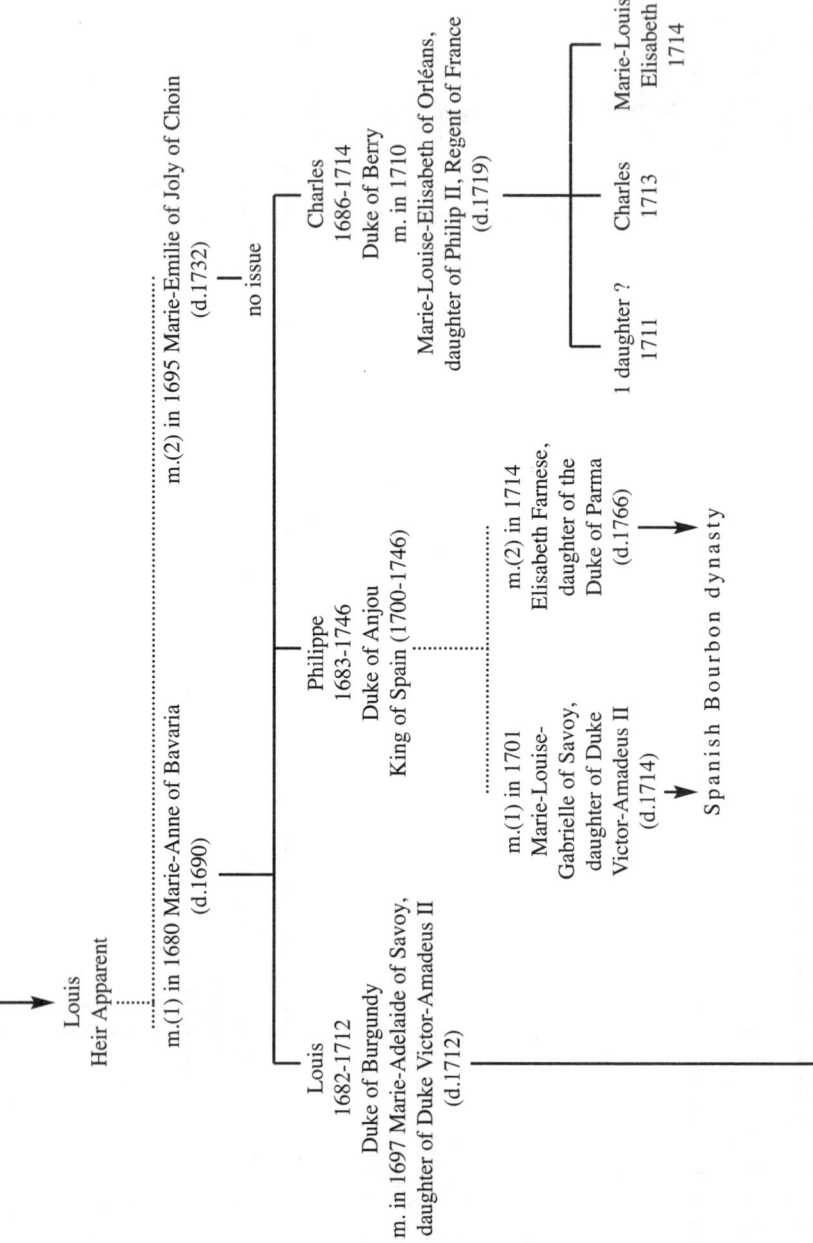

Louis
Heir Apparent

m.(1) in 1680 Marie-Anne of Bavaria
(d.1690)

m.(2) in 1695 Marie-Emilie of Joly of Choin
(d.1732)

no issue

Louis
1682-1712
Duke of Burgundy
m. in 1697 Marie-Adelaide of Savoy,
daughter of Duke Victor-Amadeus II
(d.1712)

Philippe
1683-1746
Duke of Anjou
King of Spain (1700-1746)

m.(1) in 1701
Marie-Louise-
Gabrielle of Savoy,
daughter of Duke
Victor-Amadeus II
(d.1714)

m.(2) in 1714
Elisabeth Farnese,
daughter of the
Duke of Parma
(d.1766)

Spanish Bourbon dynasty

Charles
1686-1714
Duke of Berry
m. in 1710

Marie-Louise-Elisabeth of Orléans,
daughter of Philip II, Regent of France
(d.1719)

1 daughter ?
1711

Charles
1713

Marie-Louise-
Elisabeth
1714

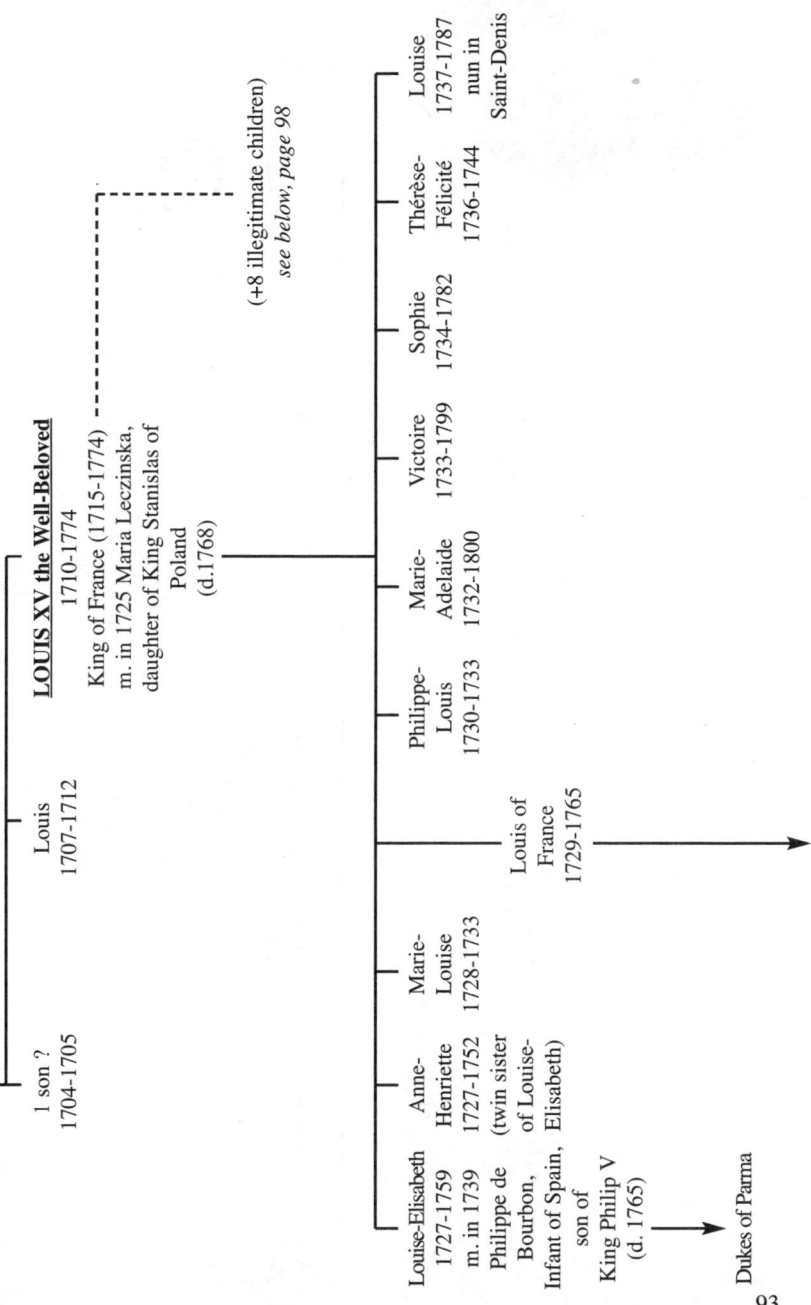

1 son ?
1704-1705

Louis
1707-1712

LOUIS XV the Well-Beloved
1710-1774
King of France (1715-1774)
m. in 1725 Maria Leczinska,
daughter of King Stanislas of
Poland
(d.1768)

(+8 illegitimate children)
see below, page 98

Louise-Elisabeth
1727-1759
m. in 1739
Philippe de
Bourbon,
Infant of Spain,
son of
King Philip V
(d. 1765)

→ Dukes of Parma

Anne-
Henriette
1727-1752
(twin sister
of Louise-
Elisabeth)

Marie-
Louise
1728-1733

Louis of France
1729-1765 →

Philippe-
Louis
1730-1733

Marie-
Adelaide
1732-1800

Victoire
1733-1799

Sophie
1734-1782

Thérèse-
Félicité
1736-1744

Louise
1737-1787
nun in
Saint-Denis

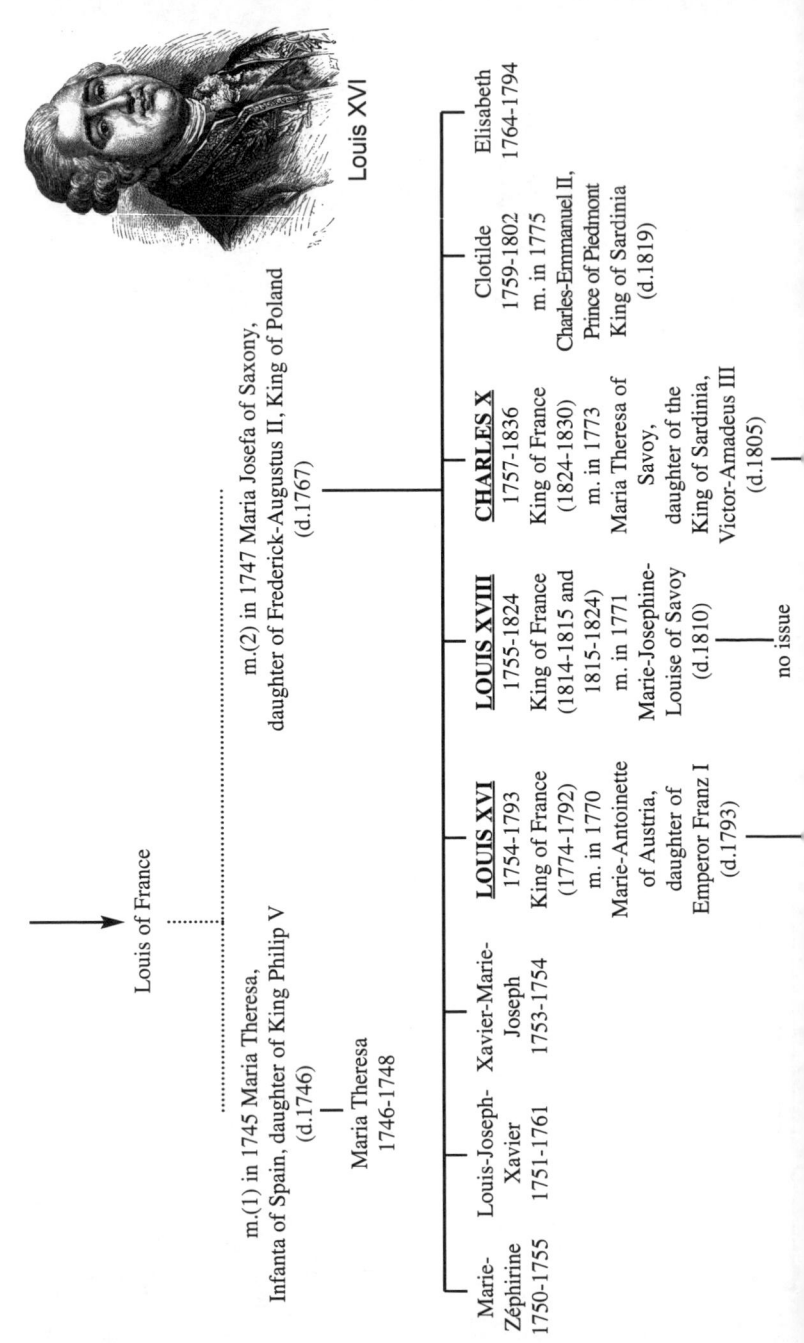

Louis of France

m.(1) in 1745 Maria Theresa, Infanta of Spain, daughter of King Philip V (d.1746)

Maria Theresa 1746-1748

m.(2) in 1747 Maria Josefa of Saxony, daughter of Frederick-Augustus II, King of Poland (d.1767)

Louis XVI

Marie-Zéphirine 1750-1755

Louis-Joseph-Xavier 1751-1761

Xavier-Marie-Joseph 1753-1754

LOUIS XVI
1754-1793
King of France (1774-1792)
m. in 1770
Marie-Antoinette of Austria, daughter of Emperor Franz I (d.1793)

LOUIS XVIII
1755-1824
King of France (1814-1815 and 1815-1824)
m. in 1771
Marie-Josephine-Louise of Savoy (d.1810)

no issue

CHARLES X
1757-1836
King of France (1824-1830)
m. in 1773
Maria Theresa of Savoy, daughter of the King of Sardinia, Victor-Amadeus III (d.1805)

Clotilde
1759-1802
m. in 1775
Charles-Emmanuel II, Prince of Piedmont King of Sardinia (d.1819)

Elisabeth
1764-1794

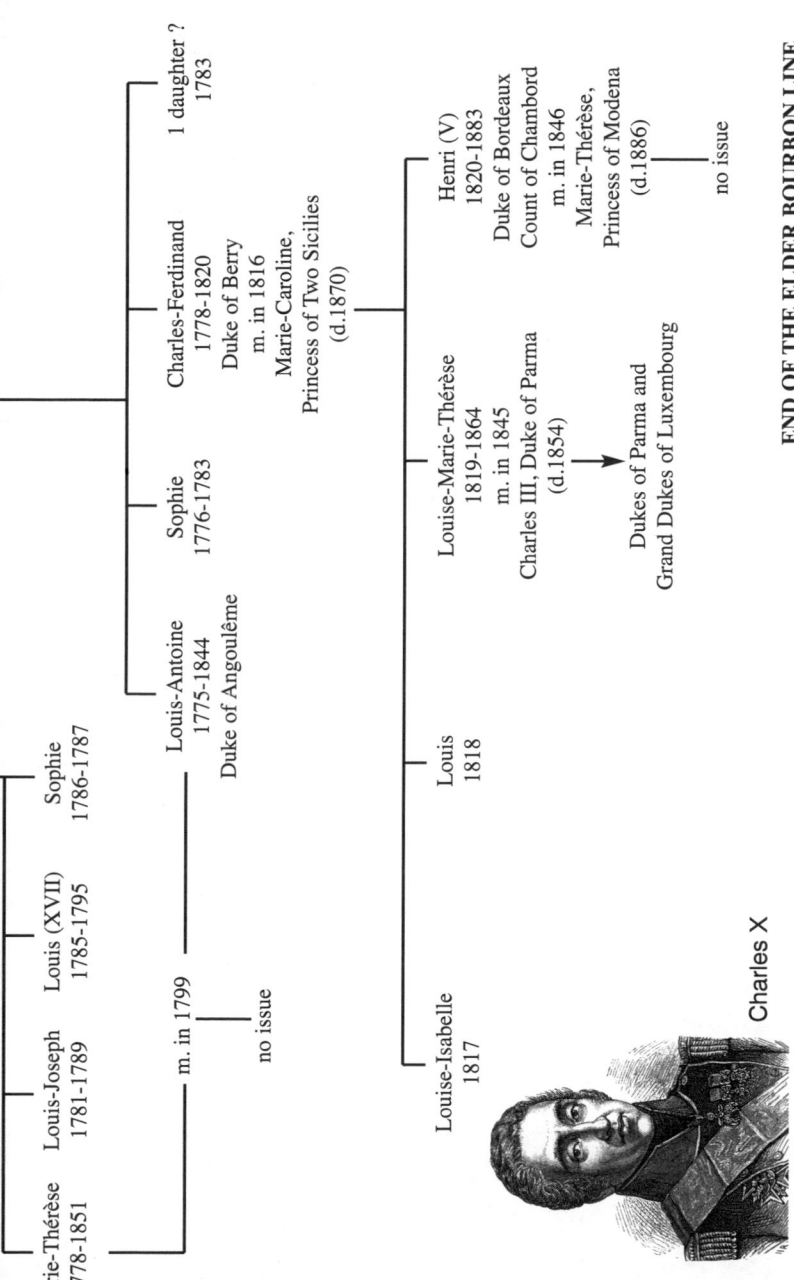

Marie-Thérèse
1778-1851

Louis-Joseph
1781-1789

Louis (XVII)
1785-1795

Sophie
1786-1787

— m. in 1799 —

no issue

Louis-Antoine
1775-1844
Duke of Angoulême

Sophie
1776-1783

Charles-Ferdinand
1778-1820
Duke of Berry
m. in 1816
Marie-Caroline,
Princess of Two Sicilies
(d.1870)

1 daughter ?
1783

Louise-Isabelle
1817

Louis
1818

Louise-Marie-Thérèse
1819-1864
m. in 1845
Charles III, Duke of Parma
(d.1854)

→ Dukes of Parma and
Grand Dukes of Luxembourg

Henri (V)
1820-1883
Duke of Bordeaux
Count of Chambord
m. in 1846
Marie-Thérèse,
Princess of Modena
(d.1886)

no issue

END OF THE ELDER BOURBON LINE

Charles X

THE ILLEGITIMATE DESCENDENTS OF THE BOURBONS

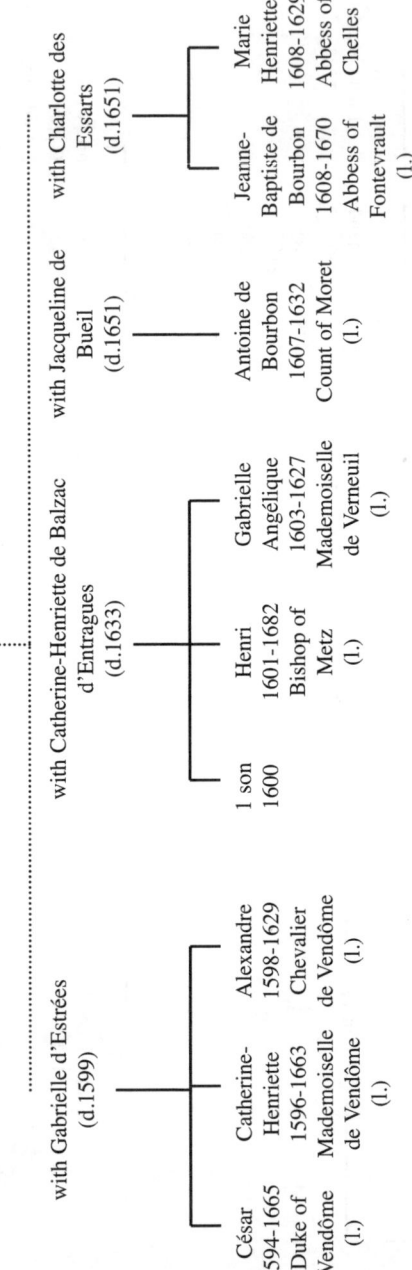

HENRI IV
1553-1610

with Gabrielle d'Estrées (d.1599)

- César 1594-1665 Duke of Vendôme (l.)
- Catherine-Henriette 1596-1663 Mademoiselle de Vendôme (l.)
- Alexandre 1598-1629 Chevalier de Vendôme (l.)

with Catherine-Henriette de Balzac d'Entragues (d.1633)

- 1 son 1600
- Henri 1601-1682 Bishop of Metz (l.)
- Gabrielle Angélique 1603-1627 Mademoiselle de Verneuil (l.)

with Jacqueline de Bueil (d.1651)

- Antoine de Bourbon 1607-1632 Count of Moret (l.)

with Charlotte des Essarts (d.1651)

- Jeanne-Baptiste de Bourbon 1608-1670 Abbess of Fontevrault (l.)
- Marie Henriette 1608-1629 Abbess of Chelles

96

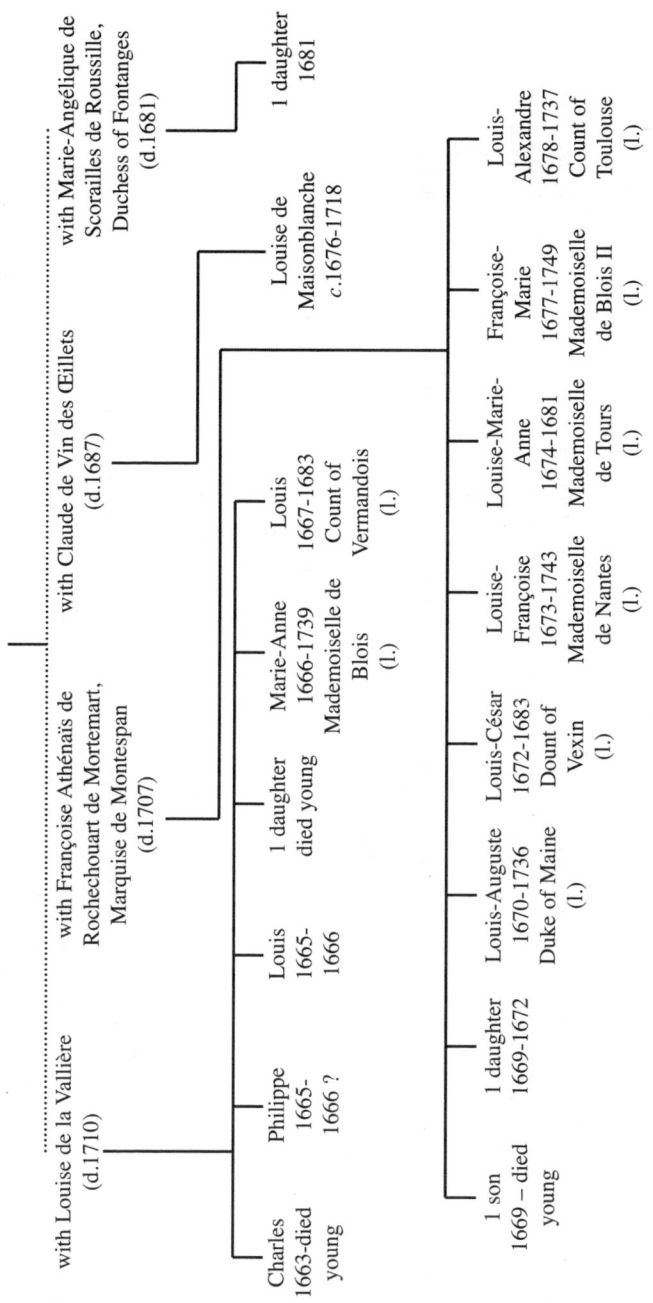

LOUIS XIV
1638-1715

with Louise de la Vallière
(d.1710)

with Françoise Athénaïs de
Rochechouart de Mortemart,
Marquise de Montespan
(d.1707)

with Claude de Vin des Œillets
(d.1687)

with Marie-Angélique de
Scorailles de Roussille,
Duchess of Fontanges
(d.1681)

Charles
1663–died
young

Philippe
1665-
1666 ?

Louis
1665-
1666

1 daughter
died young

Marie-Anne
1666-1739
Mademoiselle de
Blois
(l.)

Louis
1667-1683
Count of
Vermandois
(l.)

Louise de
Maisonblanche
c.1676-1718

1 daughter
1681

1 son
1669 – died
young

1 daughter
1669-1672

Louis-Auguste
1670-1736
Duke of Maine
(l.)

Louis-César
1672-1683
Dount of
Vexin
(l.)

Louise-
Françoise
1673-1743
Mademoiselle
de Nantes
(l.)

Louise-Marie-
Anne
1674-1681
Mademoiselle
de Tours
(l.)

Françoise-
Marie
1677-1749
Mademoiselle
de Blois II
(l.)

Louis-
Alexandre
1678-1737
Count of
Toulouse
(l.)

N.B. Kings Henri IV and Louis XIV legitimised some of their illegitimate children (l.).

97

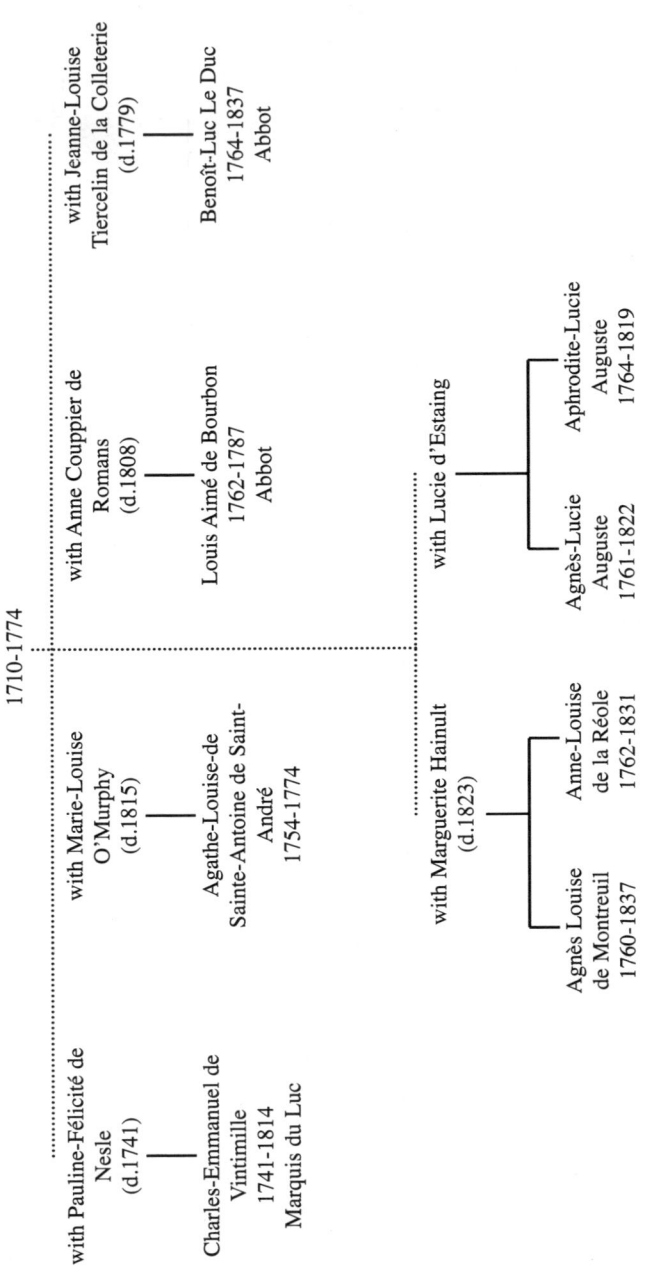

LOUIS XV
1710-1774

with Pauline-Félicité de Nesle
(d.1741)

Charles-Emmanuel de Vintimille
1741-1814
Marquis du Luc

with Marie-Louise O'Murphy
(d.1815)

Agathe-Louise-de Sainte-Antoine de Saint-André
1754-1774

with Anne Couppier de Romans
(d.1808)

Louis Aimé de Bourbon
1762-1787
Abbot

with Jeanne-Louise Tiercelin de la Colleterie
(d.1779)

Benoît-Luc Le Duc
1764-1837
Abbot

with Marguerite Hainult
(d.1823)

Agnès Louise de Montreuil
1760-1837

Anne-Louise de la Réole
1762-1831

with Lucie d'Estaing

Agnès-Lucie Auguste
1761-1822

Aphrodite-Lucie Auguste
1764-1819

Henri IV (1553-1610). King of Navarre (1572-1610), King of France (1589-1610).

Henri IV, the son of Antoine de Bourbon and Jeanne d'Albret, became the leader of the Calvinist party at the age of 16, after the death of Condé. When his mother died, he became King of Navarre (1572) and was married, that same year, to Marguerite de Valois, the sister of Charles IX, as a sign of reconciliation between Catholics and Protestants. Six days later, he escaped death and injury during the St. Bartholomew's Day massacre by tardily converting to the Roman Catholic faith. In 1576, Henri of Navarre fled the court, abjured Catholicism, and took over the leadership of the Protestant army. He then fought the Catholics for several years. When Henri II's last son died in 1584, leaving Henri III on the throne but childless, Henri of Navarre became Heir Presumptive and this led to another war. After Henri III's murder on the outskirts of Paris in 1589, Henri IV became King of France but his first aim was to conquer his kingdom, where some of the population had rejected him because of his Protestant religion. He fought the Leaguers and their ally, Philip II of Spain. Henri IV defeated Mayenne, the head of the League, in Arques in 1589 and again in Ivry in 1590 but was unable to take either Paris or Rouen. Realising that religion prevented his acceptance by the entire population of France, he eventually abjured Protestantism one last time in July 1593 and had himself anointed king in Chartres in February 1594. This enabled him to make an official entry into Paris (March 1594). He had, however, to fight the last Leaguers for some considerable time before obtaining their submission. He also fought Philip II of Spain. Henry IV was victorious in Fontaine-Française (1595) but fighting continued in the north of France until 1598. The two monarchs then signed the Treaty of Vervins which confirmed the conditions laid down in Cateau-Cambrésis and restored peace between Spain and France. In the same year, Henri IV brought religious peace to a country tired of fighting, through the Edict of Nantes (April) which gave Protestants freedom of conscience and freedom of worship. From 1598 onwards, royal authority was gradually restored, after being seriously called into question during 36 years of civil war. The king showed his authority by refraining from convening the States General, reducing claims from Parliaments and putting down, with great severity, any attempted revolt on the part of the nobility (Maréchal de Biron was executed in 1602). In order to ensure that he had the loyalty of his public servants, he promulgated the Edict of La Paulette which required them to pay for what then became hereditary offices (1604). His work to redress the situation in France also affected the economic and financial sectors. Thanks to Sully, the situation rapidly improved through a policy aimed at limiting expenditure, encouraging agriculture, developing industries and introducing a mercantile system that would enrich the country. Henri IV also worked to develop maritime trade and signed a treaty with England. Finally, he encouraged the colonial conquest of Canada where Champlain founded the town of Quebec (1608). As far as foreign policy was concerned, the second part of his reign was marked only by one short war against the Duke of Savoy (1600). France was victorious and acquired the Bresse, Bugey, Valromey and Gex areas. In 1610, Henri

IV intended to launch a new war against the imperial army but he was assassinated by a fanatic, Ravaillac. In 1599, he had obtained the annulment of his marriage to Marguerite de Valois; he married Marie de Medici in the following year. This marriage produced Louis XIII and Gaston d'Orléans. The "gay old spark" also had a number of mistresses including Gabrielle d'Estrées and Henriette d'Entragues, and a large number of illegitimate children whom he legitimised. Henri IV has remained the most popular of the French monarchs.

Louis XIII the Just (1601-1643). King of France (1610-1643).

Louis, the elder son of Henri IV and Marie de Medici, succeeded his father in 1610 at the age of 9 and his mother acted as Regent. Although he was declared to have come of age in 1614, Louis XIII continued to be strongly influenced by her and by her favourite, Concini, until 1617. The policy implemented by the Regent was contested by the kingdom's leading aristocrats, among them Condé, and they fomented an uprising in 1614-1616. In 1617, Louis XIII showed his authority by having Concini murdered and removing his mother from power. From 1617 to 1621, he left government in the hands of his favourite, Luynes, and after warring against his mother in 1619-1620, the king was reconciled with her. The year 1624 marked the beginning of cooperation between Louis XIII and Richelieu; it was to last until 1642. Although the king was particularly carefully to maintain royal authority and although all decisions were made with his approval, he let the Cardinal govern the country. Richelieu had three major aims – within France, he wanted to ruin the Huguenot party and subject the seditious nobility to the power of the absolute monarchy once and for all; his foreign policy was designed to fight the House of Austria. In religious matters, Richelieu wanted to overturn the privileged political position granted to the Protestants by the Edict of Nantes. The Peace of Montpellier (1622), signed after initial rebellion on the part of the Protestants, placed restrictions on their military potential. The struggle started again in 1625. The most symbolic act was the siege and capture of La Rochelle in 1627-1628, since this was the place through which Protestants received assistance from foreign powers, in particular England. The struggle ended with the Treaty of Alès (1629) confirming the Protestants' right of worship but leading to the destruction of their strongholds and fortresses. As far as the kingdom's leading nobility was concerned, Richelieu repressed any attempt at revolt and punished any obvious failure to comply with royal edicts e.g. after the Chalais plot in 1626, the Montmorency rebellion in 1632 or the conspiracy instigated by Louis XIII's brother, Gaston d'Orléans, in 1642. Richelieu's position came under attack on several occasions but the king never lost his trust in the Cardinal, as was evident in the Day of the Dupes (November 1630). His reign was marked by the institution of a strong, centralised, all-powerful State which intervened in every possible field (promulgation of the Michau Code in 1629, founding of the *Académie française* in 1635). In foreign policy areas, the Cardinal re-opened the hostilities against Austria, the country's traditional enemy since the reign of François I. Richelieu began by signing an alliance with England against Spain (1625) but domestic difficulties and the threat from Protestants forced him to reverse the alliances in 1627. The problems inherent to the succession in the Duchy of Mantua led to French military intervention in the north of Italy in 1629-1630 and the occupation of Savoy. The Thirty Years' War provided Richelieu with an opportunity to take direct action against the imperial army. France entered the fray in 1635. Although the war began with a string of defeats (Corbie, 1636) and with anti-fiscality revolts in a France crushed by the burden of taxation, it later enabled France to occupy the Artois and Roussillon areas. The war was not quite over when Richelieu died, in 1642, and Louis XIII in 1643. Louis XIII's reign was also marked by the building of a colonial empire in Canada, Africa and the West Indies. He married Anne of Austria in 1615 and had only one heir, the future Louis XIV who was born in 1638.

Louis XIV the Great (1638-1715). King of France (1643-1715).

Louis XIV, Louis XIII's only son and his successor in 1643, was a mere 5 years old when he mounted the throne and his mother, Anne of Austria, became Regent until 1651. In fact, it was her right-hand man and adviser, Mazarin, who governed until his death in 1661. Mazarin's first aim was to continue the war against the imperial army that had begun during the reign of Louis XIII. The French army won the Battle of Rocroi (1643), conquered the left bank of the Rhine (1644) and was victorious in Nördlingen (1645). The Treaties of Westphalia signed in 1648 put an end to the war and France obtained a number of bases in Alsace. The conflict, however, had caused increasing economic and financial difficulties and Mazarin had been content to use expedients to bring money into the State's coffers. In 1648, his policies led to opposition; this was the beginning of the Fronde Revolt, the last brutal, disorganised manifestation of armed opposition to royal authority. Its failure resulted in the triumph of absolute monarchy. The Fronde was initially a rebellion on the part of the Parliamentarians in Paris, forcing the royal family to flee (January 1649) and Mazarin to negotiate (Peace of Saint-Germain). In 1650, however, it became a revolt on the part of the princes and a veritable civil war broke out. It was all the more serious because the Prince de Condé allied himself with Spain which was still at war. Mazarin was forced into exile on two occasions, in 1651 and 1652, in order to pave the way for peace. However, the excesses of the princes and the terror instigated by Condé in Paris led to final victory for Mazarin and royal authority. The Cardinal returned to the capital in February 1653; this was the end of the Fronde. All that remained for Louis XIV and Mazarin to do was to end the war with Spain. It continued until 1659, marked by battles on the Spanish border and in the north of France, with successive victories and defeats. Eventually, the French victory at the Battle of the Dunes in 1658 led to the signature of the Treaty of the Pyrenees in 1659 under which France obtained the Roussillon, Cerdagne and Artois areas as well as numerous places in Flanders. It also provided for Louis XIV's marriage with Maria Theresa, Infanta of Spain; the wedding took place in 1660. Mazarin died in 1661, leaving the young king a country at peace, healthy finances and stronger royal power. The political education that Louis XIV had received was to serve him in his efforts to instigate an absolute monarchy in France. His personal reign began in 1661 and lasted for an exceptionally long time (54 years). During it, Louis XIV left his mark on France. He was aware of his royal prerogatives at a very early age and, when Mazarin died, Louis XIV announced that he would no longer be appointing a prime minister. He then removed the influential Fouquet from power. The king was aided by ministers in his search for grandeur, among them Colbert in charge of finances and the Navy, Le Tellier and Louvois at the Ministry of War and Lionne who dealt with foreign affairs, but all of them merely carried out the monarch's orders. The aristocracy lost all influence and power. It was excluded from political life, especially after the court moved to Versailles (1682). The parliaments became no more than rubber stamps, the States General were never convened and administrative centralisation was strengthened through the use of intendants. Gradually, the cult of royal majesty developed. Louis became the "Sun King" in a system based on the theory of monarchy by divine right. Thanks to a major economic boom (within an authoritarian State-based regime), wealth for the country as a whole because of Colbert's ideas and the strongest army in Europe led by great generals such as Condé and Turenne, Louis XIV was able to impose his law on Europe. His aggressive foreign policy and territorial ambitions led to four wars during his reign for other European countries were worried by his attitude. The War of Devolution (1667-1668) against Spain led to the conquest of fortresses in Flanders, including Lille. The Dutch War (1672-1678), which was marked by the invasion of the Low Countries, produced an anti-French coalition but enabled the country to obtain Franche-Comté and Artois under the terms of the Treaty of Nijmegen and push back the northern and eastern borders. The policy of "reunions" implemented by Louis XIV during peace time, i.e. annexation of other territories including Strasburg (1681) led to a second coalition and the War of the League of Augsburg (1688-1697) in which France found it more difficult to stand up to its enemies. When the Peace of Rijswick was signed, Louis XIV was obliged to give back all the land he had obtained after 1679, with the exception of Strasburg. The question of the Spanish succession caused the last war since King Charles II, who had no heir, had designated as his successor the Duke of Anjou, Louis XIV's grandson. The War of the Spanish Succession (1701-1714) was particularly difficult for France which suffered serious defeats. The northern part of France was invaded and the country seemed to be on the point of succumbing but the victory at the Battle of Denain (1712) gave it one final burst of energy and paved the way for the signature of a peace treaty which left Louis XIV with all his territories except for his lands in North America (Treaties of Utrecht and Rastadt). France emerged from these numerous wars impoverished and in ruins. As far as religion was concerned, Louis XIV behaved as the head of the Church of France, opposing the Pope's views in the royal prerogative concerning revenue from vacant sees and abbacies, persecuting the Jansenists and, more particularly, the Protestants. This latter policy led to the Revocation of the Edict of Nantes and the emigration of thousands of followers of the Reformed Religion. In cultural matters, Louis XIV was a patron of the arts and both letters and arts blossomed during his reign thanks to the protection afforded by the monarch to numerous people e.g. Molière, Racine, Boileau or Lully, the creation of academies, and the numerous building projects launched (Versailles). He married Maria Theresa of Austria but soon tired of her. He had numerous mistresses including Mademoiselle de la Vallière and Madame de Montespan, and produced numerous children, all of whom were legitimised. After the queen's death in 1683, the king secretly remarried with Madame de Maintenon. By the end of his reign, he had lost all his children and grandchildren and he was succeeded on his death by his only living great-grandson, Louis XV, in 1715.

Louis XV the Well-Beloved (1710-1774). King of France (1715-1774).

Louis XV, the son of the Duke of Burgundy and Marie-Adelaide of Savoy, was the great-grandson of Louis XIV whom he succeeded in 1715 at the age of five. Philippe d'Orléans acted as Regent, assisted by Cardinal Dubois. The first years of the Regency saw general reaction against Louis XIV's policy of absolute monarchy – reform of government councils and founding of the Polysynodie, re-establishment of the Parliament's right of remonstrance, return of the Regent to Paris and development of a degree of moral laxity. In 1718, given the financial difficulties and the carelessness of the councils, the Regent returned to a more authoritarian policy, ended the Polysynodie and called upon the services of Law. The system instigated by this financier, based on a Western Company for the exploitation of Louisiana, led to the setting up of a state bank but feverish speculation led to its eventual downfall and was deeply traumatic for French public opinion (1720). In external affairs, the Regent, who feared that Philip V of Spain would lay claim to the French throne, allied himself with England and Holland and declared war on Spain in 1719. France was quickly victorious and Philip V gave up his claim. The Regent died in 1723 just after Louis XV had been declared to have come of age, but the monarch was happy to leave the government of the country in the hands of the Duke of Bourbon who arranged the king's marriage to Maria Leczinska, the daughter of the dethroned King of Poland (1725). Louis XV dismissed Bourbon in 1726 and replaced him with Cardinal Fleury who directed affairs of State until 1743. He implemented a moderate policy and stringent economies in order to redress the State's finances and bring prosperity back to the kingdom but he was also faced with a return of parliamentary unrest, especially in the matter of religion. Despite his desire for peace, Fleury had to involve France in the War of Polish Succession in order to support the king's father-in-law (1733-1738). It was a failure but Stanislaus Leczinska was granted a life interest in Lorraine. When Fleury died in 1743, Louis XV announced his intention of governing by himself. In fact he never really undertook his work as king and left his ministers to govern, maintaining rivalries, bowing to the influence of his mistresses (e.g. Madame de Pompadour) and spending his time in pleasurable pursuits.

The king took the country into the War of Austrian Succession in 1741 but, despite a number of victories, handed back all the territories he had conquered when he signed the Treaty of Aix-la-Chapelle (1748). From 1749 onwards, the financial situation worsened again and the Controller-General, Machaut d'Arnouville, created a tax called *"le vingtième"* (one-twentieth of the value of all possessions). The reign was entering its second phase. The king was no longer "Well Beloved", the critical new ideas of the Age of Enlightenment were beginning to gain ground (Louis XV condemned the *Encyclopaedia*) and the parliaments again opposed the king's wishes (quarrel over confessional "tickets", 1752-1756). Having negotiated a reversal of alliances, the king took the country into another conflict, the Seven Years' War (1756-1763) which was disastrous for France. The country was forced to hand almost all its colonial empire over to England. The end of Louis XV's reign was marked by further parliamentary unrest, which the king tried to end by supporting Maupeou's judicial reform (1771). He left a country that was exsanguinated and a greatly weakened monarchy. It was during his reign that the country was extended by two new provinces – Lorraine in 1766 and Corsica in 1768. Louis XV's marriage to Maria Leczinska brought him two sons, both of whom predeceased him, and it was his grandson, Louis XVI who succeeded him when he died in 1774.

Louis XVI (1754-1793). King of France (1774-1792).

Louis XVI, the third son of the *Dauphin*, Louis, and his wife Marie-Josèphe of Saxony and grandson of Louis XV, fell heir to the throne when his father died in 1765, since his two elder brothers had already died. Louis XVI married Marie-Antoinette of Austria in 1770 and succeeded his grandfather in 1774. He inherited a difficult financial situation and a badly impaired image of the monarchy. Filled with the very best of intentions and a will to do his utmost for his people, he was a cultured, educated man who was open to the ideas of the Age of Enlightenment. Louis XVI, however, was not the man for the job. He lacked authority, had a weak, irresolute character and was easily influenced, sometimes with disastrous results. His indecision and contradictory behaviour were his undoing. From the beginning of his reign, he realised that there was a need for reform. He therefore recalled the parliaments and brought in reformist ministers to assist him. Turgot attempted to implement a major reform including the creation of a tax payable by all and free trade in cereals. However, faced with strong opposition from parliaments and court alike, and with the resultant increase in the price of cereals (known as the "flour war"), Louis XVI dismissed Turgot in 1776. Thereafter, no more reforms were possible. Neither Necker nor Calonne were able to change the course of history. Louis XVI's decision to involve France in the War of American Independence on the side of the Insurgents (1780-1783) led to a further worsening of the financial situation because of the use of loans. In 1787, Loménie de Brienne submitted a new fiscal reform policy to the Parliament, but in vain. Eventually, faced with the hostility of Parliamentarians (unrest in Rennes and Grenoble), Louis XVI gave in and convened the States General in 1788. Their meeting, at Versailles on 5th May

1789, was considered as the start of the French Revolution. The conflict regarding the voting procedure opposing the king and the Third Estate from the outset led to a breakdown of the system and the States General became a National Assembly in June 1789. The Assembly soon gave itself constituent powers. This was the monarchy's first defeat and the end of absolutism. Louis XVI's ambiguous attitude (dismissal of Necker, arrival of troops in Paris) led to the popular uprising on 14th July and the fall of the Bastille then, in October 1789, to the days of unrest which resulted in the Parisian people bringing the royal family back to Paris. The Constituent Assembly gradually set up a constitutional monarchy and ended the old social order known as the *Ancien Régime* (abolition of privileges on 4th August 1789, acceptance of the Declaration of the Rights of Man and the Citizen on 26th August 1789). Louis XVI appeared to accept these changes but, in fact, found it difficult to cope with the loss of his absolute power. The vote on the Civil Constitution for the clergy (July 1790) reinforced his mistrust of the new regime. Counting on the assistance of loyal foreign troops and emigrant aristocrats, the king decided to flee in June 1791. He was caught in Varennes, set back on the throne by a moderate assembly careful to preserve the constitutional monarchy, but gradually lost his last supporters, even though he swore an oath of fidelity to the Constitution in September 1791. Once the Constitution became operational, it merely led to repeated conflicts between the legislative assembly and the monarch who held a right of veto. The outbreak of war against Austria (April 1792), which the king had ardently desired in the hope that a French defeat would give him back his power, discredited him once and for all. The defeats of the revolutionary armies and the sending of the threatening Brunswick Manifesto to the Parisian people revealing the king's secret negotiations with foreign sovereigns led to an uprising in Paris on 10th August 1792 and the end of the constitutional monarchy. Louis XVI was suspended from his functions, deposed and imprisoned in the Temple with his family. The National Convention, which met in September 1792, abolished royalty, proclaimed a Republic, and decided to send the king to trial. He was found guilty of conspiracy and treason, sentenced to death and guillotined on 21st January 1793. The monarchy ceased to exist but Louis XVI left a son, Louis XVII, who was imprisoned in the Temple and two brothers, the Counts of Provence and Artois, who had fled abroad.

Louis XVIII (1755-1824). King of France (1814-1815 and 1815-1824).

Louis XVIII, grandson of Louis XV and younger brother of Louis XVI, was initially known as Count of Provence. He emigrated in 1791, at the beginning of the French Revolution then took the title of "King" on the death of his nephew (Louis XVII) in the Temple Prison in 1795. He worked for the restoration of the monarchy but the military victories of the revolutionary troops, Bonaparte's rise to power and the proclamation of the Empire in 1804 removed him from the public eye. He had to wait for Napoleon's first defeats before beginning his diplomatic activity again. He finally mounted the throne after Napoleon's abdication in April

1814. This was the first period of restoration of the monarchy. On 4th June, he promulgated a charter instituting a constitutional monarchy and confirming the main political and social advantages of the Revolution. Napoleon's return to France in March 1815 forced him to flee to Ghent where he spent the period known as the "Hundred Days". Once Napoleon had been defeated at Waterloo and forced to abdicate for the second time (July 1815), Louis returned to power. Under the terms of the second Treaty of Paris (November 1815), the Allies set French borders back where they had been in 1790 and decided to implement military occupation (it lasted until 1818). The second Restoration, with the election of an assembly that had an ultra-royalist majority (known as the "Unavailable Chamber") in August 1815, reflected a violent royalist reaction called the "White Terror", but Louis XVIII succeeded in containing it by dissolving the Chamber in September 1816 and supporting the moderate policies of ministers Richelieu and Decazes. Wide-sweeping liberal laws were passed. After the assassination of the Duke de Berry, the king's nephew, in 1820, more royalist reaction was felt, leading to the nomination of Minister Villèle (1821). Laws restricting individual liberties and the electoral body and re-establishing censorship were passed in 1820-1822. Louis XVIII died in 1824 without leaving an heir and the crown passed to his brother, Charles X.

Charles X (1757-1836). King of France (1824-1830).

The younger brother of Kings Louis XVI and Louis XVIII was originally known as Count of Artois. He emigrated in 1789, at the outbreak of the Revolution, and tried to rally support among European courts in order to fight the new regime. He attempted to land on the Island of Yeu in 1795. He spent the entire Napoleonic period in England, returning to France in 1814 when the monarchy was re-established. Charles X became King of France in 1824, upon the death of his brother, Louis XVIII. He left Villèle to govern but the minister was unpopular because of the reactionary measures he introduced (vote on indemnities for émigrés in 1825). The king was less flexible than his brother had been and he totally ignored the progress of the liberal opposition. Instead, he gave the impression that he wanted to return to the old pre-revolutionary regime. After Villèle's downfall and the failure of the moderate government instigated by de Martignac, Charles X nominated Polignac, an ultra-royalist, and this was seen as a provocation (1829). Despite the Address of the 221 (members of parliament) reminding the king of the principles laid down in the Charter (March 1830), the monarch published the Four Ordinances on 25th July, restricting voting rights, limiting the freedom of the press and dissolving the Assembly. These laws led to a popular uprising on 27th, 28th and 29th July 1830, the "Three Glorious Days", which caused Charles X to abdicate. During his reign, French foreign policy led the country to intervene militarily in Greece in 1827 in support of the Greek push for independence from Turkey. France also began the colonial conquest of Algeria (capture of Algiers in July 1830). After his abdication, Charles X lived in England then in Austria where he died in 1836. His downfall marked the end of the French Bourbon line.

THE ORLÉANS

The Orléans line was the last line from the Capetian dynasty. It mounted the throne of France in 1830 and provided only one monarch, Louis-Philippe I, the last king to reign in France. The line descended from Philippe, Duke of Orléans and brother of Louis XIV, a fifth-generation forebear of Louis-Philippe I.

His reign lasted for eighteen years, from 1830 to 1848, and was known as the "July Monarchy".

The 1848 Revolution and the abdication of the king finally put an end to monarchy in France and to the Capetian dynasty.

Louis-Philippe I's descendent, Henri, Count of Paris, was born in 1933 and is currently the head of the House of Orléans and pretender to the throne of France.

Louis-Philippe I

THE ORLEANS DYNASTY

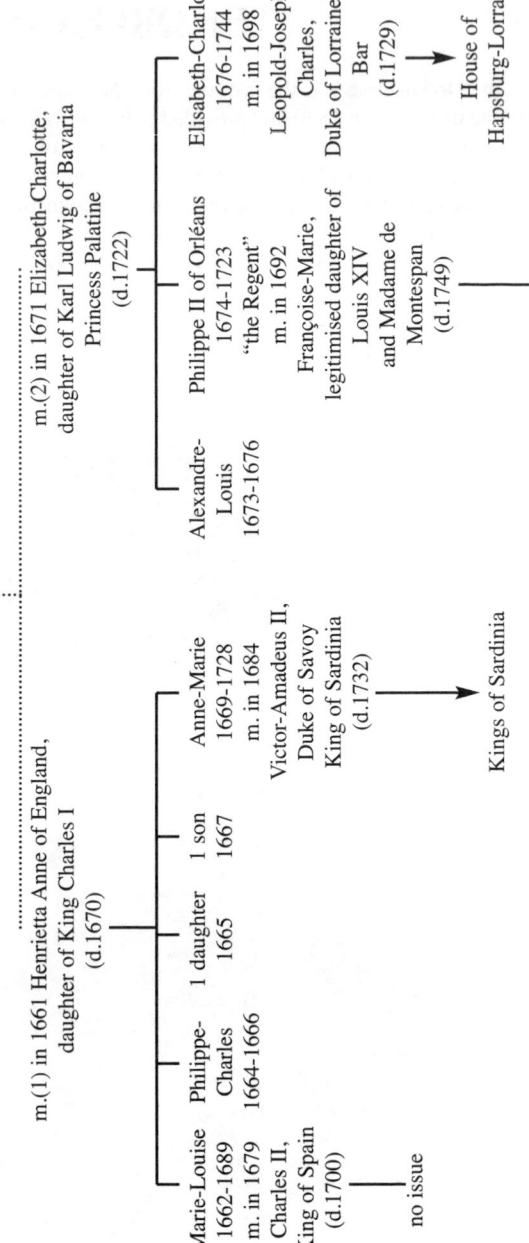

Philippe
1640-1701
Duke of Orléans, brother of King Louis XIV

m.(1) in 1661 Henrietta Anne of England, daughter of King Charles I (d.1670)

m.(2) in 1671 Elizabeth-Charlotte, daughter of Karl Ludwig of Bavaria Princess Palatine (d.1722)

Marie-Louise
1662-1689
m. in 1679 Charles II, King of Spain (d.1700)
no issue

Philippe-Charles
1664-1666

1 daughter
1665

1 son
1667

Anne-Marie
1669-1728
m. in 1684 Victor-Amadeus II, Duke of Savoy King of Sardinia (d.1732)
Kings of Sardinia

Alexandre-Louis
1673-1676

Philippe II of Orléans
1674-1723
"the Regent"
m. in 1692 Françoise-Marie, legitimised daughter of Louis XIV and Madame de Montespan (d.1749)

Elisabeth-Charlotte
1676-1744
m. in 1698 Leopold-Joseph-Charles, Duke of Lorraine and Bar (d.1729)
House of Hapsburg-Lorraine

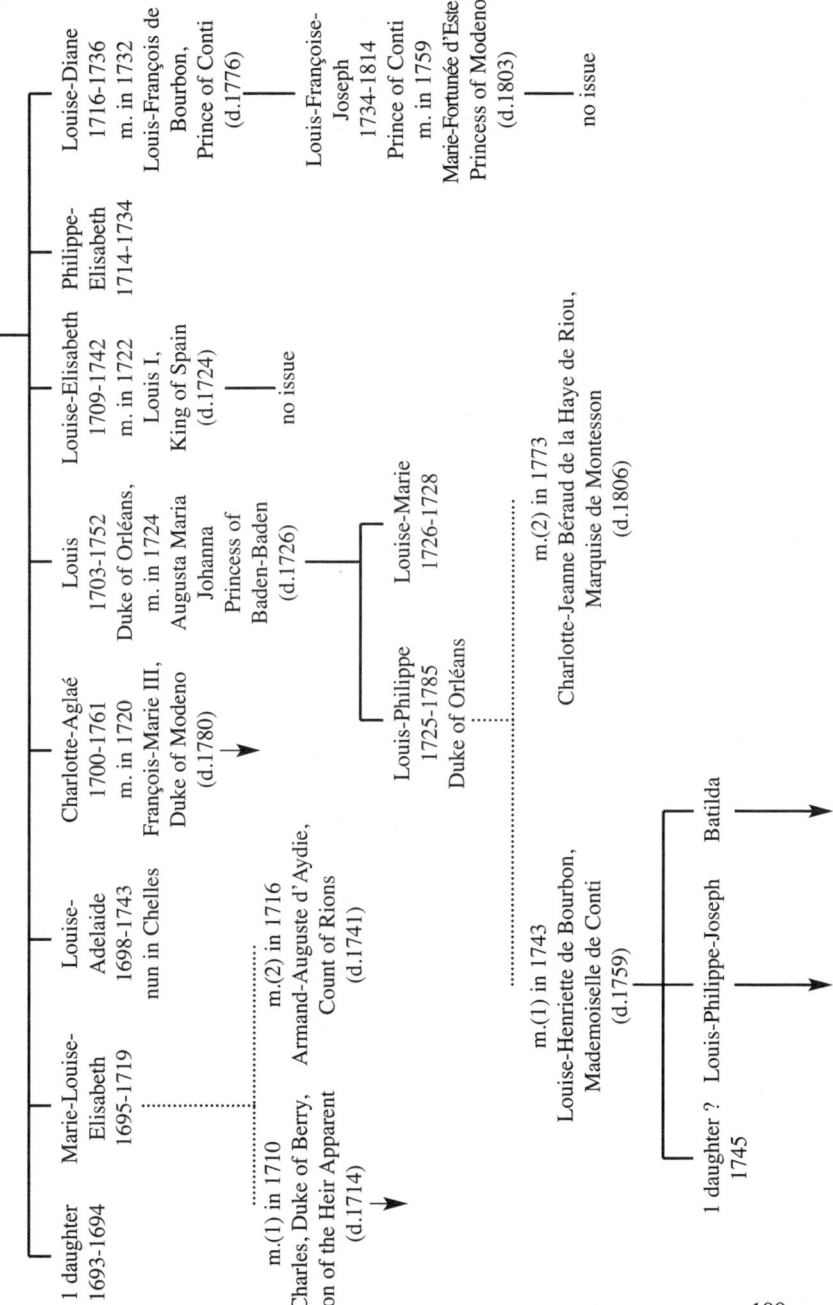

1 daughter
1693-1694

Marie-Louise-
Elisabeth
1695-1719

m.(1) in 1710
Charles, Duke of Berry,
son of the Heir Apparent
(d.1714) →

m.(2) in 1716
Armand-Auguste d'Aydie,
Count of Rions
(d.1741)

Louise-
Adelaide
1698-1743
nun in Chelles

Charlotte-Aglaé
1700-1761
m. in 1720
François-Marie III,
Duke of Modeno
(d.1780) →

Louis
1703-1752
Duke of Orléans,
m. in 1724
Augusta Maria
Johanna
Princess of
Baden-Baden
(d.1726)

Louise-Marie
1726-1728

Louis-Philippe
1725-1785
Duke of Orléans

m.(1) in 1743
Louise-Henriette de Bourbon,
Mademoiselle de Conti
(d.1759)

m.(2) in 1773
Charlotte-Jeanne Béraud de la Haye de Riou,
Marquise de Montesson
(d.1806)

1 daughter ?
1745

Louis-Philippe-Joseph →

Batilda →

Louise-Elisabeth
1709-1742
m. in 1722
Louis I,
King of Spain
(d.1724)

no issue

Philippe-
Elisabeth
1714-1734

Louise-Diane
1716-1736
m. in 1732
Louis-François de
Bourbon,
Prince of Conti
(d.1776)

Louis-Françoise-
Joseph
1734-1814
Prince of Conti
m. in 1759
Marie-Fortunée d'Este,
Princess of Modeno
(d.1803)

no issue

109

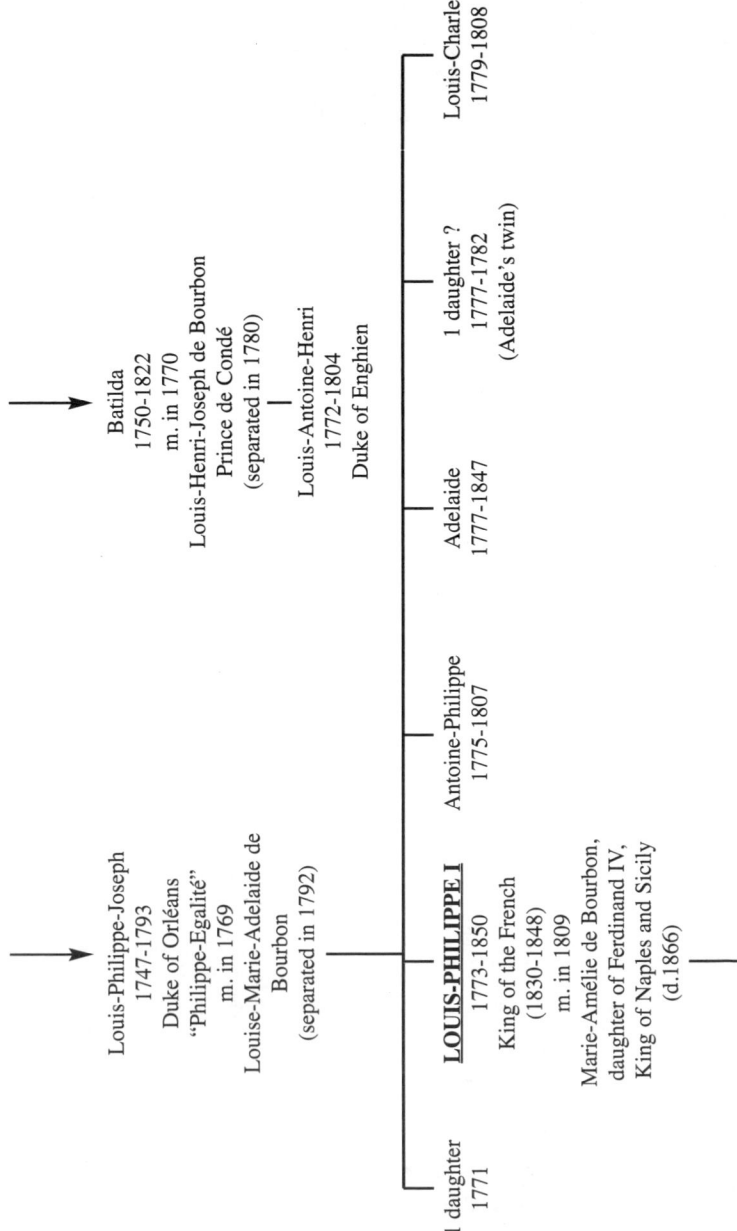

Louis-Philippe-Joseph
1747-1793
Duke of Orléans
"Philippe-Egalité"
m. in 1769
Louise-Marie-Adelaide de
Bourbon
(separated in 1792)

Batilda
1750-1822
m. in 1770
Louis-Henri-Joseph de Bourbon
Prince de Condé
(separated in 1780)

Louis-Antoine-Henri
1772-1804
Duke of Enghien

1 daughter
1771

LOUIS-PHILIPPE I
1773-1850
King of the French
(1830-1848)
m. in 1809
Marie-Amélie de Bourbon,
daughter of Ferdinand IV,
King of Naples and Sicily
(d.1866)

Antoine-Philippe
1775-1807

Adelaide
1777-1847

1 daughter ?
1777-1782
(Adelaide's twin)

Louis-Charles
1779-1808

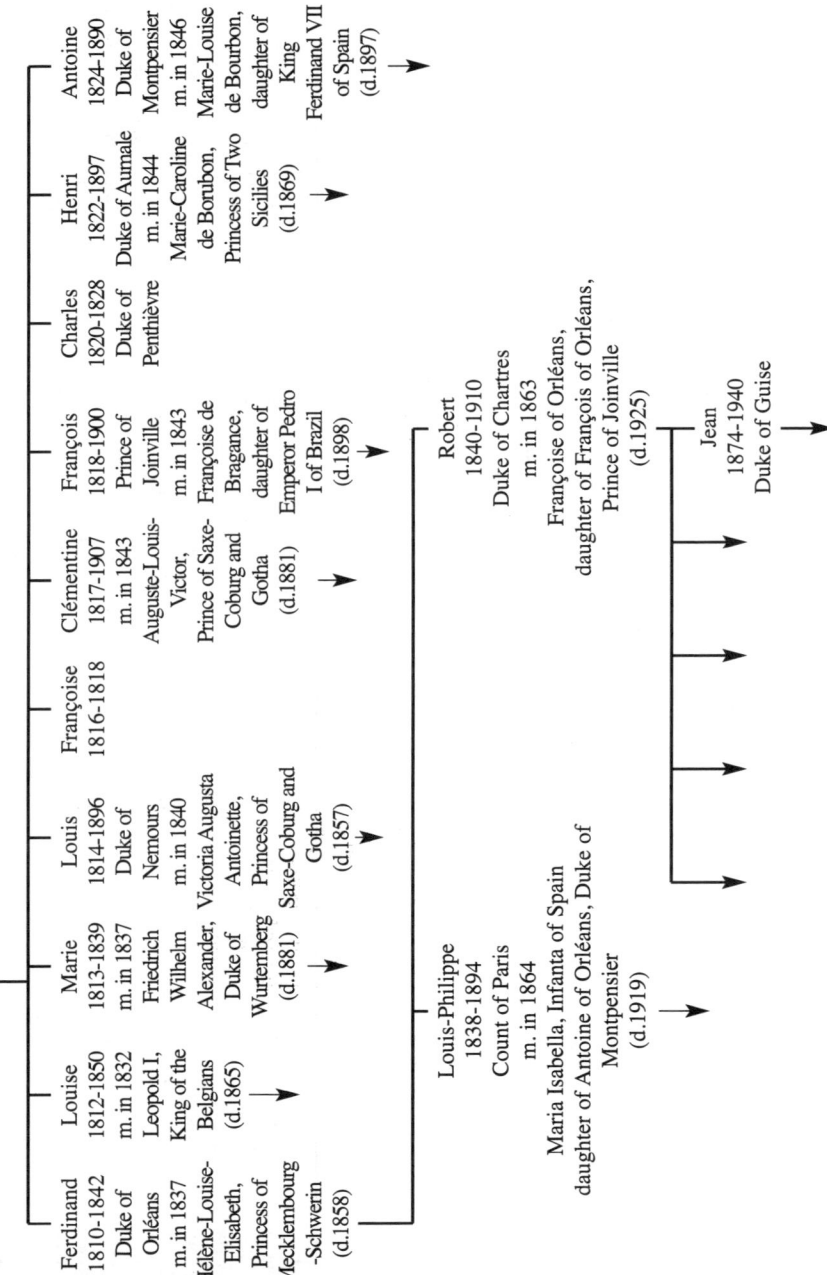

Ferdinand
1810-1842
Duke of
Orléans
m. in 1837
Hélène-Louise-
Elisabeth,
Princess of
Mecklembourg
-Schwerin
(d.1858)

Louise
1812-1850
m. in 1832
Leopold I,
King of the
Belgians
(d.1865)

Marie
1813-1839
m. in 1837
Friedrich
Wilhelm
Alexander,
Duke of
Wurtemberg
(d.1881)

Louis
1814-1896
Duke of
Nemours
m. in 1840
Victoria Augusta
Antoinette,
Princess of
Saxe-Coburg and
Gotha
(d.1857)

Françoise
1816-1818

Clémentine
1817-1907
m. in 1843
Auguste-Louis-
Victor,
Prince of Saxe-
Coburg and
Gotha
(d.1881)

François
1818-1900
Prince of
Joinville
m. in 1843
Françoise de
Bragance,
daughter of
Emperor Pedro
I of Brazil
(d.1898)

Charles
1820-1828
Duke of
Penthièvre

Henri
1822-1897
Duke of Aumale
m. in 1844
Marie-Caroline
de Borubon,
Princess of Two
Sicilies
(d.1869)

Antoine
1824-1890
Duke of
Montpensier
m. in 1846
Marie-Louise
de Bourbon,
daughter of
King
Ferdinand VII
of Spain
(d.1897)

Louis-Philippe
1838-1894
Count of Paris
m. in 1864
Maria Isabella, Infanta of Spain
daughter of Antoine of Orléans, Duke of
Montpensier
(d.1919)

Robert
1840-1910
Duke of Chartres
m. in 1863
Françoise of Orléans,
daughter of François of Orléans,
Prince of Joinville
(d.1925)

Jean
1874-1940
Duke of Guise

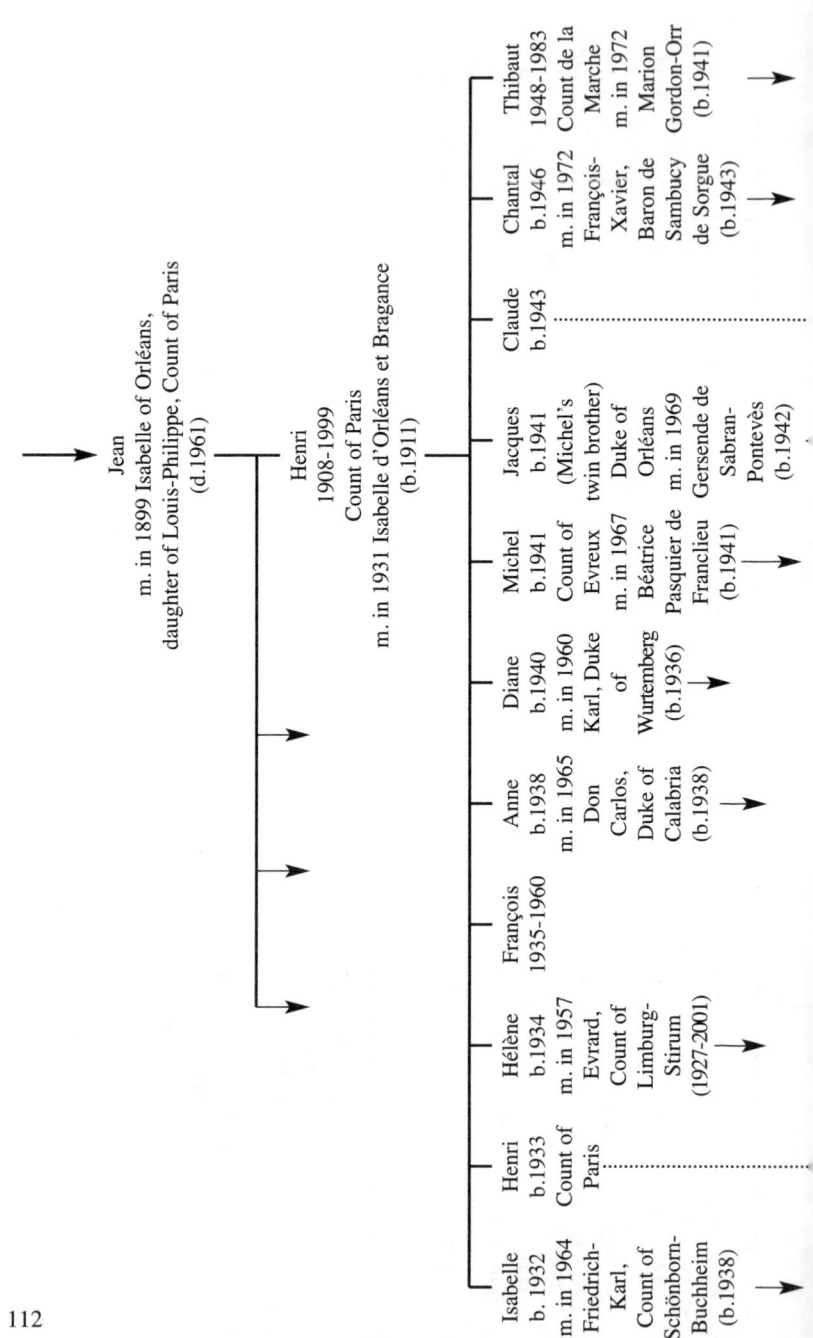

Jean
m. in 1899 Isabelle of Orléans,
daughter of Louis-Philippe, Count of Paris
(d.1961)

Henri
1908-1999
Count of Paris
m. in 1931 Isabelle d'Orléans et Bragance
(b.1911)

Isabelle
b. 1932
m. in 1964
Friedrich-
Karl,
Count of
Schönborn-
Buchheim
(b.1938)

Henri
b.1933
Count of
Paris

Hélène
b.1934
m. in 1957
Evrard,
Count of
Limburg-
Stirum
(1927-2001)

François
1935-1960

Anne
b.1938
m. in 1965
Don
Carlos,
Duke of
Calabria
(b.1938)

Diane
b.1940
m. in 1960
Karl, Duke
of
Wurtemberg
(b.1936)

Michel
b.1941
Count of
Evreux
m. in 1967
Béatrice
Pasquier de
Franclieu
(b.1941)

Jacques
b.1941
(Michel's
twin brother)
Duke of
Orléans
m. in 1969
Gersende de
Sabran-
Pontevès
(b.1942)

Claude
b.1943

Chantal
b.1946
m. in 1972
François-
Xavier,
Baron de
Sambucy
de Sorgue
(b.1943)

Thibaut
1948-1983
Count de la
Marche
m. in 1972
Marion
Gordon-Orr
(b.1941)

112

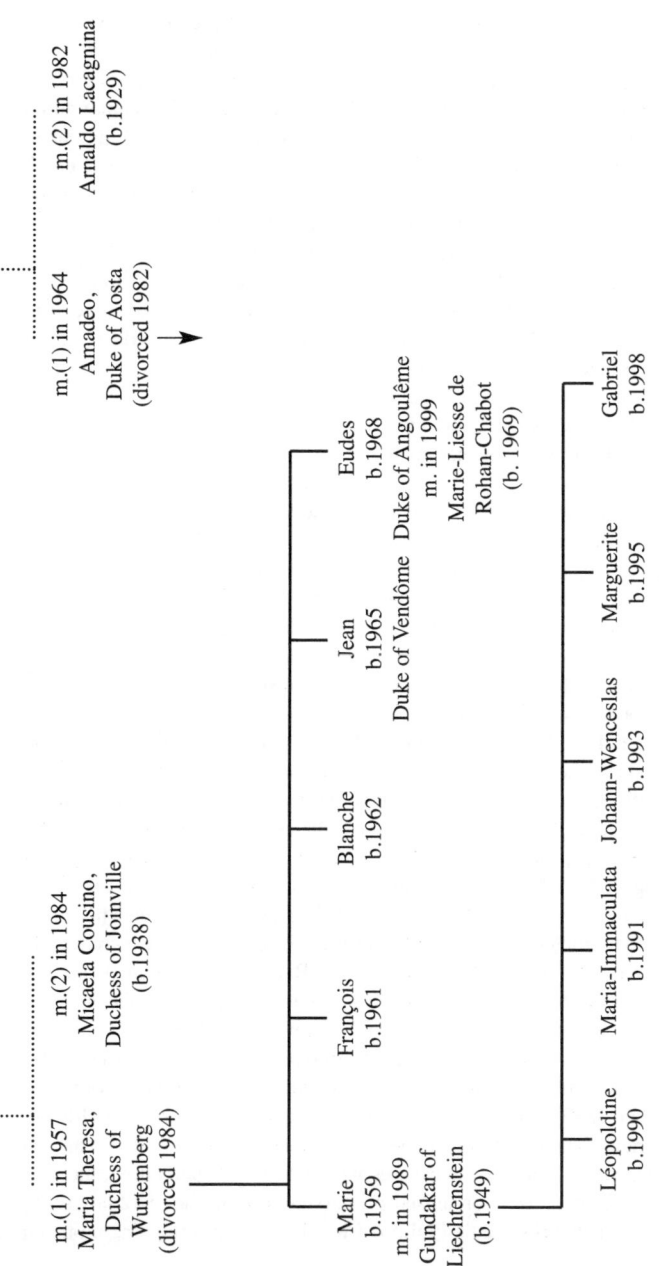

m.(1) in 1957
Maria Theresa,
Duchess of
Wurtemberg
(divorced 1984)

m.(2) in 1984
Micaela Cousino,
Duchess of Joinville
(b.1938)

m.(1) in 1964
Amadeo,
Duke of Aosta
(divorced 1982)

m.(2) in 1982
Arnaldo Lacagnina
(b.1929)

Marie
b.1959
m. in 1989
Gundakar of
Liechtenstein
(b.1949)

François
b.1961

Blanche
b.1962

Jean
b.1965
Duke of Vendôme

Eudes
b.1968
Duke of Angoulême
m. in 1999
Marie-Liesse de
Rohan-Chabot
(b. 1969)

Léopoldine
b.1990

Maria-Immaculata
b.1991

Johann-Wenceslas
b.1993

Marguerite
b.1995

Gabriel
b.1998

Louis-Philippe I (1773-1850). King of the French People (1830-1848).

Louis-Philippe, the eldest son of the Duke of Orléans, "Philippe-Egalité", was the leader of the younger branch of the Bourbons which descended from Philippe of Orléans, the brother of Louis XIV. In 1789, he enthusiastically supported the Revolution, took part in the battles of 1792-1793 but passed over to the enemy after the defeat at Neerwinden (March 1793). He sought refuge in Switzerland then travelled through various countries (Germany, Scandinavia, the USA, England and Sicily). He returned to France upon the Restoration of the monarchy (1814) but remained distant from the Bourbons who disliked his progressive ideas. He frequented bourgeois circles, owners of immense property and wealth who saw him as a hope for the future. The 1830 revolution which removed his cousin, Charles X, from the throne led to his accession. He was proclaimed Lieutenant General of the Kingdom and accepted the crown. He swore an oath of allegiance to the revised Charter and became King of the French People at the beginning of August. Louis-Philippe I's reign was a true constitutional monarchy but was especially favourable to wealthy businessmen at a time when France was undergoing its own industrial revolution. The first years of the reign were troubled by legitimist opposition reflected in the uprising led by the Duchess de Berry in 1832, by Republican riots (in Paris in 1832, 1834 and 1839), by unsuccessful attempts on the part of Louis-Napoléon Bonaparte to instigate insurrection (1836 and 1840), by social unrest (revolt by silk workers in Lyon in 1832, Parisian workers' movement in 1840) and by attempts on the king's life (1835). In government, Louis-Philippe I sought support among the conservatives in the "Resistance" party such as Casimir Périer, Soult, Thiers or Guizot. Suffrage restricting the vote to landowners allowed for the election of Assemblies that reflected the policies implemented by the king and annihilated any attempt at opposition. The 1840's were a more peaceful period, marked by the long ministry of Guizot. Economic growth was strong and many people made fortunes, but at the cost of worsening conditions for the workers. However, Guizot's conservative policies and Louis-Philippe's determination to maintain peace on the international scene at a time when the people were dreaming of Napoleonic glory added to an economic crisis that shook the country led to manifestations of discontent. When the monarch and his prime minister refused to implement an electoral reform which would have increased the number of voters, the opposition organised the Banquet Campaign (from July 1847 onwards). In February 1848, a banquet was banned in Paris. The situation degenerated and became a riot then, eventually, a revolution. Louis-Philippe abdicated on 24th February and went into exile in England where he died in 1850. The Republic was proclaimed. During his reign, the conquest of Algeria had continued. It had begun in 1830 and was marked by the struggle against Abd-el-Kadir. Meanwhile, France began to build another colonial empire in black Africa and the Pacific islands. Major legislative measures were taken as regards domestic policies. The Guizot Law of 1833 organised primary education; the 1842 law set up the major railway networks. Louis-Philippe I was France's last reigning monarch.

114

THE BONAPARTES

The Bonapartes, a Corsican family of Lombard origin, stepped onto the historical stage of France at the end of the 18th century thanks to their most illustrious member, Napoleon I.

After a period as a victorious General in the revolutionary army from 1796 to 1799, First Consul in 1799 then Emperor of the French People in 1804, Napoleon I established a hereditary imperial regime. His two-stage abdication (in 1814 and again in 1815 after the "Hundred Days") put an end to his attempt at instigating this system since his son, the King of Rome, did not succeed him.

The Bonaparte family also gave Europe several kings or princes from among Napoleon's brothers and sisters.

One of their children, Charles-Louis-Napoleon Bonaparte had himself elected President of the French Republic in 1848 after the revolution that ended the July monarchy. He then re-established the empire in 1852, as his uncle's heir. Napoleon III remained Emperor of the French People until 1870 when military defeat during the Franco-Prussian War led to his downfall and the proclamation of the Republic.

This being so, the Bonaparte dynasty had only two members on the throne of France. At present, the claimant to the throne from the Bonaparte family is Charles Napoléon Bonaparte, who was born in 1950.

Napoleon

THE BONAPARTE DYNASTY

Charles-Marie Bonaparte 1746-1785 —— m. in 1764 —— Maria Letizia Ramolino 1750-1836

Napoleon Bonaparte 1765

Marie-Anne Bonaparte 1767

Joseph Bonaparte 1768-1844
King of Naples (1806-1808)
King of Spain (1808-1813)
m. in 1794 Julie Clary (d.1845)

NAPOLEON I 1769-1821
Emperor of the French (1804-1814 and 1815)

m.(1) in 1796 Joséphine de Tasher de la Pagerie, Viscountess de Beauharnais (marriage annulled in 1810)

m.(2) in 1810 Marie-Louise of Austria, daughter of Emperor Franz I (d.1847)

Marie-Anne Bonaparte 1771

1 daughter ? 1773

Lucien Bonaparte 1775-1840 (see children, page 118)

Elisa Bonaparte 1777-1820

Louis Bonaparte 1778-1846

Pauline Bonaparte 1780-1825

m.(1) in 1797 General Leclerc (d.1802)

Louis-Napoléon 1798-1804

Caroline Bonaparte 1782-1839 (see children, pages 121-123)

m.(2) in 1803 Prince Borghese (d.1832)

no issue

Jérôme Bonaparte 1784-1860

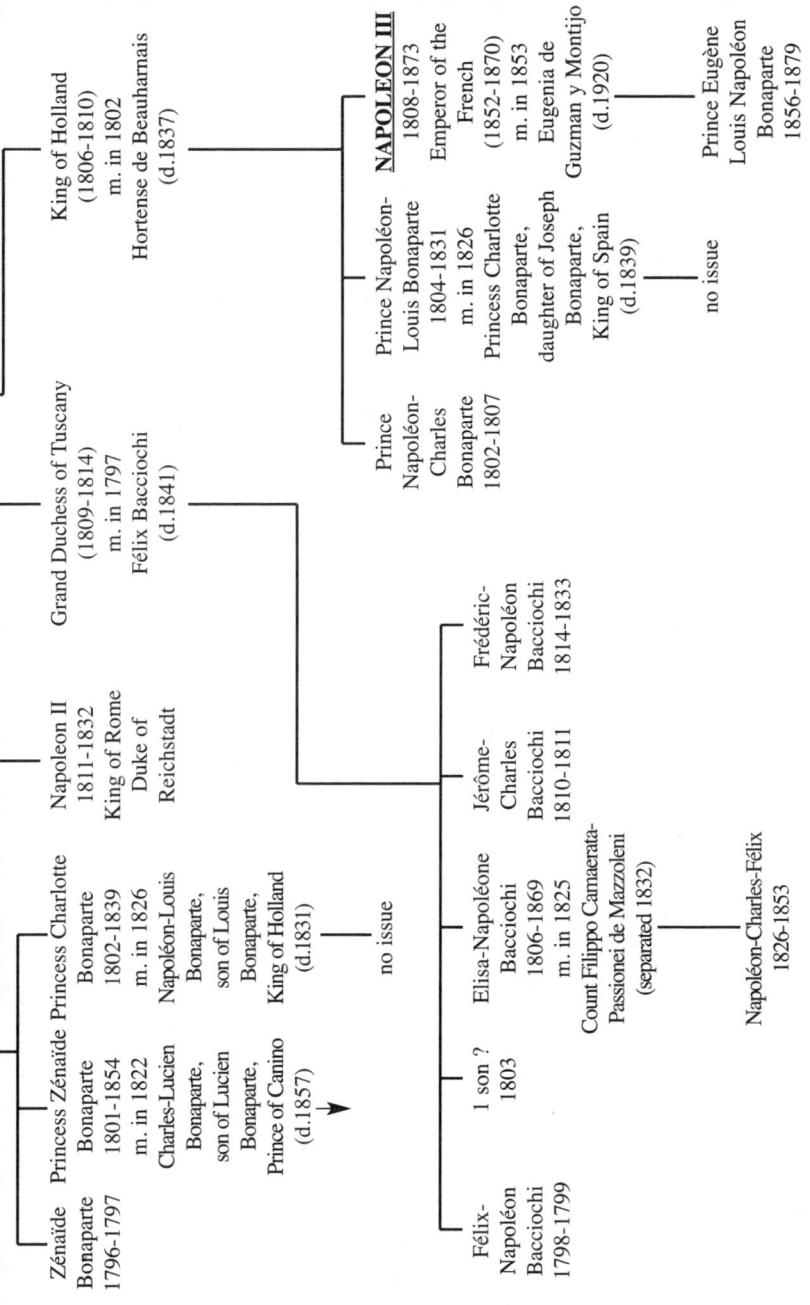

King of Holland
(1806-1810)
m. in 1802
Hortense de Beauharnais
(d.1837)

Grand Duchess of Tuscany
(1809-1814)
m. in 1797
Félix Bacciochi
(d.1841)

Napoleon II
1811-1832
King of Rome
Duke of
Reichstadt

Princess Charlotte
Bonaparte
1802-1839
m. in 1826
Napoléon-Louis
Bonaparte,
son of Louis
Bonaparte,
King of Holland
(d.1831)

Princess Zénaïde
Bonaparte
1801-1854
m. in 1822
Charles-Lucien
Bonaparte,
son of Lucien
Bonaparte,
Prince of Canino
(d.1857)

Zénaïde
Bonaparte
1796-1797

NAPOLEON III
1808-1873
Emperor of the
French
(1852-1870)
m. in 1853
Eugenia de
Guzman y Montijo
(d.1920)

Prince Napoléon-
Louis Bonaparte
1804-1831
m. in 1826
Princess Charlotte
Bonaparte,
daughter of Joseph
Bonaparte,
King of Spain
(d.1839)

Prince
Napoléon-
Charles
Bonaparte
1802-1807

Prince Eugène
Louis Napoléon
Bonaparte
1856-1879

no issue

Frédéric-
Napoléon
Bacciochi
1814-1833

Jérôme-
Charles
Bacciochi
1810-1811

Elisa-Napoléone
Bacciochi
1806-1869
m. in 1825
Count Filippo Camaerata-
Passionei de Mazzoleni
(separated 1832)

Napoléon-Charles-Félix
1826-1853

1 son ?
1803

Félix-
Napoléon
Bacciochi
1798-1799

no issue

117

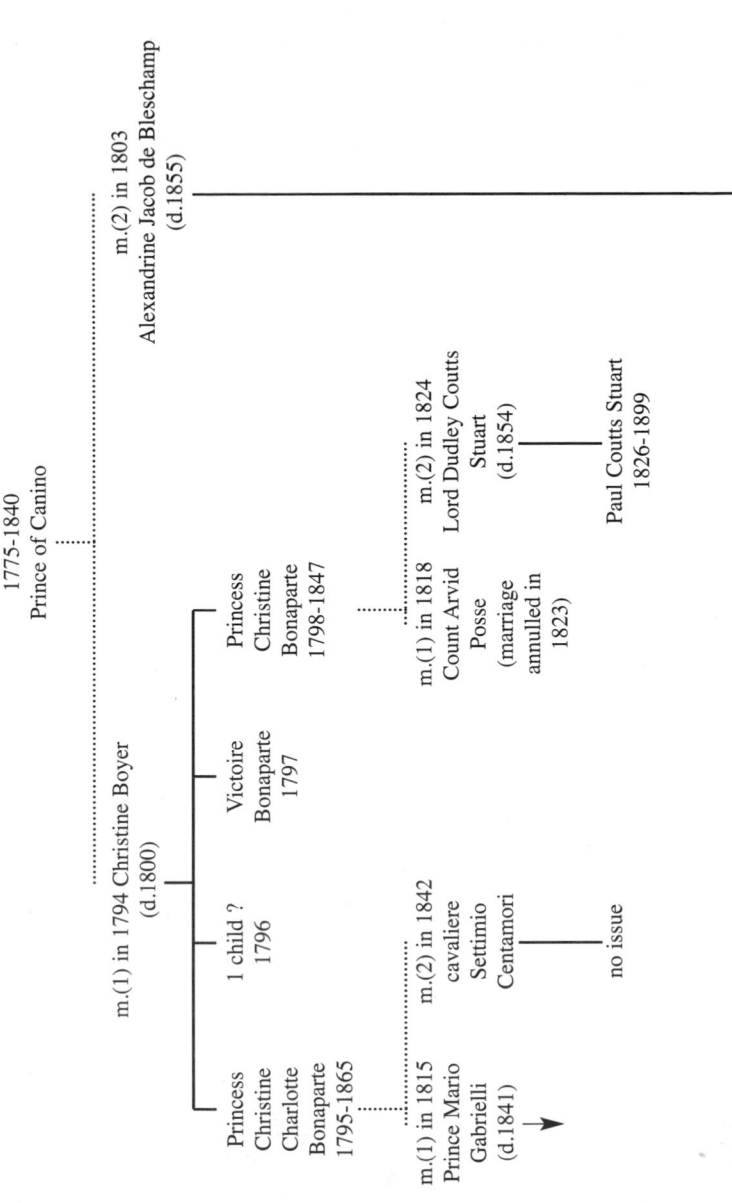

Lucien Bonaparte
1775-1840
Prince of Canino

m.(1) in 1794 Christine Boyer
(d.1800)

m.(2) in 1803
Alexandrine Jacob de Bleschamp
(d.1855)

Princess
Christine
Charlotte
Bonaparte
1795-1865

1 child ?
1796

Victoire
Bonaparte
1797

Princess
Christine
Bonaparte
1798-1847

m.(1) in 1815
Prince Mario
Gabrielli
(d.1841)

m.(2) in 1842
cavaliere
Settimio
Centamori

m.(1) in 1818
Count Arvid
Posse
(marriage
annulled in
1823)

m.(2) in 1824
Lord Dudley Coutts
Stuart
(d.1854)

no issue

Paul Coutts Stuart
1826-1899

Prince
Charles-
Lucien
Bonaparte
1803-1857
m. in 1822
Princess
Zénaïde
Bonaparte,
daughter of
Joseph
Bonaparte,
King of Spain
(d.1854)

→

Princess
Laetizia
Bonaparte
1804-1871
m. in 1821
Sir Thomas
Wyse
(d.1862)

→

Joseph
Bonaparte
1806-1807

Princess
Jeanne
Bonaparte
1807-1829
m. in 1825
Marquis
Honoré
Honorati
(d.1856)

Prince Paul
Bonaparte
1809-1827

Prince
Louis-
Lucien
Bonaparte
1813-1891
m. in 1833
Maria-Anna
Cecchi
(separated
in 1850)

Prince
Pierre-
Napoléon
Bonaparte
1815-1881
m. in 1867
Justine-
Eléonore
Ruflin
(d.1905)

Prince
Antoine
Bonaparte
1816-1877
m. in 1839
Maria-Anna
Cardinali
(d.1879)

Princess
Marie-
Alexandrine
Bonaparte
1818-1874
m. in 1836
Vincenzo,
Count
Valentini di
Laviano
(d.1858)

→

Princess
Constance
Bonaparte
1823-1876
Abbess

Clélia
Honorati
1827-1886
m. in 1847
Camiloo
Romagnoli
di Cesena
(d.1890)

no issue

no issue

no issue

Roland Bonaparte
1858-1924
m. in 1880
Marie Blanc
(d.1882)

Jeanne Bonaparte
1861-1910
m. in 1881
Marquis Christian de
Villeneuve-Escalpon
(d.1931)

Marie Bonaparte
1882-1962
m. in 1907
Prince George of Greece and Denmark
(d.1957)

→

119

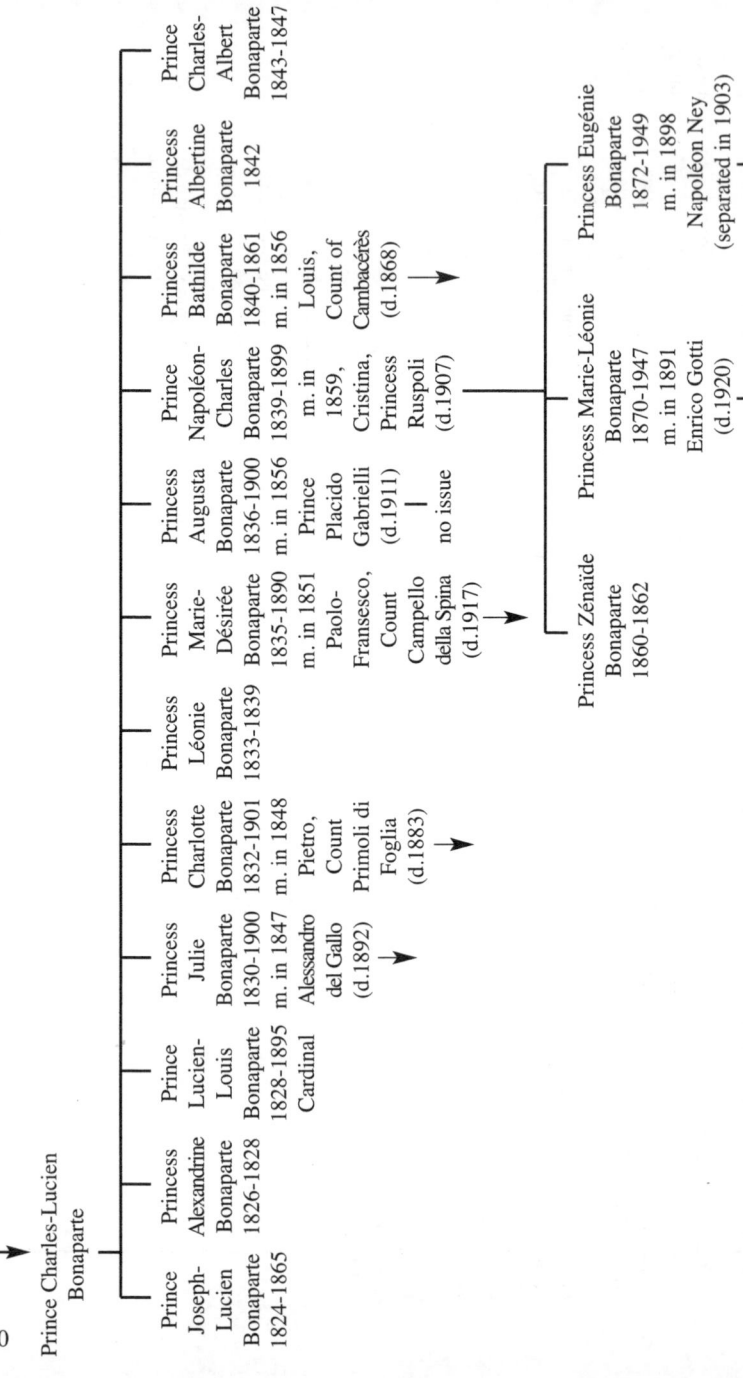

Prince Charles-Lucien Bonaparte

Prince Joseph-Lucien Bonaparte 1824-1865

Princess Alexandrine Bonaparte 1826-1828

Prince Lucien-Louis Bonaparte 1828-1895 Cardinal

Princess Julie Bonaparte 1830-1900 m. in 1847 Alessandro del Gallo (d.1892) →

Princess Charlotte Bonaparte 1832-1901 m. in 1848 Pietro, Count Primoli di Foglia (d.1883) →

Princess Léonie Bonaparte 1833-1839

Princess Marie-Désirée Bonaparte 1835-1890 m. in 1851 Paolo-Fransesco, Count Campello della Spina (d.1917) →

Princess Augusta Bonaparte 1836-1900 m. in 1856 Prince Placido Gabrielli (d.1911) — no issue

Prince Napoléon-Charles Bonaparte 1839-1899 m. in 1859, Cristina, Princess Ruspoli (d.1907)

Princess Bathilde Bonaparte 1840-1861 m. in 1856 Louis, Count of Cambacérès (d.1868) →

Princess Albertine Bonaparte 1842

Prince Charles-Albert Bonaparte 1843-1847

Princess Zénaïde Bonaparte 1860-1862

Princess Marie-Léonie Bonaparte 1870-1947 m. in 1891 Enrico Gotti (d.1920)

Princess Eugénie Bonaparte 1872-1949 m. in 1898 Napoléon Ney (separated in 1903)

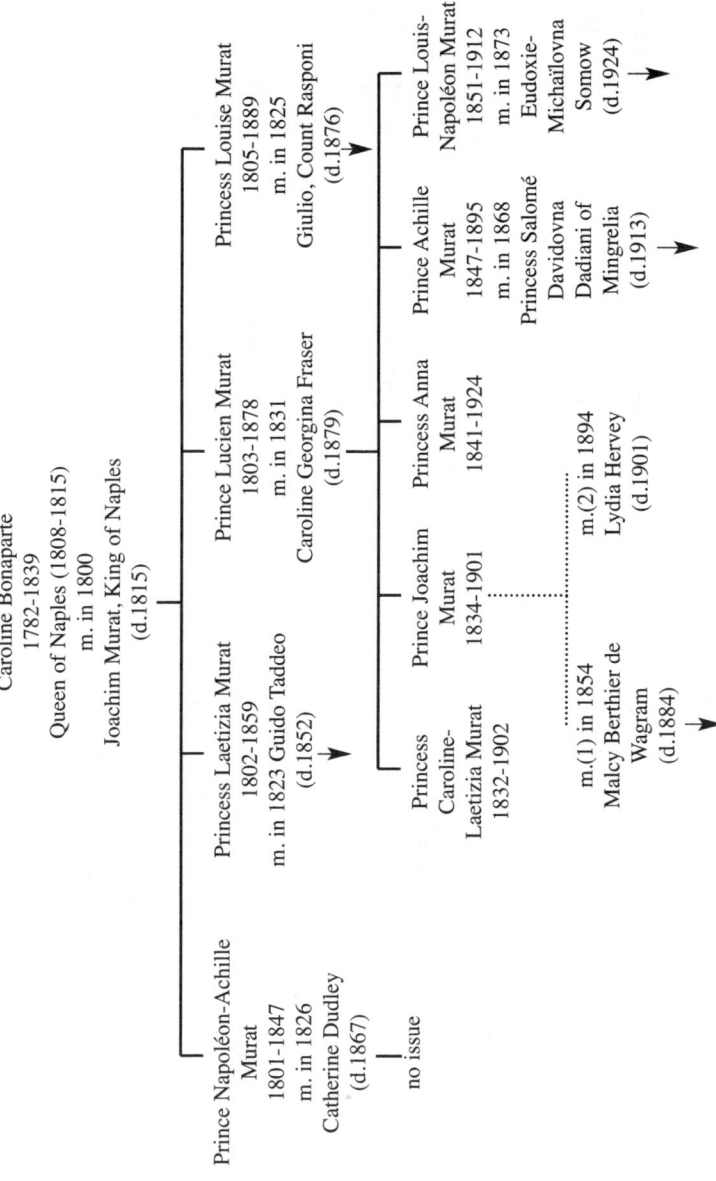

Caroline Bonaparte
1782-1839
Queen of Naples (1808-1815)
m. in 1800
Joachim Murat, King of Naples
(d.1815)

Prince Napoléon-Achille Murat
1801-1847
m. in 1826
Catherine Dudley
(d.1867)

no issue

Princess Laetizia Murat
1802-1859
m. in 1823 Guido Taddeo
(d.1852)

Prince Lucien Murat
1803-1878
m. in 1831
Caroline Georgina Fraser
(d.1879)

Princess Louise Murat
1805-1889
m. in 1825
Giulio, Count Rasponi
(d.1876)

Princess Caroline-Laetizia Murat
1832-1902

Prince Joachim Murat
1834-1901

Princess Anna Murat
1841-1924

Prince Achille Murat
1847-1895
m. in 1868
Princess Salomé Davidovna Dadiani of Mingrelia
(d.1913)

Prince Louis-Napoléon Murat
1851-1912
m. in 1873
Eudoxie-Michaïlovna Somow
(d.1924)

m.(1) in 1854
Malcy Berthier de Wagram
(d.1884)

m.(2) in 1894
Lydia Hervey
(d.1901)

Descendents of the Murat Princes

121

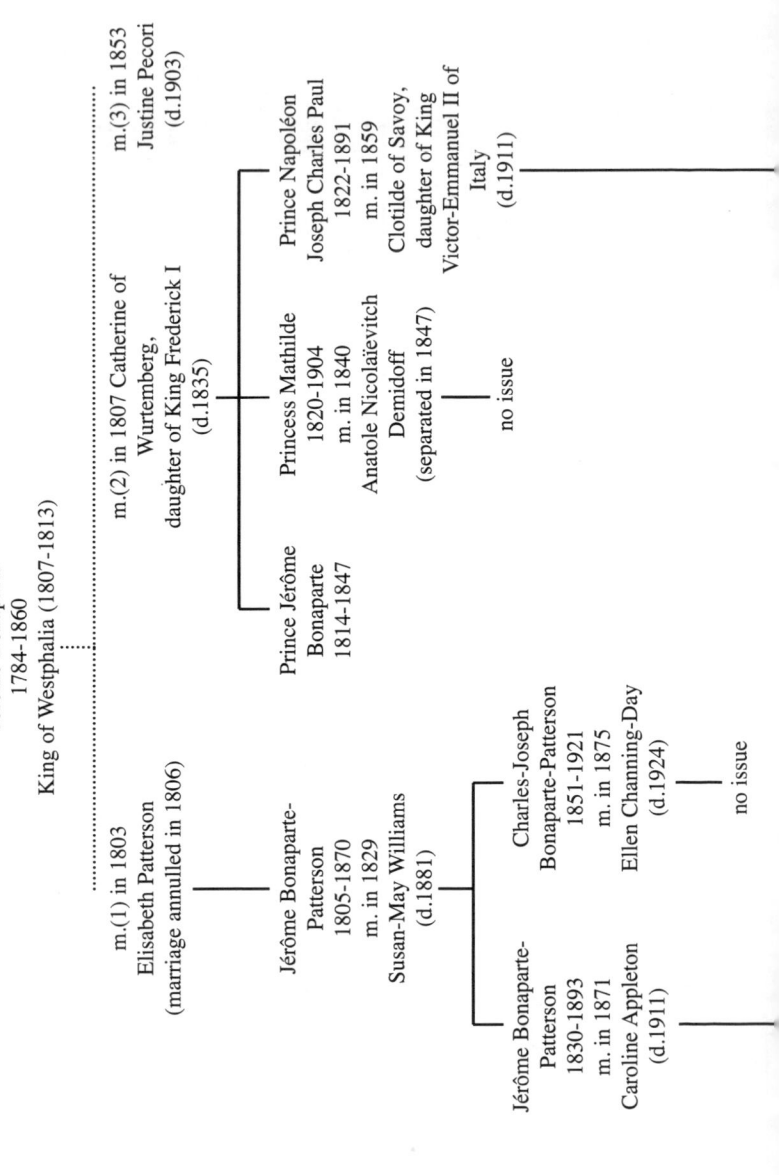

Jérôme Bonaparte
1784-1860
King of Westphalia (1807-1813)

m.(1) in 1803
Elisabeth Patterson
(marriage annulled in 1806)

m.(2) in 1807 Catherine of
Wurtemberg,
daughter of King Frederick I
(d.1835)

m.(3) in 1853
Justine Pecori
(d.1903)

Jérôme Bonaparte-
Patterson
1805-1870
m. in 1829
Susan-May Williams
(d.1881)

Prince Jérôme
Bonaparte
1814-1847

Princess Mathilde
1820-1904
m. in 1840
Anatole Nicolaïevitch
Demidoff
(separated in 1847)

Prince Napoléon
Joseph Charles Paul
1822-1891
m. in 1859
Clotilde of Savoy,
daughter of King
Victor-Emmanuel II of
Italy
(d.1911)

no issue

Charles-Joseph
Bonaparte-Patterson
1851-1921
m. in 1875
Ellen Channing-Day
(d.1924)

Jérôme Bonaparte-
Patterson
1830-1893
m. in 1871
Caroline Appleton
(d.1911)

no issue

Louise Bonaparte-
Patterson
1873-1923
m. in 1896
Adam, Count of
Moltke-Huitfeldt
(d.1944)

Jérôme Bonaparte-
Patterson
1878-1945
m. in 1914
Blanche Peirce
(d.1950)

no issue

Victor, Prince Napoléon
1862-1926
m. in 1910
Clémentine of Belgium,
daughter of King
Leopold II
(d.1955)

Prince Louis
Napoléon
1864-1932

Princess Laetitia
Napoléon
1866-1926
m. in 1888
Prince Amadeo of
Savoy,
Duke of Aosta
(d.1890)

Prince Humberto de
Savoie-Aosta
(1889-1918)

Princess Marie-Clotilde Napoléon
1912-1996
m. in 1938
Count Serge de Witt
(d.1990)

Louis, Prince Napoléon
1914-1997
m. in 1949
Alix de Foresta
(b.1926)

Princess Catherine
Napoléon-Bonaparte
b.1950

m.(1) in 1974
Marquis Nicolo San Martino
d'Aglie di San Germano
(marriage annulled)

Princess Laure Napoléon-Bonaparte
b.1952
m. in 1982
Jean-Claude Lecomte
(b.1948)

m.(2) in 1982
Jean-Claude Dualé
(b.1936)

Prince Jérôme Napoléon-
Bonaparte
b.1957

Prince Charles-Napoléon-Bonaparte
b.1950

m.(1) in 1978
Béatrice de Bourbon-Siciles
(divorced in 1989)

m.(2) in 1996
Jeanne Françoise
Valticcionni
b.1958
|
Catherine
b.1992

Princess Caroline
Napoléon-
Bonaparte
b.1980

Prince Jean
Napoléon-
Bonaparte
b.1986

123

Napoleon I (1769-1821). Emperor of the French People (1804-1814 and 1815).

The son of a Corsican family, Napoleon Bonaparte entered the military academy in Brienne in 1779 then, in 1784, joined the academy in Paris. He became a lieutenant in the artillery and was garrisoned in various places. He was an ardent supporter of the new revolutionary ideas in 1789. He distinguished himself at the Siege of Toulon and his tactics enabled the successful recapture of the rebellious town (December 1793). In October 1795, he foiled a royalist plot against the Convention. A few months later, he was given command of the army in Italy. This military campaign showed him to be a great war leader. From March 1796 to April 1797, he defeated the Italian and Austrian armies and obliged Austria to seek peace. The Treaty of Campio-Formio (October 1797) was Bonaparte's work and it showed his independence vis-à-vis the Directory. With the Egyptian Expedition (1798-1799), his popularity reached a new peak. In October 1799, he returned to France where the Directory was faced with enormous difficulties. For all those who wanted to put an end to the existing regime, Bonaparte represented the armed forces. He joined Sieyès in organising the coup d'état of 18th and 19th Brumaire (November 1799) and became provisional consul. The Constitution of Year VIII (December 1799), which was his work, named him First Consul and granted him considerable power. Within France, the Consulate achieved wide-ranging pacification and reorganisation. The signature of the Concordat with Pope Pius VII in 1801 brought religious peace back to the country. France was given new administrative, legal and financial institutions ("Prefects" were appointed in 1800, the Banque de France was set up in 1800, the *germinal* franc came into being in1803, and the Civil Code was promulgated in 1804). Outside France, war continued. Bonaparte led a second campaign against Austria in Italy, while another army was fighting in Germany (1800). Austria was defeated and signed the Treaty of Lunéville on 9th February 1801. The whole of Italy came under French domination. Great Britain, which was isolated, signed a peace treaty in March 1802. For the first time in ten years, France could enjoy general peace. Bonaparte took advantage of this and had himself appointed Consul for life in August 1802. The peace, however, lasted only just over one year – Britain opened hostilities again in May 1803. The royalists, who were seeking to overthrow Bonaparte, plotted with Cadoudal in 1804. Feelings ran high and this provided an opportunity to change the regime yet again. On 18th May 1804, Bonaparte became Emperor of the French People under the name Napoleon I and, on 2nd December in Notre-Dame in Paris, he was crowned by Pope Pius VII. This was a return to a hereditary monarchy with a court, an imperial nobility and an order of chivalry, the Legion of Honour. The regime became increasingly authoritarian. Liberties were suppressed, in particular the freedom of the press. Assemblies no longer had any power and education was shaped to suit the emperor's will, with the opening of an imperial university (1808). The population did not react; it was under close surveillance by an omnipresent police force. Napoleon I was nevertheless supported by the French people as long as he won military victories. The Third Coalition, formed in 1805, was marked by the disastrous defeat at Trafalgar which destroyed Napoleon's plans to invade Britain but on the mainland of Europe the Emperor led a crushing campaign (victory at the Battle of Austerlitz in December 1805). Austria was forced to sign the Treaty of Presburg and lost vast territories. Germany underwent major change with the setting up of the Confederation of the Rhine (July 1806), marking the end of the Holy Roman Empire. Napoleon led two campaigns against the Fourth Coalition. Prussia was defeated at the Battles of Jena and Auerstadt (14th October 1806) and lost territories to a newly-created Poland (Grand Duchy of Warsaw). Russia was defeated at Friedland (14th June 1807) and Czar Alexander I had to accept both peace and an alliance with France (Treaty of Tilsitt, July 1807). Great Britain stood alone and at war. In order to asphyxiate the country in economic terms, Napoleon instigated the Continental Blockade in November 1806 but, if it was to be totally effective, he had to have control of the entire coastline of Europe. He therefore annexed Portugal in 1807 and the Papal States in 1808. To achieve this, France had to invade Spain. Napoleon overthrew King Charles IV and placed his brother, Joseph Bonaparte, on the throne. This led to a popular uprising and a long, difficult, and ultimately unsuccessful war for the French army. When Austria saw Napoleon in difficulty in Spain, it took up arms again and formed the Fifth Coalition with Great Britain. A lightning campaign led by the Emperor resulted in victory at the Battle of Wagram (6th July 1809). The Treaty of Vienna dismembered Austria while, at the same time, making it one of France's allies. Napoleon divorced Joséphine de Beauharnais and married Marie-Louise of Austria in April 1810. The annexation of the Low Countries in 1810 and of the north of Germany in 1811 gave France a territorial expansion never before achieved (France had 130 *"départements"*). The birth of an heir for the emperor, the King of Rome (March 1811), provided a dynastic successor and the Napoleonic Empire reached the pinnacle of its success at this point. However, the total lack of liberty within the country and the economic and financial consequences of the war eventually led to general discontent. Added to this was the opposition of the clergy and Catholics when Napoleon, in dispute with the Pope, had the Holy Father kidnapped in Rome in 1809 and kept him prisoner for four years. In Europe, the countries that had been defeated began to raise their heads again. French domination was increasingly seen with hostility and the Continental Blockade was rejected. In 1812, relations were broken with Russia and Napoleon launched yet another campaign. He was unable to defeat the Russian army but succeeded in reaching Moscow in September. He was, however, forced to retreat and his withdrawal turned into a veritable debacle with the crossing of the Beresina River. The defeat caused all the European countries to band together against France. A Sixth Coalition was formed at the beginning of 1813. Forced to fight with a decreasing number of forces against enemies who were numerically superior, Napoleon nevertheless began by winning battles but he was defeated at Leipzig (October 1813) and France was invaded. This marked the beginning of the French Campaign during which the Emperor was unable to withstand the influx of troops from the coalition countries. They reached Paris in March 1814 and Napoleon I was forced to abdicate on 6th April. Under the terms of the Treaty of Paris (May 1814), France re-established its 1792 borders and the Emperor was exiled to the Island of Elba. Louis XVIII mounted the throne. Less than one year later, Napoleon returned to France by stealth (1st March 1815) and seized power again. This new period, however, lasted for only three months (it is known as the "Hundred Days"). The European powers formed a new coalition to fight the Emperor. War broke out again and led to the French defeat at Waterloo (18th June 1815). Napoleon abdicated a second time and the British deported him to a tiny island in the Atlantic, St. Helena, where he died in 1821. The second Treaty of Paris (November 1815) took the borders of France back to their 1790 position.

Napoleon III (1808-1873). Emperor of the French People (1852-1870).

Charles-Louis-Napoléon Bonaparte was the son of Louis Bonaparte, King of the Low Countries, and nephew of Napoleon I. He lived in exile after the fall of the Empire and, having secretly become a member of the *carbonari*, became involved in revolutionary movements in the Papal States in 1831. The death of Napoleon I's son, the Duke of Reichstadt, in 1832 made him the leader and hope of the dynasty. He twice attempted to overthrow King Louis-Philippe I (1836 and 1840). After the failure of his second attempt, he was sentenced to life imprisonment and interned in Ham Fort. He escaped in 1846 and reached Britain. The 1848 revolution enabled him to return to France. Taking advantage of the popularity and prestige linked to the name of his uncle, the Emperor, Louis-Napoleon Bonaparte was elected to the Constituent Assembly then, on 10th December 1848, he became President of the Republic with a crushing majority. He manoeuvred skilfully and let the Assembly fall into disrepute through its conservative measures. He then took centre stage as the defender of universal suffrage. He ensured that his popularity was maintained by touring the provinces. Once the Assembly had rejected a constitutional change which would have enabled the President to stand for re-election, Louis-Napoleon organised the *coup d'état* of 2nd December 1851, facing only token resistance. The January 1852 Constitution gave him full power. The Prince-President then had to re-establish the Empire. Having sounded out French public opinion by travelling throughout the country and having reassured an anxious Europe, Louis-Napoleon Bonaparte declared himself to be Emperor of the French People under the title Napoleon III on 2nd December 1852. Until 1860, the Empire was authoritarian – the dictatorial regime that had been created by the *coup d'état* of 2nd December 1851 remained in place, unchanged. Despite the re-establishment of universal suffrage, the principle of an official candidate in fact suppressed any opposition. Moreover, any discontent was quickly quashed by the police or by exile. The press was subject to controls and universities were under close surveillance. On an economic level, the Second Empire marked the arrival of the industrial era in France (leading banks were set up, the transport system developed, free trade was instigated, industrial output rose sharply and major construction work was undertaken in Paris under Baron Haussmann) yet the new prosperity did not benefit the working classes whose working and living conditions remained very difficult. In foreign policy, Napoleon III quickly took up arms again and involved France in foreign conflicts, firstly in the Crimean War where it fought alongside Britain to support the Ottoman Empire against Russia (1854-1856) then in Italy where it helped the Piedmont to achieve Italian unity and fight Austria (1859). These successes strengthened the Emperor's prestige, especially as France annexed Savoy and Nice in 1860 in the face of more marked opposition within the country. The Catholics were hostile to his Italian policy, industrialists were unhappy about the free trade treaty signed with Britain in 1860, Republican opposition began to become apparent again, and there was general unrest within the working classes as a result of the creation of the First International. Napoleon III changed course and aimed at establishing a liberal Empire. He granted the Chambers the right of address (1860), another law granted workers the right to strike and form coalitions (1864), the press was liberalised and a right of meeting was granted (1868). These measures led to strong progress for the opposition during the elections of 1869 and, in April 1870, Napoleon III proclaimed a liberal Empire, a change that received massive approval in a plebiscite organised in May. However, it was on the international scene that the Empire was beginning to suffer its greatest defeats. Although colonial expansion continued (Indochina, New Caledonia), Napoleon III was singularly unsuccessful abroad. The Mexico Expedition (1862-1867) led to a humiliating defeat and the Emperor's prestige suffered badly as a result. His European policy, which involved encouraging German unity to the detriment of Austria, merely reinforced Prussian power, especially as Napoleon III brought discredit on himself by asking for compensation. This policy inevitably led to confrontation between France and the German States which Bismarck dreamt of unifying. The Emperor then made a mistake in 1870 by involving France, without adequate military preparation (the Niel Law was only passed in 1868) or diplomatic efforts, alone and without any allies, in a war against Prussia with the whole of Germany behind it. The beginning of the war was marked by numerous defeats for the French army. The Emperor himself was encircled in Sedan on 2nd September. He was forced to capitulate and the military disaster led to the downfall of the imperial regime. On 4th September 1870, the Republic was proclaimed. Napoleon III, who was freed after the end of the war, went into exile in Britain where he died in 1873.

Napoleon III

TABLE OF CONTENTS